Interactions in
Online Education

Interactivity is the core of learning, and is evident at all levels of engagement, whether between fellow students, students and tutors, online learning materials or interfacing with the learning environment. This book critically examines and contributes to the crucial debate about interactions in online education.

Expert contributors provide international perspectives on theory and pedagogy, design and the learning environment, implications for practice, and professional development. Key topics covered include:

- Analysing and designing e-learning interactions
- Social and conceptual dimensions of learning
- Interactions in online discussions
- Interactions in peer learning
- Professional development of online facilitators.

Interactions in Online Education shows how interactions enhance learning, consolidate students' knowledge, and improve reflection, questioning and deeper understanding. It will be essential reading for all those involved in the design, implementation, management and use of open and flexible learning.

Charles Juwah is Senior Educational Development Officer and Deputy Head, Centre for the Enhancement of Learning and Teaching, The Robert Gordon University, Aberdeen, UK.

Open and Flexible Learning Series
Series editors: Fred Lockwood, A. W. (Tony) Bates and Som Naidu

Activities in Self-Instructional Texts
Fred Lockwood

Assessing Open and Distance Learners
Chris Morgan and Meg O'Reilly

Changing University Teaching
Terry Evans and Daryl Nation

The Costs and Economics of Open and Distance Learning
Greville Rumble

Delivering Digitally
Alistair Inglis, Peter Ling and Vera Joosten

Delivering Learning on the Net
The why, what and how of online education
Martin Weller

The Design and Production of Self-Instructional Materials
Fred Lockwood

Developing Innovation in Online Learning
An action research framework
Maggie McPherson and Miguel Baptista Nunes

Exploring Open and Distance Learning
Derek Rowntree

Flexible Learning in a Digital World
Betty Collis and Jef Moonen

Improving Your Students' Learning
Alistair Morgan

Innovation in Open and Distance Learning
Fred Lockwood and Anne Gooley

Integrated E-Learning
Implications for pedagogy, technology and organization
Wim Jochems, Jeroen van Merriënboer and Rob Koper

Key Terms and Issues in Open and Distance Learning
Barbara Hodgson

The Knowledge Web
Learning and collaborating on the Net
Marc Eisenstadt and Tom Vincent

Learning and Teaching in Distance Education
Edited by Som Naidu

Making Materials-Based Learning Work
Derek Rowntree

Managing Open Systems
Richard Freeman

Mega-Universities and Knowledge Media
John S. Daniel

Mobile Learning
A handbook for educators and trainers
Edited by Agnes Kukulska-Hulme and John Traxler

Objectives, Competencies and Learning Outcomes
Reginald F. Melton

Online Education Using Learning Objects
Edited by Rory McGreal

The Open Classroom
Distance learning in and out of schools
Edited by Jo Bradley

Open and Distance Learning
Case studies from education, industry and commerce
Stephen Brown

Open and Flexible Learning in Vocational Education and Training
Judith Calder and Ann McCollum

Planning and Management in Distance Education
Santosh Panda

Preparing Materials for Open, Distance and Flexible Learning
Derek Rowntree

Programme Evaluation and Quality
Judith Calder

Reforming Open and Distance Learning
Terry Evans and Daryl Nation

Reusing Online Resources
Alison Littlejohn

Student Retention in Online, Open and Distance Learning
Ormond Simpson

Supporting Students in Online, Open and Distance Learning, 2nd edition
Ormond Simpson

Teaching with Audio in Open and Distance Learning
Derek Rowntree

Teaching Through Projects
Jane Henry

Towards More Effective Open and Distance Learning
Perc Marland

Understanding Learners in Open and Distance Education
Terry Evans

Using Communications Media in Open and Flexible Learning
Robin Mason

The Virtual University
Steve Ryan, Bernard Scott, Howard Freeman and Daxa Patel

Interactions in Online Education

Implications for theory and practice

Edited by Charles Juwah

Routledge
Taylor & Francis Group

LONDON AND NEW YORK

First published 2006
by Routledge
2 Park Square, Milton Park, Abingdon, Oxon OX14 4RN

Simultaneously published in the USA and Canada
by Routledge
270 Madison Ave, New York, NY 10016

Routledge is an imprint of the Taylor & Francis Group, an informa business

© 2006 selection and editorial matter, Charles Juwah; individual
chapters, the contributors

Typeset in Times by
HWA Text and Data Management, Tunbridge Wells
Printed and bound in Great Britain by
The Cromwell Press, Trowbridge, Wiltshire

British Library Cataloguing in Publication Data
A catalogue record for this book is available from the British Library

Library of Congress Cataloging-in-Publication Data
A catalog record for this book has been requested

ISBN10: 0–415–35741–1 (hbk)
ISBN10: 0–415–35742–x (pbk)
ISBN10: 0–203–00343–8 (ebk)

ISBN13: 978–0–415–35741–8 (hbk)
ISBN13: 928–0–415–35742–5 (pbk)
ISBN13: 978–0–203–00343–5 (ebk)

Contents

List of figures   ix
List of tables   xi
List of contributors   xii
Series editor's foreword   xiv
Acknowledgements   xvi

Introduction   1

PART I
Theoretical and pedagogical perspectives   7

1 Theoretical perspectives on interactivity in e-learning   9
   TERRY MAYES

2 Encounter theory: a model to enhance online communication,
   interaction and engagement   27
   ROD SIMS AND JOHN HEDBERG

3 Analysing and designing e-learning interactions   46
   ATSUSI HIRUMI

PART II
Design and learning environment   73

4 Designing interaction as a dialogue game: linking social and
   conceptual dimensions of the learning process   75
   ANDREW RAVENSCROFT AND SIMON McALISTER

5 A model of authentic activities for online learning 91
JAN HERRINGTON, THOMAS C. REEVES AND RON OLIVER

6 Learning designs, learner interactions and learning objects 104
SUE BENNETT, LORI LOCKYER AND BARRY HARPER

7 Methods of learning in simulation environments 117
RIK MIN

PART III
Practice **139**

8 Interaction in learning and teaching on the Educational
Semantic Web 141
TERRY ANDERSON

9 Interactions in online discussions: a pedagogical perspective 156
SANJAYA MISHRA AND CHARLES JUWAH

10 Interactions in online peer learning 171
CHARLES JUWAH

11 Interactions in teaching by videoconferencing 191
WOLFGANG GRELLER

PART IV
Professional development **205**

12 Professional development of online facilitators in enhancing
interactions and engagement: a framework 207
SANTOSH PANDA AND CHARLES JUWAH

13 Developing competencies for online and distance education
teaching 228
RAMESH C. SHARMA AND CHARLES JUWAH

Conclusion 247
CHARLES JUWAH

Index 252

Figures

2.1	Different and/or imbalanced encounters	37
2.2	Harmonious encounters	37
2.3	An interactive negotiation	39
2.4	Online discussion with threaded replies	41
2.5	Weekly schedule of encounters devised by all participants	42
3.1	Three levels of planned e-learning interactions	49
3.2	Sample outlines of grounded instructional strategies	54
3.3	Five step process for designing and sequencing e-learning interactions	55
4.1	InterLoc interface during a Critical Discussion and Reasoning game	80
5.1	Comparison of cognitive, affective, and conative learning domains	93
5.2a	The graduate research centre in Research Preparation: Research Methods	95
5.2b	Research data accessible via a filing cabinet in Research Preparation: Research Methods	95
5.3a	North American Fiction and Film	96
5.3b	Invitation to join Editorial Board in North American Fiction and Film	96
5.4a	Presentation of main activity in Coastal and Marine Systems	97
5.4b	BlackBoard interface used in Coastal and Marine Systems	97
5.5a	Writing in Organisations	97
5.5b	Simulated interview in Writing in Organisations	97
6.1	One of the generic designs formalised in The Learning Designs Project	110
6.2	Representation of the Smart Learning Design Framework	112
7.1	A characteristic Web-based learning environment for the simulation of phenomena from reality	121
7.2	A characteristic Web-based learning environment for simulating phenomena from reality	124
8.1	A proposed model of student-paced learning at Athabasca University	150
9.1	Interactions in technology mediated teaching-learning	158

10.1	Model of self-regulated learning	174
11.1	Use of videoconferencing in UHI	199
12.1	Cognitive structure, reflection and transformative learning/ professional development	212
12.2	Constructivist online continuing professional development of online facilitators: a framework	215
12.3	Online constructivist professional development schema	221
13.1	Models of distance education and associated delivery technologies	231

Tables

3.1 Sample instructional treatment plan based on WebQuest strategy 57
3.2 Planned interaction analysis of sample treatment plan 61
3.3 Sample scoring sheet used to analyse an existing online instructional unit 63
3.4 Summary of planned interaction analysis for an existing online instructional unit 64
4.1 A CDR game demonstrating constructive conflict, explanation and partial agreement 85
9.1 Interaction technologies/media 160
9.2 Rubric for assessing online discussions interactions 166
10.1 Models of peer learning 173
10.2 Technology for peer learning 181

Contributors

Terry Anderson is Professor and Canada Research Chair in Distance Education, Athabasca University, St Edmonton, Canada. Email: terrya@athabascau.ca.

Sue Bennett is Senior Lecturer and Deputy Director of the Centre for Research in Interactive Learning Environments, Faculty of Education, University of Wollongong, Wollongong, NSW. Australia. Email: sue_bennett@uow.edu.au.

Wolfgang Greller is at the UHI Millennium Institute, Stornoway, Isle of Lewis. Email: Wolfgang.Greller@lews.uhi.ac.uk.

Barry Harper is Professor and Dean of Education, Faculty of Education, University of Wollongong, Wollongong, Australia. Email: bharper@uow.edu. au.

John Hedberg is Millennium Innovations Chair of ICT and Education, and Director of the Macquarie ICT Innovations Centre, Australian Centre for Educational Studies, Macquarie University, Australia. Email: john.hedberg@ mq.edu.au.

Jan Herrington is Associate Professor of Education and former Fulbright Scholar, Faculty of Education, University of Wollongong, Wollongong, Australia. Email: janh@uow.edu.au.

Atsusi Hirumi is Associate Professor at the Department of Educational Research, Technology and Leadership Education 320 C, University of Central Florida, Orlando, FL, USA. Email: hirumi@mail.ucf.edu.

Charles Juwah is Senior Educational Development Officer and Deputy Head at the Centre for the Enhancement of Learning and Teaching, The Robert Gordon University, Schoolhill, Aberdeen, UK. Email: c.juwah@rgu.ac.uk.

Lori Lockyer is Director, Digital Media Centre Faculty of Education, University of Wollongong, Wollongong, Australia. Email: lori_lockyer@uow.edu.au.

Terry Mayes is Professor and Director, Centre for Academic Practice, Learning Services Office, Glasgow Caledonian University, Glasgow, UK. Email: jtma@ gcal.ac.uk.

Simon McAlister is Senior Research Fellow at the Learning Technology Research Institute Learning Centre, London Metropolitan University, London, UK. Email: s.mcalister@londonmet.ac.uk.

Rik Min is retired and was formerly at the Centre for Telematics and Information Technology (CTIT), Faculty of Behavioural Sciences, University of Twente, The Netherlands. Email: F.B.M.Min@edte.utwente.nl.

Sanjaya Mishra is Reader in Distance Education at the Staff Training and Research Institute of Distance Education (STRIDE), Indira Gandhi National Open University (IGNOU), New Delhi, India. Email: sanjayamishra@hotmail.com.

Ron Oliver is Professor of Information Technology, Faculty of Communication and Creative Arts, Edith Cowan University, Perth, Australia. Email: r.oliver@ecu.edu.au.

Santosh Panda a former Fulbright Scholar, is Professor of Distance Education and Director, Staff Training and Research Institute of Distance Education, and Head, Inter-University Consortium, Indira Gandhi National Open University, New Delhi, India. Email: pandasantosh@hotmail.com.

Andrew Ravenscroft is Deputy Director and Principal Research Fellow at the Learning Technology Research Institute Learning Centre, London Metropolitan University, London, UK. Email: a.ravenscroft@londonmet.ac.uk.

Thomas C. Reeves is Professor of Information and Communications Technology, Department of Instructional Technology, The University of Georgia, Athens, GA, USA. Email: treeves@uga.edu.

Ramesh C. Sharma is Deputy Director, Regional Services Division, Indira Gandhi National Open University, New Delhi, India. Email: rc_sharma@yahoo.com.

Rod Sims is Principal Consultant with Knowledgecraft, NSW, Australia and Adjunct Professor with Capella University, Minneapolis, MN, USA. Email: rodsims@knowledgecraft.com.au.

Series editor's foreword

Interaction between students and their tutor, and between students, is at the core of learning. It has rightly been of paramount importance to those designing, producing and presenting self-instructional materials. Indeed, the success of open and distance learning world-wide has been due in no small measure to the promotion of interaction by scholars like Derek Rowntree, Ernst Rothkopt and Börje Holmberg. Rowntree's concept of a *Tutorial and Print* and *Reflective Action Guide* provided authors with a framework within which to simulate interactivity with teaching materials in various media. Rothkopt's concept of *Mathemagenic Devices*, 'behaviours that give birth of learning', marked a significant contribution to empirical research in this field. Holmberg's concept of *Guided Didactic Conversation* was one of the first to provide a theoretical framework for the process of interaction. The impact of these scholars can still be seen in materials produced today.

Thirty-five years on, the impact of Information and Communications Technology has revolutionised open and distance learning and its adoption by conventional institutions. Access 'anywhere and at any time' to a world of online resources, and synchronous and asynchronous communication has led to a spectacular growth in flexible and e-learning – and in the number of colleagues teaching online. Gilly Salmon's contribution in terms of *eModerating* and *e-Tivities* has been significant. However, if this growth is to be sustained it is vital that quality teaching materials are assembled and a quality learning experience provided. To do so requires further exploration of the theoretical and pedagogical design of teaching materials, and the influence of learners' socio-cultural perspective as well as the professional and continuing development provided to teachers and trainers. This edited collection of chapters by Charles Juwah entitled *Interactions in Online Education: Implications for Theory and Practice* does just that. It brings together respected academics from Australia, Canada, Europe, India and the United States, to share their insights and experience, current thinking and recommendations for good practice.

Whilst the contribution this book makes to the field is significant it is the start of a new phase of development – not the end. The questions that contributors pose, and which are summarised at the end, offer a challenging agenda for future work. I am sure this book will provide advice and assistance that will enable you to recognise the challenge we face and how we can further improve the quality of the experience we provide for our learners. I recommend it to you.

Fred Lockwood
Yelvertoft
January 2006

Acknowledgements

I would like to thank all the co-authors without whose contributions this publication would not have been possible. Also I wish to offer my gratitude to family, friends, and colleagues for their inspiration, encouragement and support.

I gratefully acknowledge the various institutions for their support and kindness in permitting us to reproduce in this book some of their materials in whole or part thereof. In particular, I would like to thank The Robert Gordon University, Aberdeen, UK for their entire support in producing this book; UHI Millennium Institute, Inverness, UK; London Metropolitan University, UK; Faculty of Education, University of Wollongong, Australia; Edith Cowan University, Perth, Australia; Central Queensland University, Australia; University of Western Sydney, Australia; Knowledgecraft, Australia; Athabasca University, Canada; Nanyang Technological University, Singapore; Staff Training and Research Institute of Distance Education (STRIDE), Indira Gandhi National Open University (IGNOU), India; University of Twente, Netherlands; North American Fiction and Film, USA; BlackBoard Incorporated, USA; Interloc Open software system, USA; Turkish Online Journal of Distance Education (TOJDE) and Information and Age Publishing Incorporated, USA. Many thanks to Qiong Jia for her assistance with indexing the materials in the book, and to Dr Iain Burt and Dawei Wang for the design, construction and management of the book project website.

Charles Juwah

Introduction

Charles Juwah

The rapid evolution of information and communications technologies (ICT) and the Internet has led to an explosion of online education and training (i.e. web-based education and e-learning). Interactivity and interactions have been identified by research as the key success factors underpinning the pedagogy of online education (e-learning). Interactivity and interactions are complex, multifaceted phenomena consisting of psychological, social, technical (physical), linguistic and cultural dimensions that underpin instruction and learning processes in a diverse range of contexts and situations. The diverse range of interactions, which can be learner and learner; learner and tutor; learner and content; learner and interface; and learner and designer, help to inform, to consolidate and to enhance meaning making, as well as deepen students' understanding and mastery of the subject matter. In addition, interactions help contextualise and authenticate learning and to promote reflection. Equally, research shows that the attrition (wastage) rate for online education is significantly high, ranging between 20–43 per cent (Henke and Russum, 2000; Terry, 2003). A major reason adduced for the high attrition and drop-out rates is isolationism due to lack of interactions. The importance of interactivity in online education has created a huge global interest in the topic amongst educators, instructional designers, developers of e-learning environments and researchers.

As described in Chapter 1, the concept of interactivity is ubiquitous but surprisingly elusive, since it confounds cognitive, social and behavioural components. However, if the concept of interaction is approached by distinguishing the three stages in the learning cycle – conceptualisation, construction and dialogue – the concept becomes much clearer in terms of levels of: activity, action and operation.

Put simply, interactivity in online education describes the form, function and impact of interactions in teaching and learning. Whereas interaction may be defined as a dialogue or discourse or an event between two or more participants and objects that occurs synchronously and/or asynchronously mediated by response or feedback and interfaced by technology, educational interactions can be categorised mainly as learner to learner, learner to tutor and learner to content. Each of these interactions embodies a range of secondary interactions and is associated with different temporal and space-based constraints on participants (Anderson, 2003; Wagner, 1994). Hedberg and Sims (2001) proposed that the environment experienced by the learner is also largely determined by the designer and therefore the interaction between designer and learner must also be taken into consideration when planning learning. All of these interactions contribute in providing an enhanced learning environment through the interplay between multiple agents and situations which mediate opportunities for active and participative learning. Thus, educational interactions (see Chapter 2) form a set of changing encounters which provide the means by which online facilitators develop relationships with other key stakeholders.

Technological developments, sound pedagogical underpinnings and the effective use of a diverse range of media now make it possible for designers of learning to create sophisticated modes of interactions which engage, motivate, stimulate and 'delight' the learner. These provide the socio-cultural and educational relevance and added value to learning (see Chapter 4).

For online education (e-learning) to be meaningful and purposeful, it must integrate the cognitive, affective and systemic, and be underpinned by relevant interactions. As interactions provide the link between pre-existing knowledge, the form of new information and the way in which the information is analysed and incorporated into the existing schema for making new meaning, the quality of interactions should be strongly related to the authenticity of the tasks or activities that learners are engaged in, to enable them to develop the desired knowledge, skills, and attitudes that will be appropriated in new learning contexts and situations (see Chapter 5). Interactions also impact on the affective domain of learning and achievement of particular learning outcomes. To ensure that educational interactions contribute towards achieving intended learning outcomes, it is important that the design, planning and management of the learning situation is adequately systematised. There is the need to provide the appropriate pedagogy, a robust learning environment with the necessary learning objects, materials and media adequately contextualised to effectively impact on the quality of learning (see Chapter 7).

This book critically examines as well as contributes to the debate on the important phenomenon of interactions in online education from the theoretical, pedagogical, design, educational and socio-cultural perspectives. Also, it provides insights into relevant frameworks, current trends and practices, and drawing from evidence-based learning, suggests strategies and principles that inform professional knowledge and practice. The book consists of 13 chapters arranged in four sections: Theoretical and Pedagogical Perspectives; Design and Learning Environment; Practice; and Professional Development. Each section focuses on a unique perspective. However, the sections are arranged in such a way to provide a logical sequence in structure and content.

Chapter 1 examines the concept of interactivity in online education within the contex of the three stages in the learning cycle – conceptualisation, construction and dialogue. For each stage of the cycle, the chapter considers the essential dynamic of interaction between learners, representations, tutors and peers – all mediated through online tools. As the concept emerges more clearly from this analysis so the role of the social dimension becomes increasingly emphasised. The chapter also highlights the important fact that online learning environments must integrate the cognitive, affective and systemic.

Chapter 2 uses the concept of encounter theory in proposing that learners progress through a series of encounters between other 'players' in the collaborative environment. The chapter identifies the key elements of encounter theory, the different encounters involved within different contexts of human–computer interaction and the implications for the design of online learning environments.

In Chapter 3, the author contends that whilst published taxonomies for learning interactions give valuable insights into the nature and range of potential interactions that may be used to facilitate e-learning, existing taxonomies neither depict the relationship between, nor provide practical guidelines for planning and managing a comprehensive set of interactions necessary to achieve a specified set of objectives. This chapter posits a three-level framework for classifying e-learning interactions. It illustrates how the framework may be used to (a) design e-learning interactions and alternative e-learning environments, (b) analyse planned interactions to optimise learning and reduce the need for costly revisions, and (c) organise research on interactivity and e-learning to help interpret findings and guide future studies.

In Chapter 4, the authors contend that designing engaging and meaningful interactions within online learning contexts remains a significant challenge for e-learning. This chapter describes the use of digital gaming approaches as part of a learning landscape to support the development of social or conceptual processes that are involved in learning. Drawing on computational and empirical studies on a prototype socio-cognitive tool called InterLoc, the authors describe how the 'dialogue game' approach to e-learning mediates, structures and scaffolds the development of dialogical and reasoning skills that lead to improved conceptual understanding and collaborative knowledge refinement.

Chapter 5 presents evidence that the critical dimensions of authentic activities are not constrained to learning in face-to-face classrooms, but can be implemented in ways that maximise learning in online contexts. The chapter provides a description of the underlying theory, research and development initiatives for this design model, including specific case studies from Australia, North America and Europe. The theory, research and practice examples cited are integrated into a model for authentic activities in online courses. The chapter concludes with guidelines for the design of complex authentic activities for online learning and a suggestion for a design research agenda to further research and development in this area.

Chapter 6 explores the use of generic learning designs, driven by pedagogically sound learner interactions within the context of reusability and learning object technologies. The chapter highlights the potential that generic learning object technologies have in impacting on the quality of learning.

Chapter 7 describes the use of simulation in e-learning based on Min's design theory (the PI theory) for learning environments and how interactions and feedback in simulations have contributed in enhancing students' higher order learning. The chapter concludes with envisioning how simulations can be used to make learning more operationally dynamic, engaging and motivating for the learner.

Chapter 8 highlights interaction both as a critical component of the educational process and as a critical variable in achievement, persistence, enjoyment and approach to learning in formal educational contexts. It goes on to define the many types of educational interactions, how each interaction is associated with different temporal and space-based constraints on participants and their different impacts on learning. This chapter explores the types of existing and emerging educational interactions involving learners and focuses on those enhanced by the emergence of the Educational Semantic Web.

Chapter 9 discusses from a pedagogical perspective the importance of synchronous and asynchronous discussions as a key interaction in online learning. Also, the chapter explores the concept of 'talk' in learning, as well as methods, techniques and competencies for facilitating synchronous and asynchronous discussions in online learning. The chapter provides hints and techniques for creating interactions in online courses and for managing instructor time.

In Chapter 10, the author discusses the various and diverse forms of interactions in online peer learning. Drawing on ethnographic research, the author critically explores the practice and pedagogical importance of interactions in enhancing quality peer learning. The chapter highlights the role of technology in promoting peer learning through permitting interactions via shared spaces (data and resource sharing).

Chapter 11 focuses on the use of videoconferencing as the mode of delivery in the dispersed network environment of the University of the Highlands and Islands Project. The chapter highlights the importance of the UHI's pedagogic model of blended learning – a mix of online provision (including videoconferencing), face-to-face and traditional distance learning methods. The chapter describes the complexity of different settings, the challenges to overcome isolation of students and examples of cases on how to promote active student engagement in learning by videoconferencing, including the use of peripheral tools such as document cameras or fax machines.

Chapter 12 examines the professional development models from the works of Schon and Moon, and discusses an online constructivist professional development framework comprising context (situated learning, culture and community of practice), collaboration (in online learning community), and knowledge construction and negotiation of meaning (i.e. change in cognitive structure, and professional identity and practice). Drawing on current research and practice, the authors propose a professional development strategy for online facilitators to help inform as well as enhance effective interactions and engagement in online learning.

In Chapter 13, the penultimate chapter, the authors discuss the important issue of competencies required for the effective facilitation of interactions and engagement of learners in an online environment. The chapter highlights how enabling technologies foster the development of appropriate competencies for online teaching. Lastly, the authors compare a range of identified competencies to those developed by the International Board of Standards for Training, Performance and Instruction (IBSTPI).

Finally, the concluding chapter pulls together the key issues raised in the various chapters. It highlights major aspects of interactions in online education which need to be further investigated by research.

References

Anderson, T. (2003) 'Getting the mix right again: an updated and theoretical rationale for interaction', *The International Review of Research in Open and Distance Learning*, Vol. 4, No. 2. Online. Avaiable at: http://www.irrodl.org/index.php/irrodl/article/view/149/230 (Accessed 20 October 2004).

Hedberg, J.G. and Sims, R. (2001) 'Speculations on design team interaction', *Journal of Interactive LEarning, Research*, 12(2/3): 189–214.

Henke, H. and Russum, J. (2000) 'Factors influencing attrition rates in a corporate distance education', *The Journal*, November issue, Vol. 14, 11. Online. Available at: http://www.usdla.org/html/journal/NOV00_Issue/story03.htm.

Terry, N. (2003) 'Assessing enrollment and attrition rates for the online MBA', *The Journal*, February issue. Online. Available at: http://www.thejournal.com/articles/15251_1.

Wagner, E.D. (1994) 'In support of a functional definition of interaction', *American Journal of Distance Education*, 8(2): 6–26.

Part I
Theoretical and pedagogical perspectives

This first section of the book explores the ubiquitous but important phenomenon of interactivity and interactions in online education. It attempts to provide a definition for interactivity and interactions and types of interactions from a variety of perspectives. Also, the section provides relevant information on the theoretical principles underpinning interactions including new frameworks for conceptualising, designing and evaluating learning interaction and communication. These frameworks are: the model of encounter theory which details elements and encounters that learners progress through to engage and interact with other 'players' in the collaborative environment; and a three-level framework for classifying e-learning interactions. The framework for classifying e-learning may be used to (a) design e-learning interactions and alternative e-learning environments, (b) analyse planned interactions to optimise learning and reduce the need for costly revisions, and (c) organise research on interactivity and e-learning to help interpret findings and guide future studies. In addition, this section highlights the focus by practitioners towards more behavioural and motivational approaches that are emerging in this field, and considers how these relate to more socio-cognitive and socio-cultural perspectives on learning and interactions.

Chapter 1

Theoretical perspectives on interactivity in e-learning

Terry Mayes

> The concept of interactivity has become so firmly entrenched within the discourse of educational computing that it is a truism to say that instructional software is interactive and that interactivity promotes learning, and a kind of heresy to dispute it.
>
> (Rose, 1999, p. 44)

Introduction

The term *interactivity* is used so loosely that, in the field of e-learning, it has become almost synonymous with the notion of learning itself. Nevertheless, there is a widely-shared feeling that if only we could bring the concept into sharper focus we would gain real insight into the nature of learning in general, and of e-learning in particular. Usually, when asked to define the term, colleagues refer to the implication that there are two agents involved in some action, and there is an influence of both on the outcome. However, we also frequently refer to the idea that learners interact with learning materials, so we cannot restrict the concept by defining an agent as necessarily an active participant: one of the agents may be passive information which cannot itself do anything except make itself accessible (note how rapidly one falls into a kind of teleological trap here). In this chapter I will approach the concept by examining the way it is employed generally in e-learning contexts, by discussing its explanatory function at three levels: interaction with *concepts*, *tasks*, and *people*. These three levels correspond to the three stages of learning described in the framework for understanding courseware set out by Mayes and Fowler (1999).

A framework for interactive learning

It is quite uncontroversial to describe conceptual learning as the cyclical development and gradual deepening of understanding (Dewey, 1938; Kolb, 1984). The notion of cyclical development involves the continual testing of a current conceptualisation for adequacy of understanding, which requires testing against criteria of application. In their attempt to provide a theoretical account of learning on which to base an understanding of where technology might add real value, Mayes and Fowler described a cycling through three stages:

- *Conceptualisation* (interacting with concepts)
  – the contact the learner has with *other people's conceptualisations*. This involves an interaction between the learner's pre-existing framework of understanding and a new exposition. This stage is supported by *primary* courseware.
- *Construction* (interacting with tasks)
  – the application and testing of new conceptualisations in the performance of meaningful tasks. This stage involves the building of the learner's own framework of understanding. The task performance is mediated by *secondary* courseware.
- *Dialogue* (interacting with people)
  – the creation and testing of new conceptualisations during conversation with both tutors and fellow learners, and the reflection on these. Dialogue is facilitated through *tertiary* courseware.

Interactivity with concepts

First, then, we interact with information, or the representations of subject matter, or, in educational computing shorthand, with 'content'. Conceptualisation refers to the learner's current state of understanding about some subject matter. The current stage of development of the learner's understanding (rather than the attributes of the information) will determine the amount of meaning extracted from the information that the learner is presented with, or accesses. A simple example makes this point clear, and encourages us to think even of this stage as the outcome of a genuine interaction.

A large number of experiments on human learning have demonstrated what seems like an obvious point: we remember only what is meaningful to us (Baddeley, 1996). Yet this seems to beg the important question: how does some to-be-learned material become meaningful? Take the case of a football fan. Hearing football results does not seem like an act of learning: the information slots effortlessly into place, and when the fan is asked later about a particular result he or she will experience no difficulty in recalling it. The information is meaningful because of what is already known: a framework of understanding is already in place. A particular result will convey a great deal of meaning to a fan, and almost none to a football-hater or an American, because of the knowledge (involving a complex network of facts, expectations and opinions) that it activates. In fact, listening to the football results does not seem like the deliberate, effortful kind of learning that we associate with education because in this case most of the learning has already occurred. It has occurred in building the knowledge structures about football that allow meaning to be extracted from the information; the real learning involved here has probably taken place over hundreds of encounters with other people, and in numerous events experienced personally, as well as in the reading of sports pages in newspapers. It is evident in this example that the important variable here is not how the football results are presented to the fan (one can imagine some pointless experiments comparing multimedia presentation of the results with reading text) but how much, and what kind of, football knowledge the fan already has. We only have to observe the problems we have in remembering a telephone number for long enough to be able to dial it, to realise that where the symbols carry no meaning for us, as in a digit-string telephone number, then we have to resort to trying to maintain the information in working memory through conscious attention. We all have a fairly standard limit on how well we can do this: the famous 'magic number seven plus or minus two' (Miller, 1956, p. 81–97). However, another famous study (Chase and Ericsson, 1982) revealed that this limit can be completely overcome by activating existing knowledge to make the numbers meaningful. Many other observations of apparently prodigious memory feats have been made (see Neisser, 1982); all turn out to depend on making the to-be-recalled information meaningful by employing pre-existing knowledge.

In the theoretical formulation of human learning in cognitive psychology, the notion is one of *levels of processing*. Craik and Lockhart (1975) argued for the understanding of human memory as a by-product of perceptual analysis and that the durability of memory would be a positive function of the depth to which the stimulus has been analysed. Normally only the results of deeper analyses can be regarded as learning, the by-products of preliminary or 'surface' analysis are discarded. What is needed later is meaning, and the extraction of meaning involves the deeper levels of processing. Craik and Lockhart viewed processing levels as a continuum of analysis. At one extreme, sensory analysis in the visual or auditory analysis systems will give rise to memory traces that are transient and easily disrupted. At the other end of the continuum, the process of semantic analysis will lead to deep learning and permanent memory.

So the match, or *interaction*, between pre-existing knowledge, and the information offered in the learning materials, is all-important. The medium of expression of that information is likely to be of only marginal importance for learning. It is not the way in which the information is received that represents the crucial interaction, but the way in which it is interpreted by existing knowledge structures. It was essentially this point that underpinned Clark's (1983) argument that there were no differences in learning benefits due to employing a specific medium for instruction. Even the opposite position adopted during that famous 'media debate' (Kozma, 1991; Koumi, 1994) accepted that the different benefits for learning between media, if they exist, will be due to differences in the way in which information can be located and operated on, rather than to differences in the way the information is represented in the medium. The crucial interaction here is between the form of the new information and the way in which the knowledge that will make sense of it is internally structured. In a sense, the learner *acts* on the new information by activating an already established schema or knowledge structure. To the extent that the form of representation of the new information can suggest a particular activation, then the possibility exists that a primary exposition – an effective lecture, a powerful notation, an animated illustration – will be immediately effective. Nevertheless, in the learning cycle, the interaction between the learner's prior understanding and the primary exposition produces only an initial interpretation. Subsequent work must be done to build the new concept into the existing framework.

At first it seems self-evident that multimedia will support more effective learning, but a closer consideration of the arguments and evidence begins to raise some doubts. The combination of media in state-of-the-art courseware carries with it a *vividness* that cannot be questioned. However, Taylor and Thomson (1982) attempted to pin this down in a comprehensive meta-review of work on the 'vividness' effect. The research failed to show that concrete descriptions had any greater impact than dull ones; that pictorially illustrated information was more effective than that which was not illustrated; or that videotaped information had more impact than oral or written. The point, of course, is that vividness can never be simply a function of the presentation. The impact will always depend on what the user brings to the interaction. The attempt to use computers to somehow give the learning experience more impact by providing a vivid sensory experience is unlikely to succeed. Information that is poured into the learner's head through the 'Nurnberg Funnel' (Carroll, 1990) is only likely to be better learned as a consequence of being presented through multimedia if it is thereby better understood. For that to happen the initial interpretation must be integrated into the underlying knowledge structure so that subsequent interactions with new information will then involve the new concept. In the learning cycle that happens through the stage we labelled construction: the learner performs a task which requires the concept to be used in some way.

The essential requirement for the kind of interaction that builds new understanding is that the learner should be given feedback on his or her use of the concept. Laurillard (1993) regards simply exploring hypermedia as a non-interactive task because there is no intrinsic feedback on the user's actions. The student is not made aware of making an inappropriate link. Laurillard makes the case for multimedia as an aid to understanding by suggesting that it is the associative link between image and argument that is crucial. Where a learner is helped by visualisation to *conceptualise*, by comparing the visual nature of exemplars and non-exemplars, for example, or where a dynamic process, like the operation of the internal combustion engine, is explicated through movement, then multimedia will be performing a valuable role. It will allow a concrete representation of the teacher's conception to be better interpreted by the learner's own underlying knowledge, and a tentative modification of the learner's understanding to be formed for testing through subsequent use.

The effectiveness of what we have called primary courseware depends on the initial interaction: the matching of the new information to the existing knowledge. Adjustment of the level of description of this learning material to match the current needs of the individual learner is one of the primary goals of tutoring. This can be achieved through offering the learner a range of descriptions and allowing choice, as in hypertext/hypermedia, or through discussion, where tutors can adjust their descriptions according to the conceptualisations revealed by the learner. Primary courseware, were it developed on a sufficiently comprehensive scale to cover all possible levels, might achieve the flexibility to allow this to occur through the learner's initial interaction. However, this is to imagine a scale of courseware development that we are unlikely to experience, without a major change in the way educational institutions work. Nevertheless, there will be important differences between disciplines here. Some tutorial software, of the kind requiring problem solving and self-testing, will permit intrinsic feedback to be achievable from the underlying model of the subject matter.

So far we have considered the interaction that occurs at the level of internally-derived meaning. Yet primary courseware can be classified along a dimension ranging from linear presentations at one end to virtual worlds at the other. Even in primary courseware the learner can engage in a kind of dialogue with the expository material. Some simulations will involve genuine interaction, where 'what if' questions can be answered. The answers to the learners' questions are provided through the (re)action of the simulation software. Here we begin to encounter the idea of the computer as a virtual laboratory.

This is a dimension of *overt* interactivity, where the courseware may require the learner to make active choices. However, probably the most important single function of the primary exposition is to *orient* the learner towards the subject matter. This, too, can be regarded as a kind of interaction. It gives the learner a map of what is to be learned and understood; it sets out the conceptual parameters. It denotes the boundaries of the topic to be studied, and it should also make clear its relevance, both to a course of study, and to the wider body of knowledge to which it relates.

Orientation should also influence *affective* variables; the excitement associated with learning is largely set at this early stage in the conceptualisation cycle. Since this is the main function of the orientation stage, overtly interactive technology is probably of little importance. A live lecture can be highly effective for orientation. Similarly, the traditional media of print, film and video achieve the goal of providing an engaging and compelling primary exposition of the subject matter without the learner making any apparent overt choices or responses at all. The power of narrative (Plowman *et al.*, 1999) may be regarded as working at the level of asking continuous 'what if' questions: 'what is going to happen next?'. It is clear that the importance of engagement in the initial act of comprehension is a live research issue.

Interactivity in learning tasks

It can be argued that constructivist pedagogy has been influenced by all three of the major traditions in learning theory. In its emphasis on learning-by-doing, and the importance of feedback, it leans partly towards the *associationist/behaviourist* tradition, which underpinned the instructional systems design (ISD) approach. In placing the creation of meaning at the centre of the approach it follows the mainstream approach of cognitive psychology, and in its emphasis on authentic tasks it takes much from the influence of the *situative* tradition (Lave and Wenger, 1991). A useful distinction is made by Duffy and Cunningham (1996) between cognitive constructivism, deriving from the Piagetian tradition (Piaget, 1970), and socio-cultural constructivism, deriving from the Vygotskian approach (Vygotsky, 1962).

Piaget's constructivist theory of knowledge was based on the assumption that learners do not copy or absorb ideas from the external world, but must construct their concepts through active and personal experimentation and observation. This led Piaget to oppose the direct teaching of disciplinary content – although he was arguing against the small-components-first approach of ISD, rather than the kind of meaningful learning advocated by Bruner (1960). In this view, which emphasises general conceptual understanding and thinking ability, a rejection of didactic teaching is based on evidence that it simply does not produce generic understanding. Constructivism can be seen to have developed as a reaction to the persistence in practice of a transmission-based didactic mode of teaching, for which there is no real theoretical base, but a strong folk tradition that compelling explanations will lead to better learning. This reiterates the point for e-learning: the presentation of subject matter using multimedia is based on a discredited idea – that more vivid and naturalistic representations of knowledge would lead to better learning. This misconception was responsible for much of the disillusionment that resulted from computer-based learning in the 1980s and 1990s (Mayes, 1995).

In the constructivist view, then, the learner actively constructs knowledge, achieving deeper understanding through the performance of learning activities. Steeples *et al.* (2002) make a helpful distinction between tasks, which are designed and set by tutors, and activities, which are performed by the learners. Since it is crucial that the learners regulate their own learning we see an increasing focus on the design of student-centred methods and environments, on problem-based, enquiry-oriented pedagogies, making frequent use of projects, and placing emphasis on reflection and feedback. The design principles for constructivist learning activities emphasise ownership of the task, coaching and modelling of thinking skills, scaffolding, guided discovery, and opportunity for reflection. The essential characteristic of all these components is feedback for the individual learner, and that is why the tasks are interactive. Learners carry out the tasks set and their performance renders visible to the agent providing feedback (this need not be a person) some aspect of the learners' state of understanding.

In her influential book, Laurillard (1993) re-emphasised the importance of feedback in learning. In Laurillard's analysis feedback has returned to centre stage through the notion of a learning dialogue. A dialogue need not be restricted to a verbal exchange; the HCI (human-computer interaction) use of the term refers to the entire pattern of user-system interaction. In this wider sense it involves the process of seeking answers and testing ideas, not just in a conversation, but also by interacting in tasks. Tasks will vary on many dimensions. The task might define a discrete event like solving an equation, or involve a long-term project which would comprise many sub-tasks. Usually a complete learning task will involve many cycles through the stages, each new conceptualisation being tested for adequacy and involving dialogue. In the design of the tasks there is a fundamental tension between what Newell (1980) called *weak* methods, a focus on generic skills, and *strong* methods, domain-specific.

At a very general level, Sternberg (1984) characterised construction as:

- Selective encoding – picking out relevant information for further encoding.
- Selective combination – putting information together in a way which has meaning for the learner.
- Selective comparison – noting relationships between new information and old.

The stage of selecting information, such as in the choosing of appropriate examples, is hugely aided by the search and retrieval tools now available through the World Wide Web. Similarly, linking and classifying are supported by the functionality in editing and authoring software in a way that traditional media cannot remotely match. Some structuring software – *mindtools* – has been explicitly designed to force users to think about the subject matter at a deeper conceptual level than would otherwise have been the case, even when the learner is writing a conventional essay or lab report (Jonassen, 2000b).

An important strand of new thinking about pedagogy has emerged over the last decade through the influence of *activity theory*. Researchers are beginning to identify how activity theory can inform the design of learning tasks and environments (Jonassen, 2000a). Activity theory focuses not on the individual learner, but on the *activity system*, a larger and more social unit of analysis. An activity system consists of a group, of any size, pursuing a specific goal in a purposeful way. A well-known example (Cole and Engestrom, 1993) is of doctors practising preventive medicine in a health-maintenance organisation. Students on a networked learning course collaborating on a project would represent an activity system. Even seemingly isolated activities are usually embedded in a larger system, as in Peal and Wilson's (2001) example of collaborating researchers who must negotiate differing approaches, and coordinate their actions with colleagues.

These activity systems can be analysed into the elements devised by Engestrom (1993). The fundamental connection is between the individual *participant* and the activity system's *purpose*; this relationship is not direct, but is mediated by *tools*. Participants are usually part of communities, a relationship mediated by *rules* for acceptable interactions. Activity systems are in constant development, always changing through the actions of new participants, purposes, and tools. Tools make activity possible in the first place. Tools can be both physical (networks, books, software) and cognitive (concepts, language, memory). Tools both enable and constrain activity through their *affordances*. To illustrate the elements in terms of teaching, pedagogical frameworks are tools that afford educators a way of approaching instructional design, thereby shaping associated ways of thinking (and not thinking) about learning. An *activity*, then, is when tools are used for a purpose within the activity system. So employing a pedagogical design tool to create an e-learning course would constitute an action within the teaching and learning activity system. Actions can be further decomposed into automatic *operations*. In the case of teaching, for example, there are moves performed through pre-planned curriculum procedures (actions) and moves carried out in response to students (operations). However, these three levels (activity, action, operation) are constantly subject to change, as the activity system develops into a community of practice. Activity theory can inform all the key aspects of e-learning design: the learning outcomes, the learning activities, and the assessments.

The groundwork for activity theory was laid by Vygotsky, the Soviet psychologist who developed the concept of the *zone of proximal development* (ZPD) in 1934; the term has become part of mainstream thinking in pedagogy since the translation of his *Mind in Society* in 1978. Vygotsky defined the ZPD as the distance between a learner's current conceptual development, as measured by independent problem solving, and that learner's potential capability, as measured by what can be accomplished 'under ... guidance or in collaboration with more capable peers' (Vygotsky, 1978, p. 86). With personal support, and with practice, novices gradually increase their relative responsibility until they are coping by themselves (Cole, 1985). Skills, rules and knowledge are internalised, creating the cognitive tools used in self-directed learning. Vygotsky's concept influenced Lave and Wenger (1991) whose socio-anthropological account of learning communities can be thought of as a situative description of the ZPD.

The constructivist theme is reflected in the way in which the ZPD idea has directly influenced the design of learning environments. Peal and Wilson (2001) summarise the design of web-based learning environments as ZPDs by employing the following features:

- Learning activities that are part of real or simulated activity systems, with close attention to the tools and interactions characteristic of actual situations.
- Structured interaction among participants.
- Guidance by an expert.
- The locus of control passes to the increasingly competent learners.

The *ZPD* is exploited through the process of *scaffolding*. The learning and teaching activities will be designed to provide scaffolding –with the tutor having the main responsibility for providing the guidance, but the wider learning group itself also playing a role. To be effective scaffolders, tutors must be sufficiently expert in their domain to judge individual learning needs, and sufficiently skilled as teachers to adjust dynamically, to switch continuously between the novice's and expert's perspectives. In the ZPD, learning is distributed: thought and intelligence being 'stretched across' the larger structures of activity (Pea, 1993; Lave and Wenger, 1991; Salomon and Perkins, 1998). Tutors will themselves need guidance in the art of scaffolding as they learn to use and monitor e-mail, discussion fora, and synchronous communication tools, to engage students supportively. An effective e-learning environment will also include a variety of performance supports and other resources to help learners pick up community practices.

Learning and teaching can be viewed at each level of an activity system – activity, action, or operation. The lower the level, the weaker the connection to a specific activity system and the more transferable the skill, since activities are unique to particular systems while operations can be generalised. E-learning itself can be seen as both a tool and as a simulated activity system within which participants learn to perform the actions and operations. Purposive, coordinated learning can be organised and led by a tutor, automated by a computer-based tutorial, or created by the learners themselves, depending on the design of the learning tasks.

To some extent, to talk abstractly of learning activity is to avoid a crucial question. What kind of task is suitable for what kind of learning? Tasks will vary very widely with the nature of the subject matter. Acquiring expertise in mathematics, literature, botany, counselling, medicine, law etc. will all require quite different kinds of tasks to be undertaken. Nevertheless, all will involve attempting to solve problems, constructing answers and reflecting on feedback. As these principles have become widely accepted, so we have seen a gradual shift in our general understanding of what the overall goal of educational technology should be. This is simply stated: it is to get the learner to act and to think.

Interactivity in dialogue

Discussion is fundamental to education. It is, of course, possible to learn without discussion, but the need to support deep learning through tutorial and peer-group dialogue is paramount. Reflective thinking has also been regarded as necessary for learning, at least since the work of John Dewey (1916).

Discussion often involves a reconceptualisation cycle itself. During discussion a learner will come into contact with other people's conceptualisations, will try to apply his or her current understanding by constructing a new argument, and will elaborate current understanding by reflection.

Learning is always situated in a social context. The nature of that context will determine what approach to learning is adopted by the individual. The most important aspects in education will usually be the nature of the assessment, and the attitudes towards learning of peers. The organisational setting will set the parameters of the learning task, and the most direct expression of this will be the 'contract' between students and teachers which will set the expectations and norms. Much of what is referred to as student motivation is determined by these factors. The effectiveness of learning technology will, like all other variables in the educational setting, be determined largely by these wider factors, rather than by the intrinsic features of the technology or the content.

Depending on this overall social context, we will often find that individuals will learn more effectively through cooperative group activity. Most theorising about cooperative learning has beFen in the context of the principles of cognitive development. Piaget emphasised the powerful influence of conflicts with peers over issues of understanding. Such conflicts lead children to construct deeper understanding. In contrast, the Vygotskian tradition has emphasised the importance of communication during instruction from a person(s) more expert than the learner. The process of group communication is eventually internalised by the individual learner in a restructuring of his or her own concepts. This has led to the question of how to scaffold the learning process to shape the internalisation in an optimal way. Wood (1989) has analysed some of the characteristics of effective tutoring in this light. Peer tutors are less effective at withdrawing assistance as the learner develops competence, or at ensuring that the learner understands the connection between an activity in immediate focus and the overall goal of the collaboration. Nevertheless, the importance of sharing a learning experience with peers who also share a perception of the overall task context cannot be overestimated.

Most online learning environments now involve the use of discussion tools. Typically these are used in an integrated way with the learning tasks themselves, so it becomes rather contrived to try to separate the performance of the explicit learning tasks from the discussion which surrounds them. Indeed, Salmon's (2002) five-stage model of teaching and learning online assumes that learning tasks will themselves all involve discussion. Salmon's model describes the stages of progressing towards successful online learning both for participants (learners) and e-moderators. It describes how to motivate online participants, to build learning through online tasks (e-tivities), and to pace e-learners through stages of training and development. Stage 1 involves essential prerequisite individual access and the induction of participants into online learning. Stage 2 involves individuals establishing their online identities, and locating others with whom to interact. At stage 3 participants exchange information and start to support other participants' goals. Course-related discussions develop at stage 4 and the interactions become more collaborative. Finally, real reflection and personal development will occur in the achievement of goals at stage 5. This model summarises what is now widely accepted as good practice in engaging learners in online discussion. It assumes a commitment to constructivist tasks and to as much dialogue as the students are willing to engage with, and the tutors are able to support. It provides guidelines for e-moderating that take account of some of the realities of tutoring in UK HE/ FE. Other assumptions are that online activity will include individual participants posting a contribution, an interactive or participative element – such as responding to the postings of others, and the provision of summary, feedback or critique from an e-moderator.

It is perhaps helpful to think of learning dialogues as attempts to deal with three fundamental questions, which flow from the three fundamental requirements for learning represented in the learning cycle. These are:

- *Have I understood?* (Feedback about meaning)
- *What should I do next?* (Guidance on action)
- *How do I use my new knowledge?* (Dialogue about the context of application)

A fundamental challenge for learning technology is to allow a learner to receive answers to these questions (and the elaborations which will facilitate transformational learning) in situations where individual discussion with human tutors is simply not possible, at least on the scale and in the depth required. The fact is that we cannot yet construct dialogue-providing computer tutors for subject-matter where discussion and reflection are important components. This is because we cannot build programs which can sufficiently-well understand the conceptual difficulties a learner is currently experiencing and which can offer direct help. So how else can advanced learning technology provide learners with an experience of dialogue? There are at least two strong candidates.

One possibility is to design supportive environments for peer tutoring/peer learning, especially in a way that will capitalise on the global availability of peers across the Internet in order to locate suitable one-to-one dialogues (see Chapter 10). The second is to take real discussion between learners and tutors as the raw material from which a new kind of courseware – tertiary courseware – can be built. This involves recording real dialogues of previous learners in equivalent situations and making these accessible at just the right moment in the conceptualisation cycle for new learners. This would imply that there is pedagogical benefit in being able to experience other people's learning dialogues, provided that an appropriate dialogue can be matched to the learner's immediate need. The idea of what we have termed *vicarious* learning is attractive because it offers a way in which computers might be able to provide a partial experience of dialogue in educational situations where it is simply not possible for teachers to engage in one-to-one conversations with students (Mayes *et al.*, 2002). The notion of evolving courseware out of real teaching and learning experiences also conveys a satisfying learner-centred approach. Essentially, the learner is told: 'here are some problems previously experienced by other learners, see if you can find one that is similar to your own difficulty'. There are many research issues here, not least is the issue of what factors will encourage a learner to identify closely enough with the experiences of another learner in order to benefit directly from them. The research questions extend all the way from database design to social identity.

The kind of interaction that occurs between people is the most important of the varieties of interactivity considered in this chapter. The significant influence of Lave and Wenger's social anthropological view of the *situativity* of learning (Lave and Wenger, 1991) was to bring into focus a wider social context for understanding how interactions between people were influenced and shaped in learning environments. For Wenger (1998) the identity of a learner is shaped by his or her relationship with a wider community of practice. Lave and Wenger's perspective, however, emphasises the stable and long-term nature of communities. Perhaps this restricts the potential usefulness of the idea for the design of learning environments, where short-term and more fragile groups may nevertheless exert a powerful influence on the motivation to learn. Indeed, the social psychological literature on social identity (Turner, 1991) seems to demonstrate that temporary but real social identities can be created through group membership. Fowler and Mayes (2000) argued that learning relationships between tutors and learners, or between peer learners, or between learners and significant others, were also key to understanding how learning was socially situated.

Goodyear (2002) discusses the creation of online learning communities. He explains how such communities emerge and shape themselves, and describes the role of the course designer in the setting up of supportive organisational forms and structures. The underlying point that Goodyear brings out is that, however well-designed the online tasks in supporting interaction, however successful the protocols in facilitating genuine discussion, in the final analysis a learning community is a social construction that will be shaped by forces that lie well outside our normal boundaries of learning design.

Individual patterns of interactivity

The conventional role of teaching is to guide the learner through a curriculum or training sequence, checking progress on the way. Since there are usually too many learners, and too few teachers, an important role of technology has been to attempt to provide individualised attention, allowing the learner to benefit from working at an appropriate pace and level. Teaching machines allowed this to happen, and the early developments of computer-based learning provided interactive environments in which the learner would be tested for developing understanding, and which provided the learner with appropriate material for studying next. In a limited sense, the computer could then be said to be providing the opportunity for a learning dialogue: the computer deduced the learner's understanding from simple choices made, and gave the learner a new task (new material to study, or a new problem to solve). Impatient with the limitations of this, however, some researchers turned to the methods and promise of artificial intelligence and cognitive science in an attempt to design systems that could offer learning dialogues which emulated the most important features of real one-to-one student–tutor discussion (Glaser and Bassok, 1989; Wenger, 1987). The assumption behind intelligent tutoring is that learning occurs through an instructional dialogue in which the learner's misconceptions, or missing conceptions, are gradually identified and corrected through individualised instructional explanation. This leads to a view that one only has to organise knowledge in an appropriate form to match the conceptual state of the individual learner and learning will occur inevitably. This view is strongly represented in the problem-solving tradition that has underpinned the Artificial Intelligence (AI) approach to learning.

A cornerstone of learning technology, then, is the attempt to programme computers to respond appropriately to the pattern of interactivity shown by an individual learner. A rather different approach from that of intelligent tutoring systems can be seen in the work of Snow and his co-workers. Cronbach and Snow (1977) developed the approach known as *Aptitude-Treatment Interaction (ATI)*, the aim of which is to predict learning outcomes from combinations of aptitudes and instructional strategies (treatments). In his work, Snow expanded the definition of aptitude from the conventional cognitive-based strategies and abilities, to include *conative* (motivational and volitional) and *affective* aspects of learning. With this broad view of aptitude, Snow's theory accounted for the interaction between an individual's personal aptitudes (e.g. experience, motivation, ability, knowledge, and regulatory processes) and task demands. Typically, the kind of research based on ATI begins with conventional psychometric measures, such as crystallised intelligence or spatial ability, and tries to relate these to variations in some kind of instructional method. Often innovative instructional methods have been employed, involving meta-cognitive methods, participative modelling, reciprocal teaching, or anxiety reduction methods. Overall, the research using this approach has produced mixed results but recent research has yielded some positive findings (Kyllonen and Lajoie, 2003).

These ideas have been introduced into the e-learning field through the work of Shute, who argues that e-learning will become greatly more effective as the selection of *learning objects* is made adaptive to the learners' profile of aptitudes. Shute and Towle (2003) review a specific system – Student Modelling Approach for Responsive Tutoring (SMART) – which attempts to select learning objects to fit the immediate needs of the learner. SMART is a student modelling system that selects learning objects according to its estimate of how much a student knows and how fast a student is learning. It estimates learning speed based on two different types of learner history. One is how quickly a student is learning in the particular learning session. This involves a *microadaptive* approach. The other is how quickly a student learns in general, not just in this session (e.g. based on how well a student performs on a separate learning task). The approach of a computer taking advantage of this kind of information is called *macroadaptive*. Combining microadaptive and macroadaptive approaches to estimate a student's current knowledge and learning speed, the SMART system selects appropriate learning objects for a particular learner at a particular moment in the instructional session.

The view of aptitude that emerges from this line of work, encompassing specific abilities, motivation and affect, is closely related to the concept of cognitive style, the characteristic ways in which people make use of their intellectual abilities. Cognitive styles are individual differences that lie in a conceptual grey area somewhere between intelligence and personality. A framework which relates abilities, cognitive controls, cognitive styles and learning styles was offered by

Jonassen and Grabowski (1993). Combinations of mental abilities comprise cognitive controls. These, in turn, define cognitive styles. At the most general level of all lie learning styles.

Cognitive *controls* are specifically concerned with the manner and typical form of learning. They are descriptions of information-processing techniques, as are cognitive styles, but they emphasise control rather than facilitation. Cognitive controls include field dependence/independence, cognitive flexibility, impulsivity/reflexivity, breadth of categorising and cognitive complexity. Cognitive *styles* are descriptions of characteristic and stable approaches adopted by individuals in acquiring information. They include styles of information *gathering* (e.g. visualiser/verbaliser) and *organising* (e.g. serialist/holist).

The construct of *learning style* has attracted a great deal of attention in recent years, particularly for its popularity with practitioners. Jonassen and Grabowski point out that learning style essentially represents an attempt to specify cognitive styles that have particular relevance in applied learning environments. All of these are based on self-reports of preferences in learning. The validity of these rests largely on the assumption that learners have insight into, and awareness of, their own learning processes. In a recent major review of the literature on learning styles Coffield *et al.* (2004) identified 71 models of learning styles from which they were able to select 13 major models, with their associated measuring instruments, for analysis. They further classified these into five 'families' along a 'fixedness' dimension:

- Constitutionally-based learning styles and preferences.
- Learning styles reflecting deep-seated features of the cognitive structure, including patterns of ability.
- Learning styles as one component of a relatively stable personality type.
- Learning styles as 'flexibly-stable' learning preferences.
- Styles as learning approaches and strategies.

The Coffield *et al.* report is highly critical of most current practice in the use of learning styles instruments, and also of the empirical underpinning of most of the assumptions made about the importance of learning styles in education. However, the report tries to deal in a balanced way with the observation that the approach is very popular with practitioners. Coffield *et al.* make a positive recommendation for learning styles instruments, at least those that stand up best to research scrutiny, particularly those of Entwistle (1998) and Vermunt (1998), to be developed as tools for encouraging reflection on learning, and further self-development. The authors recommend that the language of the concepts developed by Entwistle and others of *deep, surface and strategic approaches to learning,* and Vermunt's *meaning-directed, application-directed and reproduction-directed styles* should be widely adopted in post-16 education. These terms raise awareness of learner differences that point to important pedagogical approaches and thus provide a 'lexicon of learning for dialogue'.

The evaluation of learning styles becomes more positive as we move across the 'fixedness' categories towards a view of learning style that encompasses an individual's strategic flexibility in how they approach study. The approaches of both Entwistle and Vermunt derive from the work of Marton and his co-workers (Marton and Säljö, 1976, 1997) who described the concept of *approach to learning* with its categories of *deep* and *surface*, to which was subsequently added an *approach to studying* which could be *strategic* (Entwistle and Ramsden, 1983) and *achieving* (Biggs, 1987). This can be thought of as having broadened the concept of learning style to include aspects of the teaching–learning environment being provided.

Matching refers to the practice of linking learning styles with teaching styles. It seems a fundamental point that if we have diagnosed a learner as learning in a particular way then our pedagogy should work to provide teaching that matches the individual's preferred approach. This is the fundamental rationale for Snow's ATI approach, as well as the point of most attempts to produce learner models in intelligent tutoring. Coffield *et al.* review a large amount of research evidence on this (although not technology-based matching) and conclude that the evidence is 'equivocal at best and deeply contradictory at worst' (2004, p. 39) where controlled attempts have been made to achieve matching. However, these studies have all been based on the idea of matching to a learner's preferences and they do not take account of the point that preferred approach may not be the same as need. Indeed, there are even arguments in favour of deliberate mismatching as a way of stretching learners and encouraging them to develop a range of styles (Grasha, 1984; Vermunt, 1998; Kolb, 1984). This begins to convey a constructivist flavour. Mayes and Fowler (1999) argued that learning is fundamentally unlike any other kind of work, where the goal is normally to achieve task goals in the most direct and efficient way. To achieve deep learning it is sometimes advantageous to set barriers for the learner to overcome. The importance of challenging students' existing ideas or beliefs as a way of provoking development can be found in the classic work of Perry (1970).

Conclusion

Is interactivity a synonym for learning?

I close by returning to the question with which this chapter began. Our discussion of interactivity in learning has certainly not narrowed the descriptive scope of the concept. We have used the term to refer, first, to the way in which information is interpreted by our existing knowledge structures (which is beyond conscious awareness). Here the term might best be restricted to the situation in which an existing concept is modified, so that both agents in the interaction (the new information and the learner's existing knowledge structure) are subject to some effect from the act of comprehension. Our second case, interactivity in tasks, seems to involve a similar logic. Only where the performance of a task involves a feedback loop, so that the performance has modified both the learner and the external world of information, can we properly regard it as interactive.

In our third level of interactivity we examined the way in which learners relate to each other, and exert mutual influence, as social beings. These are unambiguously interactions. By using the same term to refer to all three levels, however, we lose some of the theoretical distinctions we have tried to explore. On the other hand, it could be argued that the use of the concept across this range of processes has encouraged us to see how the continuously dynamic nature of the goal–action–feedback cycle underlies all intentional learning, and also extends to the affective and social domains where dialogue between people plays a crucial role in providing the motive force which sustains the whole learning process.

References

Baddeley, A.D. (1996) *Human Memory: Theory and Practice*, Hove: Psychology Press.

Biggs, J. B. (1987) *Student Approaches to Learning and Studying*, Melbourne: Australian Council for Educational Research.

Bruner, J. (1960) *The Process of Education*, Cambridge, MA: Harvard University Press.

Carroll, J. M. (1990) *The Nurnberg Funnel: Designing Minimalist Instruction for Practical Computer Skill*, Cambridge, MA: MIT Press.

Chase, W. G. and Ericsson, K.A. (1982) 'Skill and working memory', in G. H. Bower (ed.), *The Psychology of Learning and Motivation* (Vol. 16), New York: Academic Press.

Clark, R.E. (1983) 'Reconsidering research on learning from media', *Review of Educational Research*, 53(4), 445–59.

Coffield, F., Moseley, D., Hall, E. and Ecclestone, K. (2004) *Learning styles and pedagogy in post-16 learning: a systematic and critical review*, Learning and Skills Research Centre Report. Online. Available http://www.lsda.org.uk/pubs/.

Cole, M. (1985) 'The zone of proximal development: where culture and cognition create each other', in J.V. Wertsch (ed.), *Culture, Communication and Cognition: Vygotskian Perspectives*, Cambridge: Cambridge University Press.

Cole, M. and Engestrom, Y. (1993) 'A cultural-historical approach to distributed cognition', in G. Salomon (ed.), *Distributed cognitions: Psychological and Educational Considerations*, New York: Cambridge University Press.

Craik, F. I. M. and Lockhart, R.S. (1975) 'Levels of processing: A framework for memory research', *Journal of Verbal Learning and Verbal Behaviour*, 11, 671–84.

Cronbach, L. and Snow, R. (1977) *Aptitudes and Instructional Methods: A Handbook for Research on Interactions*, New York: Irvington Publishers.

Dewey, J. (1916) *Democracy and Education*, New York: The Free Press.

Dewey, J. (1938) *Logic, the Theory of Inquiry*, New York: Holt, Rinehart and Winston.

Duffy, T. M. and Cunningham, D. J. (1996) 'Constructivism: implications for the design and delivery of instruction', in D. H. Jonassen (ed.), *Handbook of Research for Educational Communications and Technology*, New York: Simon and Schuster Macmillan.

Engestrom, Y. (1993) 'Development studies of work as a testbench of activity theory: the case of primary care medical practice', in S.Chaiklin and J. Lave (eds), *Understanding Practice: Perspectives on Activity and Context*, Cambridge: Cambridge University Press.

Entwistle, N. J. (1998) 'Approaches to learning and forms of understanding', in B. Dart and G. Boulton-Lewis (eds), *Teaching and Learning in Higher Education*, pp. 72–101, Melbourne: Australian Council for Educational Research.

Entwistle, N. J. and Ramsden, P. (1983) *Understanding Student Learning*, London: Croom Helm.

Fowler, C .J. H. and Mayes, J. T. (2000) 'Learning relationships: from theory to design', in D. Squires, G. Conole and G. Jacobs (eds), *The Changing Face of Learning Technology*, Cardiff: University of Wales Press.

Glaser, R. and Bassok, M. (1989) 'Learning theory and the study of instruction', *Annual Review of Psychology*, 40, 631–66.

Goodyear, P. (2002) 'Psychological foundations for networked learning', in C. Steeples and C. Jones (eds), *Networked Learning: Perspectives and Issues*, London: Springer-Verlag.

Grasha, A. F. (1984) 'Learning styles: the journey from Greenwich Observatory (1796) to the college classroom (1984)', *Improving College and University Teaching*, 32(1), 46–53.

Jonassen, D. H. (2000a) 'Revisiting activity theory as a framework for designing student-centred learning environments', in D. H. Jonassen, and S. M. Land (eds), *Theoretical Foundations of Learning Environments*, Mahwah, NJ: Lawrence Erlbaum.

Jonassen, D. H. (2000b) *Computers as Mindtools for Schools: Engaging Critical Thinking*. Columbus, OH: Prentice-Hall.

Jonassen, D. H. and Grabowski, B.L. (1993) *Handbook of Individual Differences, Learning and Instruction*, New York: Erlbaum.

Jonassen, D.H. and Land, S.M. (2000) *Theoretical Foundations of Learning Environments*, Mahwah, NJ: Lawrence Erlbaum.

Kolb, D. A. (1984) *Experiential Learning: Experience as the Source of Learning and Development*, Englewood Cliffs, NJ: Prentice-Hall.

Koumi, J. (1994) 'Media comparison and deployment: a practitioner's view', *British Journal of Educational Technology*, 25(1), 41–57.

Kozma, R. (1991) 'Learning with media', *Review of Educational Research*, 61(2), 79–211.

Kyllonen, P. C. and Lajoie, S. P. (2003) 'Reassessing aptitude: introduction to a special issue in honor of Richard E. Snow', *Educational Psychologist,* 38(2), 79–83.

Laurillard, D. (1993) *Rethinking University Teaching: A Framework for the Effective use of Educational Technology*, London: Routledge.

Lave, J. and Wenger, E. (1991) *Situated Learning: Legitimate Peripheral Participation*, Cambridge: Cambridge University Press.

Marton, F. and Säljö, R. (1976) 'On qualitative differences in learning. I – Outcome and process', *British Journal of Educational Psychology*, 46, 4–11.

Marton, F. and Säljö, R.(1997) 'Approaches to learning', in F. Marton, D. J. Hounsell and N. J. Entwistle (eds), *The Experience of Learning*, 2nd edn, Edinburgh: Scottish Academic Press.

Mayes, J. T. (1995) 'Learning technology and groundhog day', in W. Strang, V. B. Simpson and J. Slater (eds), *Hypermedia at Work: Practice and Theory in Higher Education*, Canterbury: University of Kent Press.

Mayes, J. T. and Fowler, C. J. H. (1999) 'Learning technology and usability: a framework for understanding courseware', *Interacting With Computers*, 11, 485–97.

Mayes, J. T., Dineen, F., McKendree, J. and Lee, J. (2002) 'Learning from watching others learn', in C. Steeples and C. Jones (eds), *Networked Learning: Perspectives and Issues*, London: Springer.

Miller, G. A. (1956) 'The magical number seven plus or minus two: some limits on our capacity for processing information', *Psychological Review*, 63, 81–97.

Neisser, U. (ed.) (1982) *Memory Observed: Remembering in Natural Contexts*, San Francisco, CA: W. H. Freeman.

Newell, A. (1980) 'One final word', in D.T. Tuma and F. Reif (eds), *Problem Solving and Education: Issues in Teaching and Research*, Mahwah, NJ: Lawrence Erlbaum.

Pea, R. (1993) 'Practices of distributed intelligence and designs for education', in G. Salomon (ed.), *Distributed Cognition*, New York: Cambridge University Press.

Peal, D. and Wilson, B. (2001) 'Activity theory and web-based training', in B. H. Khan (ed.), *Web-Based Training*, Englewood Cliffs, NJ: Educational Technology Publications.

Perry, W. G. (1970) *Forms of Intellectual and Ethical Development in the College Years: A Scheme*, New York: Holt, Rinehart and Winston.

Piaget, J. (1970) *Science of Education and the Psychology of the Child*, New York: Orion Press.

Plowman, L., Luckin, R., Laurillard, D., Stratfold, M. and Taylor, J. (1999) 'Designing multimedia for learning: narrative guidance and narrative construction', *Proceedings of CHI '99 (ACM Conference on Human Factors in Computing Systems)*, Pittsburgh, PA, USA.

Rose, E. (1999) 'Deconstructing interactivity in educational computing', *Educational Technology*, 39(1), 43–9.

Salmon, G. (2002) *e-Tivities: The key to Active Online Learning*, London: Kogan Page.

Salomon, G. and Perkins, D. N. (1998) 'Individual and social aspects of learning', *Review of Research in Education*, 23, 1–24.

Salomon, G., Perkins, D. and Globerson, T. (1991) 'Partners in cognition: extending human intelligence with intelligent technologies', *Educational Researcher*, 4, 2–8.

Shute, V. and Towle, B. (2003) 'Adaptive e-learning', *Educational Psychologist*, 38(2), 105–14.

Steeples, C., Jones, C. and Goodyear, P. (2002) 'Beyond e-learning: a future for networked learning', in C. Steeples, and C. Jones (eds), *Networked Learning: Perspectives and Issues*, London: Springer.

Sternberg, R. (1984) *Mechanisms of Cognitive Development*, New York: W. H. Freeman.

Taylor, S. E. and Thomson, S. C. (1982) 'Stalking the elusive vividness effect', *Psychological Review*, 89, 155–81.

Turner, J. C. (1991) *Social Influence*, Milton Keynes: Open University Press.

Vermunt, J. D. (1998) 'The regulation of constructive learning processes', *British Journal of Educational Psychology,* 68, 149–71.

Vygotsky, L. S. (1962) *Thought and Language*, Cambridge, MA: MIT Press.

Vygotsky, L. S. (1978) *Mind in Society: The Development of Higher Psychological Processes*, Harvard, MA: Harvard University Press.

Wenger, E. (1987) *Artificial Intelligence and Tutoring Systems*, Los Altos, CA: Morgan Kaufmann.

Wenger, E. (1998) *Communities of Practice: Learning, Meaning, and Identity*, Cambridge: Cambridge University Press.

Wood, D. J. (1989) *Social Interaction as Tutoring*, Hillsdale, NJ: Erlbaum.

Chapter 2

Encounter theory

A model to enhance online communication, interaction and engagement

Rod Sims and John Hedberg

Introduction

The theme of this book relates to the different ways that we understand the interactions and communications that occur between the various participants within online teaching and learning environments. The current understanding of interaction and interactivity suggests that these are the essential components through which engagement and meaning emerge (e.g. Sims, 2003a). This aspect is especially true in the context of higher education, where more and more institutions are using online environments for whole or part of the delivery of undergraduate and graduate programmes.

With this shift in educational delivery, quite frequently we find that the implementation of online learning programmes is predicated on existing models of face-to-face classroom interactions, with the result that many teachers and learners find the management of the communication and instruction complex, and limited in the flexibility they had experienced in face-to-face contexts. This lack of interactivity is further constrained by the enterprise Learning Management Systems (LMS) as the major delivery vehicle for those courses. Other key players in the educational process, specifically instructional designers, technicians and administrators, also have responsibilities for the success of the online experiences that instructors create.

In this chapter we examine the construct of interactivity from an understanding of the online dynamic that must successfully occur between the stakeholders in order to achieve a better balance between didactic and inquiry strategies within those environments. By focusing upon these aspects, we are also considering what potentially needs to be changed. For example, David Jonassen and his colleagues argue that:

> Like the chiropractor who realigns your spine, we might become healthier from a realignment of our theories. If we admit to and attempt to accommodate some of the uncertainty, indeterminism, and unpredictability that pervade our complex world, we will develop stronger theories and practices that will have more powerful (if not predictable) effects on human learning.
>
> (Jonassen *et al.*, 1997, p. 33)

Is it just a realignment of our theories of effective online interactions that is required, or have we reached a time when we must reassess the very frameworks by which online interactions are devised, implemented and acted out by the ever-growing number of online teachers and learners? As whole journal issues are now being devoted to how best to interpret and support online interactions (*Studies in Higher Education*, 2005), then the force of Robbins' (1994) assessment of the human condition, albeit fictitious, serves as a reminder of the *librettos* we use, and the assumptions we make:

> Sarah Bernhardt was such a powerfully popular, awe-inspiring actress that when she toured in North America her performances invariably sold out, even though she spoke hardly a word of English. Whatever play she did, Shakespeare, Moliere, or Marlowe, she performed in French, a language few nineteenth century Americans could comprehend. Theatre goers were provided with librettos so they might follow the action in English. Well, on at least a couple of occasions, ushers passed out the wrong libretto, a text for an entirely different drama than the one that was being staged. Yet, from all reports, not once did a single soul in those capacity crowds ever comment or complain. Furthermore, no critic ever mentioned the discrepancy in his or her review. We modern human beings are looking at life, trying to make some sense of it, observing a 'reality' that often seems to be unfolding in a foreign tongue – only we've all been issued with the wrong librettos. For a text we're given the Bible. Or the Talmud or the Koran. We're given Time magazine and Reader's Digest, daily papers and the six o'clock news; we're given school books, sitcoms and revisionist histories; we're given psychological counselling, cults, workshops, advertisements, sales pitches, and authoritative pronouncements by pundits, sold-out scientists, political activists, and heads of state. Unfortunately, none of these translations bears more than a faint resemblance to what is transpiring in the true theatre of existence, and most of them are dangerously misleading. We're attempting to comprehend the spiralling intricacies of a magnificently complex tragi-comedy with librettos that describe barroom melodramas or kindergarten skits.
>
> (Robbins, 1994, pp. 116–17)

If we are to agree with Robbins' perspective, then the current practices and frameworks used to support the design and implementation of online teaching and learning systems may not be the most appropriate to understand the dynamics of virtual, asynchronous learning environments. Our proposal in this chapter therefore is to investigate alternative ways to view online teaching and learning, taking account of both the major stakeholders as well as those responsible for design and administration. We propose, through an elaboration of existing design models, that by better understanding the encounters that are established and flourish between teachers, learners, designers and administrations, and the multifarious ways in which those encounters demand negotiation skills, we will better address the needs of all participants.

To frame our discussion, we shall address the essential research considerations that inform the construction of encounter theory, and contextualise that theory through the analysis of a case study of online teaching and learning.

Theoretical frameworks

Context

What are the issues we face in online learning today? As practising online teachers we find that a wide range of factors including the design constraints of the LMS, the prior experience of both teachers and learners, time management, time availability and the expectations of the institution all contribute to the success of the online environment. This is supported by the extensive documentation on 'good practice' for the online teacher (Palloff and Pratt, 2003) and the competencies recommended for both designers and teachers (IBSTPI, 2003).

However, it is the interactions between the key stakeholders (administrators, designers, technicians, teachers and learners) that all impact on the success of the online experience and viewing these interactions as encounters between people can enhance our understanding of the online dynamic. Different discourses result in different design outcomes, and the goals of the participants will skew the outcomes (Hedberg, 2004). Similarly, we also need to appreciate the importance of effective interactivity within the online environment. Research on interactive learning environments suggests that the key interactions are those between learner and learner, learner and teacher and learner and content (Moore, 1989; Wagner, 1994), which was extended to include that of learner and interface (Hillman et al., 1994). More recently Hedberg and Sims (2001) proposed that the environment experienced by the learner is also largely determined by the designer and therefore the interaction between designer and learner (albeit delayed) must also be taken into consideration. Other studies have proposed that we have yet to realise the true potential of computer-based and online learning environments (Sims, 2003b). From a cybernetics perspective, Whitaker (2005) has described this interaction as dynamic, not static, thus requiring the designer to understand the domains of reference and interaction of the potential users. He suggests:

> The thrust of interface design accordingly shifts from the configuration of on-screen objects per se to the circumscription of domains of interaction which should be afforded a user. These new domainal specifications are framed with regard to the given task's subject matter and the flow as engaged from the workers' first-person perspective. The former derives from analysis of referential domains, and the latter derives from analysis of domains of interaction. Interfaces come to be designed not as control panels for a particular software application but as a combination of 'windows onto the task

referential domain' plus affordances tailored to reflect an effective domain of interactions in response to what's visualised. Phrased another way, I craft and assess interface components with respect to how transparent a linkage they provide to the task-specific domain of relevance and interaction.

(Whitaker, 2005, p. 96)

It is also pertinent to note that as online teachers we have found that the expectations of learners, designers and administrators have significant effects on the way we teach and the response from learners to that teaching. And by framing our interactions as a set of changing encounters we have determined that it provides a useful means to develop our relationships with the learners and the other key stakeholders. From a different perspective, we also find that certain online environments have shifted from the one-to-many experience of the face-to-face classroom to a one-to-one set of communications between each individual participant which has resulted in extensive increases in workload both on facilitators (instructors) and participants. Why this has occurred, rather than a more collegial and collaborative many-to-many set of interactions, is one of the factors that prompted this chapter.

In saying this it is also important to note that there are a range of environments that can be termed online. The first of these is where the students and teachers are geographically separated; the second is where online activities are blended together with a face-to-face on-campus environment, and the third is where online resources are seen essentially as a supplement to a face-to-face model. For this chapter we are focusing on the online environment which is accessed by all stakeholders through the internet and in which there is little or no face-to-face contact, unless initiated independently by the individual members of the course. Importantly, these encounters can also be related to the communication that takes place between the stakeholder and the application system, typically an LMS.

Interactive encounters

The word encounter can be defined as 'a meeting, especially one that is unplanned, unexpected, or brief' (dictionary.com, 2005). This seems most applicable to what happens when learners first join an online course. While they may be familiar with the content and aims of the overriding curriculum, their first encounter with a computer-based application will potentially be confrontational. This was demonstrated by Sims (2003b), where the interactions described by research participants included both the *unplanned* and *unexpected* aspects attributed to encounters. It thus becomes critical to determine not only how to design the intended outcomes, but also how to work with unanticipated events. The importance of creating a welcoming climate to begin the learning journey is also emphasised by Salmon (2004) in her five-stage model, and participants need to be socialised into the learning culture.

The following discussion introduces a range of situations that may be described in terms of a series of different encounters between the participating stakeholders and the implications for the design and effective management of online teaching and learning environments.

Welcoming encounters

When learners and teachers first commence working within online environments, it is essential to create introductions between each of the participants. In addition, and depending on the structure of the software application which links the stakeholders, this may involve some form of communication from the design team presenting the background to the learning environment and its intended operation. In the broadest sense this also includes contributions from the administrative and technical support stakeholders. Considered as 'second order' contributions in our discussion, these are more subtle but often drive the decisions about the type of LMS the organisation employs, and the functions it provides and supports technically.

As many online facilitators have suggested, the opening gambit in a formal learning sense requires the learners to introduce themselves (Salmon, 2004). Learners must also be able to inform, in the context of negotiation, the teachers and, to a lesser extent, instructional designers of their experience and expectations. In this way the learning environment can use the information to configure the way in which the activities will be presented and the means by which the learner can progress through the content material and learning activities. While this is often achieved through formal feedback systems that are independent from the learning environment, we are recommending a more integrated form of interactive learning.

As a course progresses, the welcoming encounter can develop to more of a help function, either informational or supportive, of processes through scaffolds and cognitive tools. As a simple example, the helpful paperclip in Microsoft Office fulfils such a role (albeit at times annoying!). What makes a welcoming encounter is the concern of each stakeholder, as no other participant should be confused or 'lost' within the learning environment; through these encounters participants can manipulate that environment to achieve the required learning tasks and activities.

The notion of the welcoming encounter can also be applied in reverse to that of departing encounters, where the learner is recognised for the role played, and course information shared and exchanged. It is also relatively simple to record user responses and integrate them into future presentations of the course – placing value on the individual learner is a means to enhance the purposeful nature of the product, as well as utilise their contributions within the course.

Directing encounters

In human–human encounters, the participants may operate equitably or one may dominate the process. In the case of online environments, participants have demonstrated that the two-way exchange of information is essential (Sims, 2003b); however, based on the observations from that study, there is a need to be able to control the content beyond the selection of predetermined readings, navigation between locations or scrolling through large amounts of textual information. While learners are often quite willing and able to contribute to the creation of learning resources or recommend a change to discussion threads, there are times when the LMS (through the actual technology or indirectly through the administration) can inhibit that opportunity.

For example, the first author experienced an online environment where the institutional administration issued a directive that no changes could be made to specified discussion items. While this can be understood from a consistency perspective with respect to the same course being taught by many instructors, such directives can impact on the flexibility and individualisation that online learning environments espouse. Conversely, the second author used an open source LMS (Moodle) for several courses. The freedom of allowing students to self enrol, to facilitate the learning activities, to create resources and activities, and to comment on others' work actually meant that they took charge of their own learning and decided on what learning paths would be of interest to them individually and as groups and as a whole class. The simple design of a directed sequence of encounters provided structure and flexibility.

Thus directed encounters may be a relatively effective means to address the need for structure and interaction. If interactions are structured so that the learner and teacher can control the content then it becomes more their choice as to how the course progresses, which in turn supports the development of a learner-centred, constructivist paradigm (Reigeluth, 1999). This implies that the learner and teacher need to virtually meet and effectively debate with the designer, technician and administrator to develop and enhance the learning context. It is anticipated that these concepts can be generalised to a wide range of content domains and metaphors, independent of the technological environment, with the aim of producing even more effective learning outcomes. In fact, the more the tools become less structured around administrative controls, it might be reasonable to expect that the design will be driven by the teacher and even the student, rather than a third person designer. We realise this opens up another set of issues, but at least in some cases this might be feasible.

Other aspects of directing encounters can be the types of scaffolding that the teacher and designer place into the learning environment to support the learners achieve the intended learning outcomes. The provision of scaffolds becomes more critical if there is less informal support for the learners. Scaffolds can be provided through information structures such as FAQs or through procedural sequences or even learning activities which can be built over time during the learning experience. Typical scaffolded sequences are those provided by such products as Knowledge Forum (www.knowledgeforum.com) that provide a scaffolded discussion forum environment in which students assign the nature of their contribution according to a scaffolded argumentation structure (Scardamalia and Bereiter, 1994).

Strategic encounters

It is also important that the encounters between learner, teacher and designer be strategically positioned throughout the online environment in such a way that they can be initiated by any of the stakeholders. The activation of these encounters will be dependent on the extent to which the particular user has achieved interactive balance and control over the application. While the use of agents has been applied to personalise the environment and provide contextual advice, the responses provided by those agents are typically defined by the system to operate under prescribed conditions, rather than those conditions being negotiated by the user and designer.

Of importance is the extent to which the primary stakeholders can take the initiative in a specific course activity, and if they have the impression that they are being communicated with on an individual and personal level. Generally strategic encounters are designed to support choice and directions for subsequent learning experiences. In many environments these choices are made by the designer or teacher but they can be undertaken by the learner equally well. In fact, the match between learners' desires and teaching activities represents a major factor in achieving engagement in the course.

Ethical 'framing' encounters

A fourth mode of encounter that we wish to identify relates to the policies and codes of practice that are in place to guide behaviour within the online environment and the management or guidance of all stakeholders in the understanding and application of those policies. While at the basic level this can relate to accepted netiquette, there are significant issues related to the implementation of online learning with which all stakeholders must be acquainted. For example, the ethical and acceptable use of resources, plagiarism, and the presentation of written materials (Spinello and Tavani, 2004).

This comes to the fore with an issue like plagiarism, where from the administrative and technical perspective it can be both mandated as unethical and subject to academic penalties, and detection software can be employed routinely to scan submissions from learners. From the pedagogical perspective the designer has the responsibility to create assessments that do not promote plagiarised submission, the teacher the responsibility to watch for plagiarism and the learner the responsibility to conform to institutional policy and demonstrate personal ethics. Where cases of plagiarism arise, a series of encounters between all stakeholders also arise.

Personal narrative encounters

The encounters between learner and teacher need to manifest a level of empathy and tolerance. There is no reason why a learner in an online environment cannot indicate an inability to undertake a task, or a teacher be apologetic for limiting the range of options. The underlying argument for negotiation and encounters is one of personalising the experience, of integrating good design into the process, and continually ensuring that learners are comfortable with their progress. This can be achieved through building the environment into a narrative, such that the online teaching and learning environment is conceived as a learning journey in which all stakeholders have an integrated and valuable role.

The narrative may occur in terms of statements of what the learning has achieved or sets of questions about interpretations of communications or resources. It may also take the form of feedback on the students' assignments either from other students or the teacher, and ultimately, depending upon the personal encounters, it might be student comment on teacher ideas and strategies. In general we are suggesting that narrative encounters form the basis of metacognitive activity for each stakeholder.

As stakeholders get to know one another then the narrative encounter can shift from the formal to the informal, from professional relationships to acquaintance and possibly friendship. Recognising when it is appropriate to enable this shift is a significant part of the overall learning experience and requires the skill of an experienced facilitator.

Stakeholders

An understanding of the role of each stakeholder is critical to implementing and maintaining effective encounters in the online environment. Dringus (1999, p. 6) reminds us that

> faculty, learners, administrative and technical staff comprise the human resources that bring the OLE to life and link learners to the world of information at large ... it is particularly important that stakeholders assume responsibility for participation and engagement by proactive demonstration of accountability, accessibility, and visibility.

Any conceptualisation of encounters must therefore be considered in terms of the key stakeholders of online teaching and learning, and this focus on the participants of the online environment extends the proposals of Hedberg and Sims (2001) and Sims and Jones (2003). One of the key additions in our framework is that of the designer – the person(s) responsible for the instructional strategies that both the learner and instructor will need to negotiate. While in many instances the designer will also be the teacher, there are as many environments where the teacher is employed to teach a course developed by others. Consequently there needs to be recognition of the encounters, although displaced in time, between the designer, the learner and the teacher as well as the administration and technical support personnel.

The following brief overview of the roles of these stakeholders is documented to emphasise that the teaching and learning environment required for online

cannot be maintained as a set of discrete but different 'stages' but is in reality one dynamic experience in which the encounters and communications between all 'actors' must be well designed and documented, and equally well understood.

Learners

In any educational environment, learners are the key stakeholders; not only are they the recipients of the instruction but also those who manifest the success of the learning activities. Learners are the key stakeholders by which successful outcomes will be measured. In the online context, learners become even more critical as they will have specific expectations of the activities they will undertake and the role that the teacher/facilitator will play in assisting them achieve their outcomes.

Teachers

The teachers (instructor or facilitator) will find that their most frequent encounter is directly with the learners; however, there will also be significant communication with the administration of the institution, more than likely the designer and, with the implementation of new systems, the technical support group as well. The communication channels provided to enable the facilitation of information exchange between stakeholders will ultimately determine the success of the educational programmes being delivered. It needs also to be remembered that with the increase of part-time (adjunct) teaching positions, the teacher will also experience a range of encounters that will impact on their ability and motivation to effectively deliver the prescribed course of study.

Designers

The designers refer to those people responsible for the actual conceptualisation and construction of the online course – the discussions, the activities, the assignments and the grading. They have a responsibility to effectively communicate what is required from both the teacher and the learner and, in a course spanning 12–15 weeks, each week or learning activity will represent a new set of encounters between learner and teacher. Using an example experienced by the first author, changes recommended for a course are communicated to a central administration section for implementation. In a number of cases the mechanics of that maintenance has resulted in delivery inconsistencies that have impacted on the efficiency of learner–teacher encounters.

Administrators

The administration of an institution will often prescribe the structure and expectations for course interactions and as such have a responsibility to communicate that to all stakeholders. In some cases the administration is positioned such that communication is either to other areas of administration or to the teachers, but not directly to the learners.

Technicians

The technicians are those who support the system and ensure the integrity of the various functions supported by the institution. Again, they will have encounters with and requirements to respond to demands from all stakeholders.

Having briefly documented different roles, the following figures are provided to demonstrate the extensive set of encounters that must be considered in terms of all stakeholders and the proposed encounter types. In creating new online environments, therefore, the designers need to ensure that each of the communications' potential is catered for. For example, a welcoming encounter between technician and learner could include specific information on who to contact and the guaranteed response time in the case of system malfunction. Alternatively there might be a narrative encounter between teacher and learner to explore continuity or discrepancy within the content domain, the outcome of which would also require a communication (strategic encounter) between teacher and designer to identify key instructional strategy updates. Thus the interactions between stakeholders cannot simply be seen as a single encounter, but as a multiplicity of encounters at different levels.

Figure 2.1 represents a snapshot of an online learning environment where the different stakeholders are all experiencing different, and potentially conflicting or frustrating, encounters. The imbalance of the encounters experienced by each of the stakeholders can impact on the overall quality of the teaching and learning environment. In contrast, Figure 2.2 represents a state in which all stakeholders (in terms of their roles for a particular course) are at the same level of personal narrative encounters, a harmonious state, one that we argue is the most effective for consistent and effective online teaching and learning experiences.

At any one time there will be a number of different encounters occurring between the stakeholders and a constant state of harmony would not be realistic. However, bringing all stakeholders into a shared understanding of the individual's teaching and learning environment will require the creation of a narrative model to be successful. An important extension of working towards this concept of encounters in harmony is that it will also entail negotiation between stakeholders.

Negotiations

Dictionary.com (2005) defines negotiation as 'a discussion intended to produce an agreement' and it is in the context of this definition that we are conceptualising interactivity as a process of negotiation of encounters between stakeholders. Being involved and entering into a two-way process of communication and information exchange are integral components of the interactive process.

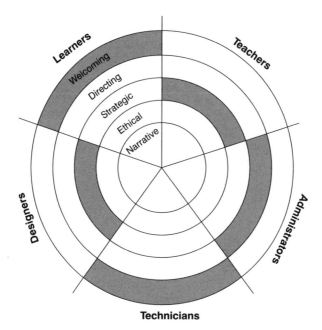

Figure 2.1 Different and/or imbalanced encounters

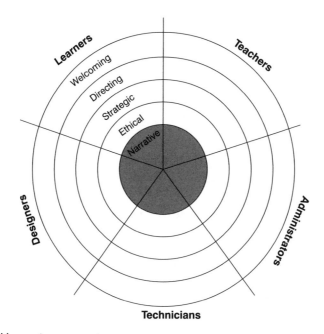

Figure 2.2 Harmonious encounters

Based on background research into narrative (Plowman, 1996), into play (Humphreys, 2003) and the potential for extending this concept to theatre and performance (Laurel, 1991), we propose that there is an opportunity to focus on online human–computer interaction as one involving all stakeholders, rather than the frequently confined focus on learners and teacher. While the learner is receiving responses from the environment, they may not be receiving input from the designer – the person who devised the programme and who expects learners to be engaged and develop knowledge and understanding. While computer technology is frequently portrayed as emancipating, providing the learner with the freedom to pursue their own learning needs, it can also be alienating and confusing if the content is difficult to locate or presented in a manner that is complex to interpret or constrained to a frustrating narrow set of options by the designer. One way to gain maximum benefit from the interaction is for the learner to be placed in a position where they are able to negotiate and maintain a conversation with other stakeholders and work within an environment that is extensible if they choose to take a particular direction or use tools in unintended ways.

From narrative to negotiation

Figure 2.3 represents a number of elements that re-focus the way in which online interactive environments might be considered to establish effective negotiation of the different encounters.

The first is to introduce the concept of the *user illusion* of a narrative-space, that is the extent to which the designer has created an environment in which the user believes (Tognazzini, 1999). Rather than perceiving this as a metaphor for a real world environment, the illusion sets up a temporary microworld that the designer will reveal to the user over time. For example, in many of the current Learning Management Systems the interface is designed around the functionality of the tasks – assignments, discussions, grading – rather than around either the process of learning (knowledge construction) or the context of learning (workplace, laboratory).

Within this narrative space the *interface* allows the learner to participate with the illusion created, having movement within and control of that space and the ability to *navigate* to preferred aspects of the discussion thread or activities along paths which provide access to discrete content areas. The user conceptually *enters* and *exits* the illusion (to negotiate the encounter), rather than beginning and finishing a prescribed activity.

When the learner is focusing on a particular component, the associated interactions come into play and support a period of *engagement*. The importance of this concept is that the environment (through designer, teacher and technician) has a significant role in providing the structure and engagement for the learner (as elaborated in Sims, 2003a). If this were to be compared to a sideshow, the user is free to move between exhibits but it is the performer at each exhibit who has the

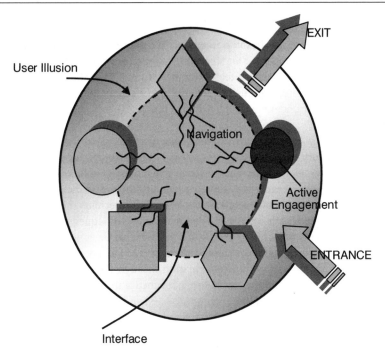

Figure 2.3 An interactive negotiation

challenge to attract and engage the audience. It is through this form of negotiation that a level of interactive balance might also be facilitated.

As the learner enters this negotiation space, information on current and past performance can be made available to the designer (either in person or as an intelligent agent) in such a way that the structure of the interaction can be adapted. It is then the designer who the learner and teacher perceives to be modifying the application to meet their current learning or informational needs. The implication is that when a learner enters the negotiation space, they bring with them a set of characteristics both personal (in terms of learning style and motivation) and archival (in terms of their preferred options as recorded through previous interactive encounters) which affect the interaction. In brief, an effective online environment should be adaptive to both user and designer characteristics.

We contend that the implementation of this structure is one of conceptual design and the ability to create the illusion to the users that the environment in which they are operating is dynamic. The environment does not need to present itself as a set of content structures accessible by navigation paths, but as an environment in which the designer, teacher, learner and other stakeholders are all involved in the communication and negotiation process.

Applying encounter theory

Having documented the basic framework, we therefore propose a theory of encounters for online teaching and learning that requires appropriate management of encounters to result in more effective online learning. To enable these encounters to be managed requires valuing the integration of stakeholders, appreciating the dynamic nature of encounters and catering for the various competencies of the stakeholders.

In the same way that Kearsley and Shneiderman (1998) proposed that an engagement theory would provide a set of prescriptions for successful computer-mediated communication, the classification of encounters in this analysis provide a framework for what we have termed encounter theory. If the development of online environments is considered as a sequence of interrelated encounters, then the interactions provided for the learner will be of consequence and contribute to meaningful engagement. Both learner and teacher/designer will have been presented with a conversational framework that should be integral to the operation of the online course. In addition, navigation through the delivery environment will be more directed and the destinations reached will be more predictable and anticipated by the learner, rather than unexpected and confusing.

Given this elaboration of an encounter theory that advocates strategies for effective negotiation between all stakeholders in the interactive process, we will underpin that analysis through the presentation of a case study.

Case study: creating effective encounters in a blended course

In one course focusing on the design of e-learning systems, the second author was challenged to provide an experience for graduate students who were learning to become effective online facilitators and designers of online learning activities, but who were required to undertake the course in a face-to-face context. The institution had a commitment to one of the traditional LMS systems and students had used the system as a discussion forum and resource dissemination device over three to four of their previous courses. Resources and expertise meant that the designer and teacher were one and the same. Technical support was provided in terms of managing the systems and the administration did not require marks and assignments to be submitted through the LMS system.

In responding to this challenge, it was decided to employ an open source LMS which the technician set up to enable students with code words to enrol themselves into the course. This meant that other participants could also contribute from remote sites, and two others, one a professor in Europe and the other a designer in New Zealand, were able to critique the students' responses to some of their learning tasks. The early tasks were to make comparisons of LMS systems and the first assignment was to compare three. Needless to say all students chose their main traditional LMS and compared it with the open source one and then had to search to find other options (in fact they were encouraged to explore blogs and wikis as well as what are more traditional LMS systems).

The opening encounters were based around a task of finding out the contributions of several well-known contributors to the field and posting details about what their contributions were on a discussion forum; this served as both a welcoming and narrative encounter. Students would comment on the personal interests of each of the high profile figures and compare them to their own contexts. The exercise also provided a range of different perspectives on the e-learning experience and collated a set of resources from the leading figures. This led to later discussions of topics such as learning objects where the background resources and discussion activities and examples were provided online by a group of two class members (Figure 2.4). (It should be noted that the simple inclusion of photographs was seen by the learners as supporting personal encounters; as the class continued they kept on mentioning the fact that they knew who they were talking with as a major factor in focusing their contributions.)

Digital Resource
by Chee Kian Teo - Wednesday, 25 August 2004, 10:54 PM

Raymond,

You got a valid point here. Wiley had also defined what he meant by digital resources. Do go to Foo Keong's new thread by topics on "definitions of LOs", I have placed some summarised points of wiley's article there.

Michael,

You are absolutely right in limiting LOs to digital format, in line with wiley's definition and all your points stated are valid. We need to limit to some extent or else everything under the sun will be considered LO according to LTSC's definitions.

Please do go over to Foo Keong's newly created thread to continue discussions. I will try to copy all your discussions here over to the new threads set up by him.

Sorry for all the mess created. My apology.

Show parent | Delete| Reply

Re: An Ideal Defintion ???
by Raymond Wong - Wednesday, 25 August 2004, 03:29 PM

But what is the definition of digital resources? That could be very broad too and doesn't really help to "limit the scope" does it? Resources could be photographs to short video clips to flash animations to java applets to text files to powerpoint slides etc etc etc.

Show parent | Delete| Reply

Re: An Ideal Defintion ???
by michael j - Wednesday, 25 August 2004, 12:28 PM

If we accept their (McGreal & Roberts, 2001) definition then virtually everything is LO.

For a definition to be useful, it has to limit the scope of what is being discussed.

Figure 2.4 Online discussion with threaded replies

The online tools also enabled the structuring of the learning activities around the weekly schedule. As the group started to make comparisons, the directing and strategic encounters were set up using the simple act of a schedule of events (Figure 2.5). The tools also enabled the format of the interactions to follow a topic format or a social networking format, options that might form the basis of alternative encounters and alternative forms of interaction.

By the end of the 14 weeks of the course, students had each run one online session, participated in seven others and had compared different systems in terms of the interactions that were not only possible but also supported more effective learning outcomes. In fact the final assignments consisted of several options which varied among students who kept their own learning blog, some students who set up their own LMS to use with others, and some students who chose to compile a CD-ROM portfolio of their collected resources, ideas, and group and personal contributions.

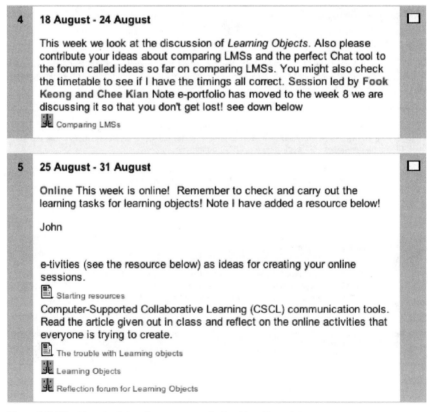

Figure 2.5 Weekly schedule of encounters devised by all participants

Conclusion

Through an analysis of online teaching and learning environments we have proposed that interaction can be framed as a recurring set of encounters and negotiations between designers, teachers, learners, technicians and administrators. These different encounter modes will change with technology as it moves from the common asynchronous to the synchronous and on to multiple realities where the learner is participating in a multi-user online environment. As we shift from online communication contexts that are frequently a series of many one-to-one negotiations to environments that are many-to-many, we need to ensure we are prepared by better understanding how all stakeholders within the online context can best cooperate and achieve. In the meantime, teachers can be conceptualised as the interpreter of design, through which significant communication and negotiation needs to take place.

We have presented these ideas as they have helped to frame a wider set of learning outcomes which are possible with online learning contexts and which will help the new online facilitator to focus the experiences so that students are supported through their learning journey. In effect, they will answer at each option point the questions around the types of encounters:

- What do I need to provide to welcome and help the learner?
- How do I show and direct learners to the best learning pathway?
- What can I do to evaluate what options make the best choice based on the evidence of their understanding?
- What are my expectations about context and how are they made explicit to the learner?
- Have I established a supportive narrative that will facilitate the relationships particularly between students and myself, and between students (and in accord with other stakeholders)?

Rethinking the way we interact with the stakeholders we encounter within online environments is akin to acknowledging Robbins' (1994) admonition that we may be working with the wrong libretto – that the principles we currently practise by may not be aligned accurately to the online context. And it also reminds us of the importance of realignment and readjustment of the theories which inform our thinking (Jonassen *et al.*, 1997). Therefore, as higher education increasingly relies on learning experiences through online environments, more teachers will be working with virtual classrooms of learners who will expect to be supported through their studies in a meaningful way. By becoming aware of how the different encounters occur during this process it is possible to maximise the opportunity for all stakeholders in these environments to experience more rewarding outcomes.

References

Dictionary.com (2005) Online. Available at: www.dictionary.com (Accessed 20 January 2005).

Dringus, L. P. (1999) 'Connecting resources in online learning environments', *Online Journal of Distance Learning Administration*, 2(2). Online. Available at: http://www.westga.edu/~distance/dringus22.html (Accessed 7 January 2005).

Hedberg, J. (2004) 'Designing multimedia: seven discourses', *Cambridge Journal of Education*, 25(3), 241–56.

Hedberg, J. and Sims, R. (2001) 'Speculations on design team interactions', *Journal of Interactive Learning Research*, 12(2/3), 189–204.

Hillman, D. C., Willis, D. J. and Gunawardena, C. N. (1994) 'Learner-interface interaction in distance education: an extension of contemporary models and strategies for practitioners', *The American Journal of Distance Education*, 8(2), 30–42.

Humpherys, S. (2003) 'Online multi-user games: playing for real'. Online. Available at: http://www.bgsb.qut.edu.au/conferences/ANZCA03/Proceedings/papers/humphreys_full.pdf (Accessed 22 January 2005).

IBSTPI (2003) International Board of Standards for Training Performance and Instruction. Online. Available at: http://www.ibstpi.org (Accessed 20 January 2005).

Jonassen, D. H., Hennon, R. J., Ondrusek, A., Samouilova, M., Spaulding, K. L., Yueh, H. P., Li, T. C., Nouri, V., DiRocco, M. and Birdwell, D. (1997) 'Certainty, determinism, and predictability in theories of instructional design: lessons from science', *Educational Technology*, 37(1), 27–34.

Kearsley, G. and Shneiderman, B. (1998) 'Engagement theory: a framework for technology-based teaching and learning', *Educational Technology*, 38(5), 20–3.

Laurel, B. (1991) *Computers as Theatre*, Reading, MA: Addison Wesley.

Moore, M. G. (1989) 'Editorial: three types of interaction', *The American Journal of Distance Education*, 3(2), 1–7.

Palloff, R. M. and Pratt, K. (2003) *The Virtual Student: A Profile and Guide to Working with Online Learners*, San Francisco, CA: Jossey-Bass.

Plowman, L. (1996) 'Narrative, linearity and interactivity: making sense of interactive multimedia', *British Journal of Educational Technology*, 27(2), 92–105.

Reigeluth, C. M. (1999) *Instructional-Design Theories and Models*, Volume II, Mahwah, NJ: Lawrence Erlbaum.

Robbins, T. (1994) *Half Asleep in Frogs Pyjamas*, New York: Bantam Books.

Salmon, G. (2004) *E-Moderating*, 2nd edn, London: Kogan Page.

Scardamalia, M. and Bereiter, C. (1994) 'Computer support for knowledge-building communities', *The Journal of the Learning Sciences*, 3(3), 265–83.

Sims, R. (2003a) 'Interactivity and feedback as determinants of engagement and meaning in e-learning environments', in S. Naidu (ed.), *E-Learning: Technology and the Development of Teaching and Learning*, London: Kogan Page.

Sims, R. (2003b) 'Promises of interactivity: aligning learner perceptions and expectations with strategies for open and flexible learning', *Distance Education*, 24(1), 87–103.

Sims, R. and Jones, D. (2003) 'Where practice informs theory: reshaping instructional design for academic communities of practice in online teaching and learning', *Information Technology, Education and Society*, 4(1), 3–20.

Spinello, R. A. and Tavani, H. T. (2004) *Readings in Cyberethics*, 2nd edn, Boston, MA: Jones and Bartlett Publishers.

Tognazzini, B. (1999) 'Magic and software design'. Online. Available at: http://www. asktog.com/papers/magic.html (Accessed 22 January 2005).

Wagner, E. D. (1994) 'In support of a functional definition of interaction', *The American Journal of Distance Education*, 8(2), 6–29.

Whitaker, R. (2005) 'Thanks for the magic, Humberto', *Cybernetics and Human Knowing*, 11(4), 93–7.

Chapter 3

Analysing and designing e-learning interactions

Atsusi Hirumi

Published taxonomies give educators valuable insights into the nature and range of interactions that may be used to facilitate e-learning. However, they fail to provide practical guidelines for designing and sequencing a comprehensive set of interactions necessary to achieve a specified set of instructional objectives. This chapter posits a three-level framework for classifying e-learning interactions and illustrates how the framework may be used to (a) design e-learning interactions and alternative e-learning environments, (b) analyse planned interaction to optimize learning and reduce the need for costly revisions, and (c) organize research on e-learning interactions to help interpret findings and guide future studies.

Introduction

Interactions are one of the most frequently discussed topics and a critical concern among distance educators (Saba, 2000). Without interactions, instruction may simply become 'passing on content as it if were dogmatic truth, and the cycle of knowledge acquisition, critical evaluation and knowledge validation, that is important for the development of higher-order thinking skills, is nonexistent' (Shale and Garrison, 1990, p. 29). While many concur with such statements, some question the significance of interactions in distance education (DE). In a review of DE research, Simonson *et al.* (2000, p. 61) conclude, 'similar to [media] comparison studies examining achievement, research comparing differing amounts of interaction showed that interaction had little effect on achievement' (Beare, 1989; Souder, 1993). Research is needed to support the intuitive sense that interactions are important and necessary (Moore, 1995) and effort must be made to synthesize what is known to guide research and practice.

This chapter posits a framework that delineates three-levels of e-learning interactions. It begins by examining existing taxonomies and defining the components of the proposed framework. It then illustrates how the framework may be used to (a) design and sequence e-learning interactions, (b) analyse the nature and quantity of e-learning interactions, and (c) organize existing literature on interactions.

Existing taxonomies

Published taxonomies for classifying e-learning interactions may be grouped into four categories: (a) communication, (b) purpose, (c) activity, and (d) tool-based taxonomies (Hirumi, 2002b).

Communication-based taxonomies

Communication-based taxonomies specify the sender and receiver of the interaction. Moore (1989) posits one of the most widely known taxonomies, defining three basic interactions: student–student, student–teacher and student–content. In Chapter 1, Mayes examines each of these interactions from a similar perspective, depicting interactions as learner–representation (content), learning–tutor (instructor), and learner–peers (learner).

With the increasing use of computers, Hillman *et al.* (1994) argued convincingly for a forth class, learner–interface interactions, where the interface acts as the means of interaction including learners' use of electronic tools and navigational aids.

Others posit additional classes of communication-based interactions. For example, in 1999, Carlson and Repman defined learner–instructional interactions as those between the learner and the content that utilize strategies such as questioning, feedback and clarification, and control of lesson pace and sequence. In 2001, Hedberg and Sims first noted the importance of considering learner–designer interactions, illustrating how learners are affected by the environment that is created, to a large extent, by the designer, and in Chapter 2, Sims and Hedberg identified additional learner–stakeholder interactions that include encounters between learners, teachers, designers, technicians and administrators.

Purpose-based taxonomies

An alternative approach codifies interactions based on purpose. For example, Hannafin (1989) posits five basic purposes for computer-based interactions; to (a) confirm, (b) pace, (c) inquire, (d) navigate, and (e) elaborate. To guide the selection of online instructional strategies and tactics, Northrup (2001) proposes five interaction attributes (or purposes); to (a) interact with content, (b) collaborate, (c) converse, (d) help monitor and regulate learning (intrapersonal interaction), and (e) support performance. With the emerging use of telecommunication technologies, Breakthebarriers.com (2001) identified nine purposes; to (a) communicate synchronously, (b) communicate asynchronously, (c) browse and click, (d) branch, (e) track, (f) help, (g) practise, (h) provide feedback, and (i) coach.

Activity-based taxonomies

Activity-based taxonomies specify the level or type of interactivity experienced by learners. For instance, to guide the development of Interactive Multimedia

Instruction, the Department of Defense (2001) distinguishes four levels of interactivity: (a) Level 1 – Passive (student acts solely as a receiver of information), (b) Level 2 – Limited Participation (student makes simple responses to instructional cues), (c) Level 3 – Complex Participation (student makes a variety of responses using varied techniques in response to instructional cues), and (d) Level 4 – Real Time Participation (student is directly involved in a lifelike set of complex cues and responses).

Others note different types of online activities and group them in three basic categories. For example, based on a wide range of literature on learning and instruction, Bonk and Reynolds (1997) list a number of activities that may be designed to promote critical thinking, creative thinking, and cooperative learning online. Similarly, Harris (1994a, 1994b, 1994c) discusses various interactivities for information searching, information sharing, and collaborative problem-solving.

Tool-based taxonomies

Bonk and King (1998) take a 'tools-based' approach, focusing on the capabilities afforded by various technologies to facilitate e-learning. They delimit five levels, ranging from basic to complex telecommunication tools: (a) electronic mail and delayed-messaging tools, (b) remote access and delayed collaboration tools, (c) real-time brainstorming and conversation tools, (d) real-time text collaboration tools, and (e) real-time multimedia and/or hypermedia collaboration tools.

Existing taxonomies provide valuable insights into the nature and range of interactions that may be used to facilitate e-learning. However, they do not provide practical guidelines for designing and sequencing a comprehensive array of interactions necessary to facilitate e-learning. Within an instructional unit or lesson, when should the instructor interact with students and what should be the nature of these interactions? When should students interact with other students, with content information or with external resources? How should each of these interactions be designed? What tools should be used to facilitate each interaction? This chapter seeks to answer these questions by proposing a framework that may be used to analyse, design and sequence e-learning interactions.

Three-level framework

The proposed framework posits three interrelated levels of interactions that may be planned as an integral part of e-learning (Figure 3.1).

Level I interactions occur within the minds of individual learners. Level II interactions occur between the learner and human and non-human resources. Level III interactions define an e-learning strategy that guides the design and sequencing of Level II interactions that, in turn, stimulate Level I interactions. It is the alignment of Levels I, II and III that is thought to be essential for the design and sequencing of meaningful e-learning interactions and the development of sound e-learning environments.

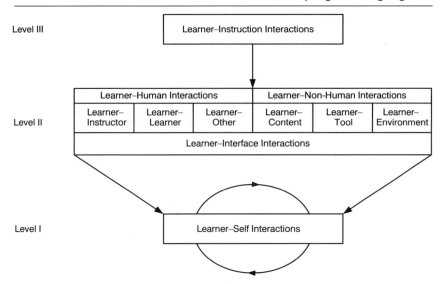

Figure 3.1 Three levels of planned e-learning interactions

Level I: learner–self interactions

Learner–self interactions consist of the cognitive operations that constitute learning and the metacognitive processes that help individuals monitor and regulate learning. The specific operations that occur within a learner's mind depend on the epistemological beliefs of the person applying the framework. A behaviourist with a positivist epistemology may recognize that learner–self interactions occur, but may choose not to attend to them, concentrating solely on Level II and Level III interactions and how they reinforce or weaken particular overt behaviours. In contrast, for someone who believes in information-processing theories of learning, key learner–self interactions may include sensory memory, selective attention, pattern recognition, short term memory, rehearsal and chunking, encoding, long-term memory and retrieval. Alternatively, a developmental constructivist may concentrate on learner–self interactions that result from adaptations to the environment that are characterized by increasingly sophisticated methods of representing and organizing information, and a social constructivist may focus on learner–self interactions that occur when individuals interact with their social and cultural environment.

Studies on self-regulation underscore the importance of distinguishing learner–self interactions (see Zimmerman and Martinez-Pons, 1988; Zimmerman and Paulsen, 1995; Corno, 1994). Self-regulated learners may have a greater potential for success than those with relatively poor self-regulatory skills because they may not need as much prompting from an instructor or help from other learners to monitor, regulate and otherwise facilitate their learning. Fortunately, self-regulation may be learned and instruction may be designed to compensate for possible deficiencies (Corno and Randi, 1999; Iran-Nejad, 1990).

In short, the proposed framework does not adhere to any particular theory or epistemology. Level I: learner–self interactions that depict beliefs about how and why people learn and regulate their learning should, however, drive the selection of Level III interaction and the subsequent design and sequencing of Level II interactions as discussed later in this chapter.

Level II: learner–human and non-human interactions

Level II interactions occur between the learner and other human or non-human resources. Seven classes of Level II interactions are presented based on a framework for comparing instructional strategies posited by Reigeluth and Moore (1999). Two recent refinements have been made to the original framework (Hirumi, 2002b). Specifically, learner–interface interactions have been repositioned to better illustrate their relationship to other Level II interactions and, like Reigeluth and Moore, learner–tool interactions have been distinguished from learner–environment interactions.

Learner–interface interactions

During e-learning, the user interface serves as the primary point, but not necessarily the sole means, of interaction with both human and non-human resources. Attention must be placed on how the interface enables learners to manipulate electronic tools, view and access content, and interact with others. Hillman *et al.* (1994) suggest that the extent to which a learner is proficient with a specific medium correlates positively with the success the learner has in extracting information from the medium. Metros and Hedberg (2002) also note that poor interface design can place high cognitive demands upon the learner that may take their attention away from the subject matter.

Learner–instructor interactions

Learner–instructor interactions are defined as student or instructor initiated communications that occur before, during and immediately after instruction. Moore (1989) characterizes learner–instructor interactions as attempts to motivate and stimulate the learner and to allow for the clarification of misunderstanding by the learner. A recent study of distance educator competencies reveals seven learner–instructor interactions, to: (a) establish learning outcomes/objectives; (b) provide timely and appropriate feedback; (c) facilitate information presentation; (d) monitor and evaluate student performance; (e) provide (facilitate) learning activities; (f) initiate, maintain and facilitate discussions; and (g) determine learning needs and preferences (Thach and Murphy, 1995).

Learner–learner interactions

Learner–learner interactions occur 'between one learner and another learner, alone or in group settings, with or without the real-time presence of an instructor' (Moore, 1989, p. 4). Typically, such interactions ask learners to work together to analyse and interpret data, solve problems, and share information, opinions and insights. They are designed to help groups and individuals construct knowledge and apply targeted skills.

Assigning individuals to groups does not mean that they will work collaboratively (Johnson and Johnson, 1993). For the most part, considerations for effective learner–learner interactions are similar in traditional classroom and e-learning environments (e.g. group size, composition, goals, roles and responsibilities, tools, contact information, grading). The challenge lies in planning and managing such interactions in a meaningful manner at a distance through the use of telecommunication technologies.

Many have written about learner–learner interactions, some in context of other key interactions (e.g. Mayes, Chapter 1), and others as the primary focus of discussion (e.g. Juwah, Chapter 10). Those particularly interested in learner–learner interactions are also referred to literature on cooperative learning (e.g. Totten *et al.*, 1991; Slavin, 1989, 1987; Johnson and Johnson, 1986) and social constructivism (e.g. Jonassen, 1999; Vygotsky, 1978; von Glasersfeld, 1989).

Learner–other human interactions

Learner–other human interactions enable learners to acquire, interpret and apply information from various resources. Increasing numbers of online courses ask learners to communicate with others outside class to promote knowledge construction and social discourse (e.g. Bonk and King, 1998). In education, such interactions may include exchanges with teaching assistants, mentors, subject matter experts, and academic support staff. In industry, learner–other human interactions may consist of communications with workplace managers and supervisors. Learner–other human interactions may occur online or face-to-face depending on the location and configuration of the learners and the other human resources.

Accrediting agencies, such as Southern Association of Colleges (SACS), also remind us that distance learners must be afforded the same services provided to local students. During the design of e-learning programmes, educators must consider how distance learners will be able to contact and garner support and services from staff such as librarians, advisors and counsellors. The pervasive use of computer technology also makes ready, if not immediate access to technical support staff essential during e-learning.

Learner–content interactions

Learner–content interactions occur when learners access audio, video, text and graphic representations of the subject matter under study. Each multimedia element may present learners with content information or other instructional events. The key distinction between Level II learner–content interactions and Level III learner–instruction interactions is that Level III presents a comprehensive sequence of instructional events that comprise an instructional or e-learning strategy, whereas Level II interactions focus on individual events and the sender and receiver of the event.

Learner–tool interactions

Learners interact with tools to complete tasks both within and outside the computer environment. Telecommunication tools, such as electronic mail, discussion forums, and chat, are often integrated within learning management systems to facilitate learner–human interactions. Productivity tools, such as word processors, databases, spreadsheets and graphic applications, may also be used to facilitate e-learning. Outside the computer environment, learners may be asked to use tools, such as a microscope, to complete specified activities. Whatever the case, the use of tools during e-learning warrants consideration. Instructors and/or support staff must ensure that learners have access to required tools during and after instruction (as a learner, it can very frustrating to be trained on a software application that is not available on-the-job). Furthermore, instructors and instructional designers must take into account the prerequisite skills and knowledge necessary to use specified tools.

Learner–environment interactions

Learner–environment interactions occur when learners visit locations or work with resources outside the computer environment. As noted earlier, not all e-learning interactions must occur online. Learners may be asked to seek or travel to specific locations to gather, observe and otherwise use external resources to complete activities and participate in planned educational events.

Learner–environment interactions may be difficult to manage at a distance, but when necessary, they can be arranged. Like planning complex learner–other human interactions, the keys are to: (a) clearly delineate the desired learning outcomes and identify when learner–environment interactions are essential for the achievement of those outcomes; (b) plan and coordinate the interactions so that learners readily understand what is expected of them and why it is important for them to interact with their environment; and (c) integrate the event with other interactions and embed them within a sound instructional strategy to optimize the experience and ensure learners reach the specified objectives.

Level III: learner–instruction interactions

Congruent with Driscoll's (1994) definition for instruction, learner–instruction interactions involve a deliberate arrangement of events to promote learning and facilitate goal achievement. Level III is considered a meta-level that transcends, and is used to guide the design and sequencing of Level II interactions. Learner–instruction interactions are distinguished to illustrate how grounded instructional strategies may be used to design and sequence vital e-learning interactions associated with an instructional unit.

Educators often fail to ground their designs in research and theory (Bonk and King, 1998; Bednar *et al.*, 1995). While there is no substitute for practical experience, difficulties occur when e-learning strategies are based solely on past practices. With little time, training or support, educators rely on what they know best (i.e. teacher-directed methods). Such methods, however, are often inadequate for facilitating e-learning.

In traditional classroom settings, key interactions that affect learners' attitudes and performance often occur spontaneously in real-time. Good instructors interpret students' body language, answer questions, clarify expectations, facilitate activities, promote discussions, elaborate concepts, render guidance, and provide timely and appropriate feedback. Good instructors also use their expertise to shed light on complex content matter and use their charisma to motivate and engage learners.

During e-learning, communications are predominately asynchronous and mediated by technology. Opportunities to address individual and group needs based on verbal and non-verbal cues are relatively confined. Key interactions that occur spontaneously in traditional teacher-directed classroom environments must be carefully planned and managed as an integral part of e-learning.

So, how do grounded instructional strategies help guide the design and sequencing of Level II interactions? Hannafin *et al.* (1997) define 'grounded design' as 'the systematic implementation of processes and procedures that are rooted in established theory and research in human learning' (p. 102). A grounded approach uses theory and research to make design decisions. It neither subscribes to, nor advocates any particular epistemology, but rather promotes alignment between theory and practice.

A cursory review of literature on teaching methods reveals a number of grounded instructional strategies that may be classified, in general, as learner-centred, experiential or teacher-directed pedagogical approaches (Figure 3.2).

Each event associated with a strategy represents an interaction; a transaction that occurs between the learner and other human or non-human resources. The application of a grounded strategy gives educators a foundation for planning and managing a comprehensive series of e-learning interactions based on a combination of research, theory and practical experience.

Learner-Centred Approaches		
Collaborative Problem-Solving (Nelson, 1992) 1. Build Readiness 2. Form and Norm Groups 3. Determine Preliminary Problem 4. Define and Assign Roles 5. Engage in Problem-Solving 6. Finalize Solution 7. Synthesize and Reflect 8. Assess Products and Processes 9. Provide Closure	WebQuest (Dodge, 1998) 1. Introduction 2. Task 3. Process 4. Resources 5. Evaluation 6. Conclusion	Eight Events of Student-Centred Learning (Hirumi, 2002c) 1. Set Learning Challenge 2. Negotiate Goals and Objectives 3. Negotiate Learning Strategy 4. Construct Knowledge 5. Negotiate Performance Criteria 6. Assess Learning 7. Provide Feedback (Steps 1–6) 8. Communicate Results
BSCS 5E Model (Bybee, 2002) 1. Engage 2. Explore 3. Explain 4. Elaborate 5. Evaluate	Case-Based Reasoning (Aamodt and Plaza, 1994) 1. Present New Case/Problem 2. Retrieve Similar Cases 3. Reuse Information 4. Revise Proposed Solution 5. Retain Useful Experiences	Problem-Based Learning (Barrows, 1985) 1. Start New Class 2. Start a New Problem 3. Problem Follow-Up 4. Performance Presentation(s) 5. After Conclusion of Problem
Experiential Approaches		
Experiential Learning (Pfeiffer and Jones, 1975) 1. Experience 2. Publish 3. Process 4. Internalize 5. Generalize 6. Apply	Simulation Model (Joyce et al., 1992) 1. Orientation 2. Participant Training 3. Simulation Operations 4. Participant Debriefing 5. Appraise and Redesign the Simulation	Learning by Doing (Schank et al., 1999) 1. Define Goals 2. Set Mission 3. Present Cover Story 4. Establish Roles 5. Operate Scenarios 6. Provide Resources 7. Provide Feedback
Teacher-Directed Approaches		
Nine Events of Instruction (Gagne, 1974, 1977) 1. Gain Attention 2. Inform Learner of Objective(s) 3. Stimulate Recall of Prior Knowledge 4. Present Stimulus Materials 5. Provide Learning Guidance 6. Elicit Performance 7. Provide Feedback 8. Assess Performance 9. Enhance Retention and Transfer	Direct Instruction (Joyce et al., 1992) 1. Orientation 2. Presentation 3. Structured Practice 4. Guided Practice 5. Independent Practice	Elements of Lesson Design (Hunter, 1990) 1. Anticipatory Set 2. Objective and Purpose 3. Input 4. Modelling 5. Check for Understanding 6. Guided Practice 7. Independent Practice

Figure 3.2 Sample outlines of grounded instructional strategies

Applying the framework

Several applications illustrate the utility of the proposed framework for (a) designing and sequencing interactions, (b) analysing planned interactions, and (c) organising research on interactions.

Designing and sequencing e-learning interactions

Over successive implementations, the original process for applying the framework (Hirumi, 2002a) has evolved into five steps as listed in Figure 3.3.

The selection of an appropriate strategy is critical. It determines the nature of the e-learning environment and guides the overall design and sequencing of e-learning interactions. It requires the instructor and/or instructional designer to consider the desired learning outcomes, learner characteristics, and contextual factors as well as his or her personal values and beliefs about teaching and learning. It may also require the instructor and/or instructional designer to step out of his or her comfort zone, applying a strategy that s/he may have yet to experience.

A fundamental systematic design principle is that the nature of the desired learning outcomes should drive the instructional design process. For instance, the specific technique used to analyse an instructional situation should be based on targeted learning outcomes (Jonassen *et al.*, 1999). Similarly, learner assessment methods should be determined by the nature of specified objectives (Berge, 2002; Hirumi, 2002d). The same principle applies to the selection of a grounded instructional strategy.

For instance, a direct instructional strategy may be effective and efficient for training people on the use of a new photocopying machine (a relatively simple procedure). If there is basically one correct answer or one method for deriving the

---

Step 1 – Select a Level III grounded instructional strategy based on specified objectives, learner characteristics, context and Level I epistemological beliefs;

Step 2 – Operationalize each event, embedding essential experiences and describing how the selected strategy will be applied during instruction;

Step 3 – Determine the type of Level II interaction(s) that will be used to facilitate each event;

Step 4 – Select the telecommunication tool(s) (e.g. chat, email, bulletin board system) that will be used to facilitate each event based on the nature of the interaction.

Step 5 – Analyse materials to determine frequency and quality of planned e-learning interactions and revise as necessary.

Figure 3.3 Five step process for designing and sequencing e-learning interactions

correct answer, learners may not have to derive meaning and construct knowledge through social discourse. In contrast, if the learning outcome requires higher-order thinking and there is more than one correct answer, or more than one way to find the answer, then learner-centred approaches that encourage learners to interact with others to help interpret, apply and otherwise construct knowledge may optimise learning.

Learner characteristics are also important to consider. In some situations, learners may have greatly varying prior knowledge of the subject matter. For example, it is not uncommon for some to begin an introductory computer course with considerable computer experience, while others may start with little to no computer skills. In such cases, a student-centred approach (e.g. Hirumi, 2002c) that allows learners to negotiate their own learning objectives, strategies and assessments based on their particular needs and interests may be useful. Other key learner characteristics may include, but are not necessarily limited to learners' level of social and cognitive development, and preferred learning style.

Key contextual factors, such as the number and nature of learning sites may also affect the selection of an instructional strategy. If there are over 50 students taking a course who are spread across a state and it is important to allow them to work at their own pace, a self-instructional strategy may be necessary. Self-instructional materials that help students monitor and regulate their own learning with few learner–instructor interactions may be more appropriate than a collaborative approach with a high degree of planned learner–learner and/or learner–instructor interactions. Some contexts may also call for the use of specific methods, such as simulations or cases, warranting the use of the simulation model or case-based reasoning as an instructional strategy.

In selecting an appropriate strategy, the instructor's educational philosophy and epistemological beliefs must also be taken into account. If the instructor believes that people derive meaning and construct knowledge through social interactions, then constructivist, learner-centred, and cooperative instructional strategies may support his or her beliefs. In contrast, if the instructor or designer believes people learn best by 'doing,' then an experiential approach may resonate with his or her educational philosophy. In cases where an instructional designer works with the instructor to create instructional materials, discussions of beliefs and values are warranted, leading to a common vision of a general instructional approach (e.g. learner-centred, experiential, teacher-directed) and then the selection of a grounded strategy.

Selecting an appropriate instructional strategy is neither simple, nor straight-forward. Much depends on the desired learning goals and objectives, but concerns for the learner, the context and fundamental beliefs about teaching and learning also mediate the selection process. Perhaps even a stronger influence is time and expertise. With insufficient time or training, educators often revert to what they know best; that is, teacher-directed methods and materials. To select an appropriate instructional strategy, the instructor and/or designer must have the time and skills necessary to analyse several important variables and consider alternative strategies. They must also have the confidence, desire and the opportunity to apply alternative instructional strategies within the context of their work environment.

Completion of Steps 2–5 is best illustrated through an example. In short, the five steps result in an instructional treatment plan (ITP). The ITP is then used to create flowcharts, storyboards and prototypes of an instructional unit before proceeding to the production of the entire course. Table 3.1 depicts an ITP created by an engineering professor during a two-day workshop on designing e-learning interactions. The instructional unit and corresponding treatment plan were designed

Table 3.1 Sample instructional treatment plan based on WebQuest strategy

Event	Description	Interaction(s)	Tools
Introduction	Present students with series of questions to establish context, need for learning and guide completion of proceeding task.	Learner–Content	WWW
	Ask learners to post message describing reports they have seen and/or written that work.	Learner–Instructor Learner–Learner	BBS
Task	End products: • feasibility report • oral debriefing report	Learner–Content	WWW
Process	1. Identify topic	Learner–Content Learner–Instructor	WWW Email/BBS
	2. Perform research	Learner–Content Learner–Environment Learner–Other (Librarian)	WWW Go to Library Online Library
	3. Generate problem statement	Learner–Content Learner–Learner Learner–Instructor	WWW BBS/Stu. Pres. BBS/Email/Stu. Pres.
	4. Identify options	Learner–Content	WWW
	5. Select criteria	Learner–Content	WWW
	6. Write communication purpose	Learner–Content Learner–Learner	WWW BBS/Stu. Pres.
	7. Write report body	Learner–Content	WWW
	8. Conduct peer reviews	Learner–Content Learner–Learner	BBS/Stu. Pres./ Email
	9. Write final report	Learner–Content Learner–Instructor	WWW Stu./Email
	10. Present debriefing	Learner–Content Learner–Learner (Synchronous) Learner–Instructor	WWW Audiobridge, Chat, Desktop Video/Audio Conferencing,

continued…

Table 3.1 continued

Event	Description	Interaction(s)	Tools
Resources	In addition to the information provided as links from each of the steps listed above, here are a series of resources that may help you complete your task: • Engineering professors • Galileo (online library) • Engineering and scholarly journals • Product Websites • Textbook • Handouts • Sample reports	Learner–Content Learner–Other (Professors) Learner–Environment (Textbook)	WWW F2f, email, phone Purchase (F2f or online)
Evaluation	The following evaluation criteria will be used to evaluate your work and to determine completion of your task. • Grading Rubric for Report • Grading Rubric for Debriefing	Learner–Content Learner–Instructor	WWW Email (feedback templates)
Conclusion	Learner to prepare and submit journal entry reflecting on experience.	Learner–Content Learner–Instructor	WWW Email

Note
BBS = Bulleting Board System; Stu. Pres. = Student Presentation

for undergraduate engineering students with the terminal objective to write and present a feasibility report. The professor selected a WebQuest (Dodge, 1998) as the Level III interaction (or instructional strategy) because the terminal objective requires students to search the World-Wide-Web and synthesize information from at least five sources to prepare their report. A WebQuest was selected as the strategy because the basic task involved the use of a number of pre-specified Web sites and considerable problem-solving skills.

Column 1 lists the key events associated with WebQuests. Column 2 provides a short description of how the professor plans to operationalize each of the events online. Italicized words represent the actual text that is to go online, plain text provides basic descriptions and underlined words indicate links to additional information or resources.

At this stage, the amount of detail to include when describing each event is frequently questioned. The answer is, 'You can do the work now or you can do the work later'. Eventually, you will have to create the images or write the words to be seen by learners. If you write general summaries at this point, significant time will be necessary later to prepare content and vice versa. In cases when a team is tasked with design and development, the more detail put into treatment plans, the less time is required later to explain designs to writers, programmers and other course developers.

Column 3 identifies the type of interaction(s) that will be used to facilitate each event based on the classes of Level II interactions posited by the framework. Does the event require learner–instructor interactions? Learner–learner interactions? Learner–content interactions? One event may require multiple interactions. This is a good time to reflect on the quantity and quality of your planned interactions to determine if you have included an appropriate combination. How many learner–instructor and learner–learner interactions are planned? Do students have sufficient opportunities to interact with one another and with the instructor? Do learners require access to others? Are there too many learner–instructor interactions, making it difficult or impossible for the instructor to manage all of the communications? You may find that you need to go back and revise your description of one or more events, illustrating the iterative nature of the five-step process.

Column 4 denotes the specific telecommunication tools that were selected to facilitate each interaction. Although your primary delivery system may have already been selected, you still have several options. Your task is to determine the appropriate tool(s) for facilitating each interaction (defined in Column 3) that also falls within the confines of available resources. Relevant questions to consider include: who are the primary senders and receivers of the communications? Do learners need audio, video, text and/or graphics? Are synchronous or asynchronous communications necessary? Are the communications one-to-one, one-to-some, or one-to-many? What kind of budget do you have? What kind of technologies and human resources are available? How much time do you have to prepare course materials?

After filling in the four columns, the resulting treatment plan can then be used to generate flowcharts, storyboards and/or prototypes of your instruction. Rather than taking the time to generate an instructional treatment plan for all units that may comprise a course or training programme, prepare a treatment plan for one instructional unit and then create flowcharts and storyboards (if necessary), and generate and test a prototype of your unit. After testing and revising your prototype, it may then be used as a template for designing and developing the remaining instructional units or modules.

Analysing planned e-learning interactions

At this point in the design process, an analysis of planned interactions (Step 5) may help improve the quality of e-learning materials and reduce the need for costly revisions during program development or implementation. Web-based courses with greater interactions can be more complicated to use (Gilbert and Moore, 1998). Berge (1999), for example, found that the overuse or misuse of interactions can lead to frustration, boredom, and overload. For novice distance learners, complex interactions may cause confusion and eventual drop-out. Experienced distance learners may become dissatisfied if they perceive online interactions as meaningless busy work. Furthermore, too many interactions may overwhelm the instructor. A common concern expressed by educators is that it takes far more time and effort to manage an online versus a traditional class. Two potential causes for such overload are (a) too many planned learner–instructor interactions, and (b) poorly designed interactions that require additional clarification, explanation and elaboration.

Table 3.2 represents a planned interaction analysis completed during the workshop of the sample treatment plan presented in Table 3.1.

Column 1 lists each type of interaction specified in the treatment plan. Column 2 denotes the frequency of each type of interaction. Column 3 provides a brief description of the quality or nature of the interaction, and column 4 specifies any required revisions in design or factors to consider during development, implementation or evaluation.

An analysis of each class of planned interactions reveals several crucial considerations. To begin with, the analysis reveals eight planned learner–instructor interactions; far too many for an instructor to handle. For each interaction, the instructor must: acknowledge receipt of the initial communication; save, organize, and track relevant documents; review learners' work; generate and send timely feedback; and ensure learners receive and understand the feedback. If you multiply the effort required to manage each interaction by the number of students and consider that the treatment plan represents just one of several units contained in the course, it is readily apparent that the instructor would be quickly overwhelmed. In such cases, it may be helpful to group or eliminate interactions to reduce the total number of required communications, to group learners to reduce the number of assignments, or to automate one or more interactions so that pre-programmed responses are provided based on users' input.

The second category of planned interactions includes five learner–learner interactions. In light of the number of planned learner–instructor interactions, five learner–learner interactions may be too much. During the workshop, the professor noted that students completed similar learner–learner interactions in her face-to-face courses. However, in conventional classrooms, such interactions occur through speaking and listening, two modes of synchronous communication that take less time than reading and writing. To reduce learner–learner interaction requirements, the professor considered either grouping the interactions (e.g. requiring learners to share and discuss problem and purpose statements as two parts of one online activity) or eliminating one or more interaction.

Analysis of learner–other human interactions identifies two worth noting; potential interactions with a librarian and planned interactions with other professors. Librarians must be informed with enough lead time to allocate resources so that they can respond in a timely fashion. The participation of other professors must also be solicited far enough in advance to ensure sufficient numbers and so they can properly plan for and address learner inquiries.

The analyses of learner–content and learner–interface interactions illustrate the predominate use of the computer to facilitate learner–instructor, learner–learner and learner–content interactions. Such reliance emphasizes the importance of the user interface, suggesting the application of heuristic and scenario-based usability tests (c.f. Neilson, 1993), particularly if the instructor

Table 3.2 Planned interaction analysis of sample treatment plan

Interaction	Quantity	Quality	Design Decision
Learner–Instructor	8	• Ask learner to post message • Review and provide feedback on topic • Review and provide feedback on problem statement • Provide guidance on writing final report • Provide guidance on preparing debriefing • Assess and provide feedback on final report • Assess and provide feedback on debriefing • Review and provide feedback on journal entries	Far too many interactions to manage. Need to review and revise by grouping two or more interactions, grouping students, eliminating or further automating interactions.
Learner–Learner	5	• Share short description of previously seen or written reports • Share and discuss problem statements • Share and discuss purpose statements • Conduct peer reviews of reports • Participate and share comments on debriefings	Maybe too much, need review and pay particular attention during testing.
Learner–Other	2	• Contact Librarian • Contact other Professors	Need to ensure Librarian prepared, need to ensure ready access to other Professors.
Learner–Content	21	• 1 lesson overview page that provides description of and links to information about intro., task, process, resources, evaluation, and conclusion • Detailed descriptions of how to complete each of the 10 tasks associated with the process • Links to 7 resources • 2 detailed evaluation rubrics • Description of how to prepare and submit journal entry	Interface very important to test prior to official course delivery.
Learner–Environment	3	• Go to Library • Acquire and read textbook • Acquire and read journal articles	Need to ensure ready access to library resource and textbook.

continued…

Table 3.2 continued

Interaction	Quantity	Quality	Design Decision
Learner–Tool	2	• Assumed that learners will use word processor to prepare feasibility report. • Assumed that learners will use PowerPoint to prepare presentation	Need to ensure learners have access to and can utilize word processor and PowerPoint.
Learner–Interface	34	• All Learner–Instructor, Learner–Learner, and Learner–Content interactions are mediated through computer interface	Interface very important to test prior to official course delivery.

chooses not to use a commercially available learning management system for course delivery.

Analysis of the learner–environment and learner–tool interactions notes several resources that must be accessible to learners. In this case, the professor must make sure that all learners have ready access to a library, and can obtain textbooks and related journal articles in a timely fashion; processes that may take additional time to establish for distance learners. In addition, the instructor must ensure that learners have access to a word processor and presentation software (e.g., Microsoft PowerPoint™), plus the skills and knowledge necessary to use the applications.

Too few, too many or poorly designed interactions can result in learner and instructor dissatisfaction, inadequate learning and insufficient performance, requiring additional time, effort and expertise to revise instruction; resources that could have been spent on other projects. Improved interface design (Metros and Hedberg, 2002) and the evolution of better Web course authoring and delivery tools may eventually make the technical aspects of online interactions transparent to learners. However, until such improvements are realized, educators must keep in mind that frequency does not equal quality (Northrup, 2001). Analysis of planned e-learning interactions specified in initial drafts of instructional treatment plans can help educators correct potential problems prior to programming as well as identify key factors to consider during development and implementation.

Planned interaction analysis of existing coursework may also help increase the overall effectiveness of e-learning materials. Table 3.3 depicts a scoring sheet used to analyse the planned interactions in one unit of an online introductory computer course designed primarily for K12 teacher candidates. The goal of the unit was to increase learners' ability to interpret and adhere to copyright and fair use policies and laws. To demonstrate acquisition of related concepts, learners were tasked with creating an online scavenger hunt.

Multiple raters were asked to examine each module to increase the reliability of the analysis. Columns 1 and 2 were included in the scoring sheet to facilitate

Table 3.3 Sample scoring sheet used to analyse an existing online instructional unit

Event	Webpage or location	Level II Interaction	Quantity	Comments
I	Lesson 2 Overview Page	L–C L–Int	I	Introduction, TEKS correlates, Resources, Instructional Events (3 paragraphs and 3 lists on 2 pages).
2	Individual Learning Venue	L–C	2	Read textbooks, 17 pages and 11 pages.
3	External Website	L–C L–Int	I	Read Fair Use guidelines on Web site (9 pages, 4,396 words).
4	External Website	L–C L–Int	2	Take online tutorial on copyright and fair use, including an online quiz (13 pages and 4,904 words).
5	Assignment 2.1 Description	L–C L–Int	I	Copyright scavenger hunt (2 paragraphs, 2 lists, links to scavenger hunt, 2 example links, rubric).
6	Assignment 2.1 Task	L–T L–Int	I	Download scavenger hunt.
7	Assignment 2.1 Task	L–T L–Int	I	Save scavenger hunt doc as html.
8	Assignment 2.1 Task	L–T L–Int	I	Upload file using Submit Assignment tool.
9	Assignment 2.1 Task	L–T L–Int	I	Create link to scavenger hunt on splash page.
10	External Website	L–C L–Int	I	Read description of Netiquette on Web site listed (12 pages, 3,290 words).
11	Course Email System	L–I L–Int	I	Learner receives feedback from the instructor via email.

communications between the raters. Column 1 (Event #) notes each time the learner is asked to interact with an item or person as they proceed through the unit. Column 2 depicts the location of the interaction, whether it occurs within the course (e.g. Lesson 2 Overview Page), on an external Web site linked to the course, or at whatever venue s/he chooses to complete the interaction. Column 3 notes the type of Level II interaction that was specified to facilitate each event. Column 4 lists the number of interactions associated with each event and column 5 describes the nature of each interaction. Table 3.4 summarizes the results of the analysis applying the same format used to report the planned interaction analysis completed during the design phase (Table 3.2).

Table 3.4 Summary of planned interaction analysis for an existing online instructional unit

Interaction	Quantity	Quality	Design Decision
Learner–Instructor	1	• Instructor reviews assignment and provides feedback	Consider adding a formative feedback cycle where the learner submits a draft of their assignment and receives feedback prior to submitting the assignment for a grade.
Learner–Learner	0	NA	Consider adding learner–learner interactions that ask learners to share and discuss alternative interpretations of copyright and fair use laws and policies.
Learner–Other	0	NA	NA
Learner–Content	8	• Introduction, TEKS correlates, Resources, Instructional Events (3 paragraphs, 3 lists on 2 pages) • Read textbooks (17 pages and 11 pages) • Read Fair Use guidelines on Web site (9 pages, 4,396 words) • Take online tutorial on copyright and fair use and take related quiz • Copyright scavenger hunt (2 paragraphs, 2 lists, links to scavenger hunt, 2 example links, rubric) • Read description of Netiquette on Web site listed (12 pages, 3,290 words)	Ensure interface facilitates ready access to and interpretation of content information. Ensure learners know how to navigate and find relevant information on external Web sites. Recommend that the instructor gather data on the user interface and learners' ability to locate and access relevant content information to optimize their time online.
Learner–Tool	4	• Download scavenger hunt • Save scavenger hunt doc as html • Upload file using Submit Assignment tool • Create link to scavenger hunt	Need to make sure learners know how to download, save and upload files, as well as create html links.
Learner–Environment	0	NA	NA

continued…

Table 3.4 continued

Interaction	Quantity	Quality	Design Decision
Learner–Interface	11	• Introduction, TEKS correlates, Resources, Instructional Events • Read Fair Use guidelines on Web site • Take online tutorial on copyright and fair use • Take quiz • Read Copyright Scavenger Hunt assignment • Download scavenger hunt • Save scavenger hunt doc as html • Upload file using Submit Assignment tool • Create link to scavenger hunt on splash page • Read description of Netiquette on Web site listed • Instructor reviews assignment and provides feedback	Important to test interface prior to implementation. Again, it is recommended that the instructor gather data on the user interface and learners' ability to locate and access relevant information to optimize their time online.

Column 4 describes recommendations for improving the instructional module based on the analysis. In short, there was only one planned learner–instructor interaction and no planned learner–learner interactions to help learners interpret and apply content information. Considering the assignment only asked learners to demonstrate that they have located relevant information, the number and nature of learner–instructor and learner–learner interactions may be sufficient. However, since the instructor wants to develop learners' ability to interpret and apply copyright and fair use laws and policies (as specified in the terminal objective for the lesson), it was recommended that the instructor add a few learner–instructor and learner–learner interactions to formatively evaluate learners' work and to help learners interpret and apply related laws and policies.

Analysis of learner–tool interactions notes the importance of ensuring that learners know how to download, save and upload files, as well as create html links. The instructor and/or support staff must make sure that learners have the necessary prerequisite skills and/or ensure that technical support is available as learners complete the assignment.

The considerable number of learner–content interactions facilitated through the computer emphasizes the need to ensure that the user interface facilitates ready access to and interpretation of content information. Links to and the use of external Web sites also highlights the importance of ensuring learners know how to navigate and find relevant information. It is recommended that the instructor gather data on the user interface and learners' ability to locate and access relevant information to optimize their time online.

The analyses of a design document and of an existing instructional unit illustrate how the proposed framework may be used to optimize both the quantity and the quality of planned interaction. The two examples were also chosen to show how the analysis may result in recommendations for reducing, as well as possibly increasing, the number of specific interactions to optimize both the learners' and the instructor's time online as well as promote achievement of specified learning outcomes.

Organizing research on e-learning interactions

In 2002, Bannan-Ritland used the original version of the framework to identify trends in a comprehensive review of literature on e-learning and computer-mediated-communications, illustrating the utility of the framework for organizing and guiding research (Bannan-Ritland, 2002). Several chapters contained in this book are examined here to further demonstrate how the framework may be used to organize literature on e-learning interactions and help direct future research.

In Chapter 1, Mayes refers to all three levels of interactions posited in the framework. Specifically, he describes three cyclical stages of learning (Level I interactions) and discusses each stage in relation to interactive tasks based on a constructivist instructional approach (Level III interactions) and interactivity with concepts (Level II learner–content interactions), and interactivity in dialogue (Level II learner–learner, learner–tool, and learner–instructor or tutor interactions).

In Chapter 2, Sims and Hedberg focus on a specific Level II interaction (learner–interface) and discuss the implications of encounter theory for the design of online learning environments, including learner–instructor, learner–learner and learner–other (designers, administrators, and technicians) interactions. Similarly, Bennett, Lockyer and Harper focus on a specific Level II interaction, detailing object-oriented approaches toward content development and relating the use of learning objects to learning designs and interactions in Chapter 6.

In Chapter 8, Anderson discusses three Level II interactions (learner–learner, learner–teacher and learner–content) in the context of an Educational Semantic Web that includes other Level II interactions (learner–tool and learner–other). In Chapter 9, Mishra and Juwah also concentrate on learner–learner, learner–teacher, and learner–content interactions, as well as the tools used to facilitate such interactions, but do so in light of online discussions and the management of instructor time.

Juwah, in Chapter 10, concentrates on learner–learner interactions and their relationship to learner–interface and learner–tool interactions, basing his discussion on key pedagogical principles related to Level I interactions, and in Chapter 12, Panda and Juwah describe constructivist learning principles (Level I interactions) and discuss the professional development of instructors designing relevant Level II interactions.

Further examination of the chapters contained in this book reveals several trends:

- Studies typically do not focus on one type of interaction, as noted by Bannan-Ritland (2002). Investigators usually concentrate on one class of interactions and discuss its affect on others.
- Some authors identify (Level III) guidelines for designing specific (Level II) learner–human and non-human interactions based on their (Level I) beliefs about how and why people learn. However, such guidelines tend to be heuristic in nature. Grounded (Level III) strategies that provide an algorithm for designing and sequencing (Level II) e-learning interactions, such as those shown in Figure 3.1, tend to be easier to transfer and apply across settings.
- Limited learner–environment interactions are considered in blended learning environments, and are not often addressed in totally online courses or training programmes. Just because a course is offered totally online, does not mean significant interactions with the environment (e.g. visiting labs and clinics) cannot be planned as an integral part of learning. However, research on e-learning interactions often neglects such opportunities, choosing to focus on online interactions, or limit discussions of learner–environment interactions to conventional face-to-face classroom meetings in blended environments. Although they may be difficult to arrange, particularly if learners are spread across the country and around the world, learner–environment interactions may enable learners to achieve learning outcomes that people argue cannot be achieved in online courses and programmes (e.g. interpersonal skills).

Conclusion

The creation of modern e-learning programmes requires research and the development of new methods that fully utilize the capabilities of telecommunication technologies and the potential they afford collaborative and independent learning (Bates, 1990; Mason and Kaye, 1990). This chapter posited a three-level framework for analysing, designing, sequencing and organizing research on planned e-learning interactions. Level III (learner–instruction) interactions were viewed as a meta-level that provides educators with a grounded approach for designing and sequencing Level II interactions that, in turn, stimulated Level I interactions that occur within the learner's mind.

Two examples illustrated how the proposed framework may be used to analyse planned e-learning interactions. First, the frequency and quality of planned interactions were inspected during design to reduce the need for costly revisions and optimize both the learners' and the instructor's time online. Second, the design and sequencing of planned interactions in an instructional unit were recorded and analysed to illustrate how the framework may be used to optimize e-learning within an existing course.

Finally, several chapters contained in this book were examined to illustrate how the proposed framework may be used to analyse, organize and guide research on planned e-learning interactions.

Key interactions that can affect student attitudes and performance must be carefully planned and managed as an integral part of e-learning. Published taxonomies reveal a plethora of interactions that may be used to facilitate e-learning. However, relatively little has been done to synthesize literature on, delimit the relationships between, and provide practical guidelines for designing and sequencing e-learning interactions. The effectiveness of the proposed framework has been demonstrated in several practical situations (e.g. workshops and in the design of secondary, undergraduate and graduate e-learning coursework), but much work remains.

Further study is required to provide empirical evidence for its utility and to optimize the design and sequencing of planned e-learning interactions.

References

Aamodt, A. and Plaza, E. (1994) 'Case-based reasoning: foundational issues, methodological variations, and systems approaches', *Artificial Intelligence Communications*, 7(1), 39–59.

Bannan-Ritland, B. (2002) 'Computer-mediated communication (CMC), e-learning and interactivity: a review of the research', *Quarterly Review of Distance Education*, 3(2), 141–60.

Barrows, H. S. (1985) *How to Design a Problem-based Curriculum for the Preclinical Years*, New York: Springer Publishing Co.

Bates, A. W. (1990) 'Third generation distance education: the challenge of new technology', Paper presented at the XV World Conference on Distance Education, Caracas, Venezuela (ERIC Document Reproduction Service No. 332-688).

Beare, P. L. (1989) 'The comparative effectiveness of videotape, audiotape, and telelecture in delivering continuing teacher education', *The American Journal of Distance Education*, 3(2), 57–66.

Bednar, A., Cunningham, D. J., Duffy, T. and Perry, D. (1995) 'Theory in practice: how do we link?', in G. Anglin (ed.), *Instructional Technology: Past, Present, and Future*, 2nd edn, Englewood, CO: Libraries Unlimited.

Berge, Z. (1999) 'Interaction in post-secondary Web-based learning', *Educational Technology*, 39(1), 5–11.

Berge, Z. (2002) 'Active, interactive, and reflective learning', *Quarterly Review of Distance Education*, 3(2), 141–60.

Bonk, C. J. and King, K. (1998) 'Computer conferencing and collaborative writing tools: Starting a dialogue about student dialogue', in C. J. Bonk and K. King (eds), *Electronic Collaborators: Learner-Centered Technologies for Literacy, Apprenticeship, and Discourse*, Mahwah, NJ: Lawrence Erlbaum.

Bonk, C. J. and Reynolds, T. H. (1997) 'Learner-centered Web instruction for higher-order thinking, teamwork, and apprenticeship', in B. Khan (ed.), *Web-Based Instruction*, Englewood Cliffs, NJ: Educational Technology Publications.

Breakthebarriers.com (2000) *What is interactivity?* Online. Available at: http://www.breakthebarriers.com/hottopic.html (Accessed 2 March 2001).

Bybee, R. W. (2002) 'Scientific inquiry, student learning, and the science curriculum', in R. W. Bybee (ed.), *Learning Science and the Science of Learning*, Arlington, VA: NSTA Press.

Carlson, R. D. and Repman, J. (1999) 'Web-based interactivity', *WebNet Journal*, 1(2), 11–13.

Corno, L. (1994) 'Student volition and education: outcomes, influences, and practices', in D. H. Schunk and B. J. Zimmerman (eds), *Self-regulation of Learning and Performance: Issues and Educational Applications*, Hillsdale, NJ: Lawrence Erlbaum.

Corno, L. and Randi, J. (1999) 'A design theory for classroom instruction in self-regulated learning', in C. M. Reigeluth (ed.), *Instructional Design Theories and Models: A New Paradigm of Instructional Theory* (Vol. II), Mahwah, NJ: Lawrence Erlbaum.

Department of Defense (DOD) (2001) 'Development of interactive multimedia' (Part 3 of 5 Parts) MIL-HDBK-29612-3, p. 45.

Dodge, B. (1998) *The WebQuest Page*. Online. Available at: http://edweb.sdsu.edu/webquest/webquest.html (Accessed on 3 April 2000).

Driscoll, M. P. (1994) *Psychology of Learning for Instruction*, Needham Heights, MA: Paramount Publishing.

Gagne, R. M. (1974) *Principles of Instructional Design*, New York: Holt, Rinehart and Winston.

Gagne, R. M. (1977) *The Conditions of Learning*, 3rd edn, New York: Holt, Rinehart

Gilbert, L. and Moore, D. R. (1998) 'Building interactivity into Web courses: tools for social and instructional interactions', *Educational Technology*, 38(3), 29–35.

Hannafin, M. J. (1989) 'Interaction strategies and emerging instructional technologies: psychological perspectives', *Canadian Journal of Educational Communication*, 18(3), 167–79.

Hannafin, M. J., Hannafin, K. M., Land, S. M. and Oliver, K. (1997) 'Grounded practice and the design of learning systems', *Educational Technology Research and Development*, 45(3), 101–17.

Harris, J. (1994a) 'People-to-people projects on the Internet', *The Computing Teacher*, February, 48–52.

Harris, J. (1994b) 'Information collection activities', *The Computing Teacher*, March, 32–6.

Harris, J. (1994c) 'Opportunities in work clothes: online problem-solving project structures', *The Computing Teacher*, April, 52–5.

Hedberg, J. and Sims, R. (2001) 'Speculations on design team interactions', *Journal of Interactive Learning Research*, 12(2/3), 189–204.

Hillman, D. C., Willis, D. J. and Gunawardena, C. N. (1994) 'Learner-interface interaction in distance education: an extension of contemporary models and strategies for practitioners', *The American Journal of Distance Education*, 8(2), 30–42.

Hirumi, A. (2002a) 'A framework for analyzing, designing and sequencing planned e-learning interactions', *Quarterly Review of Distance Education,* 3(2), 141–60.

Hirumi, A. (2002b) 'The design and sequencing of e-learning interactions: a grounded approach', *International Journal on E-Learning*, 1(1), 19–27.

Hirumi, A. (2002c) 'Student-centered, technology-rich, learning environments (SCenTRLE): operationalizing constructivist approaches to teaching and learning', *Journal for Technology and Teacher Education*, 10(4), 497–537.

Hirumi, A. (2002d) 'Get a life: six tactics for reducing time spent online', *Computers in Schools*, 20(3), 73–101.

Hunter, M. (1990) 'Lesson design helps achieve the goals of science instruction', *Educational Leadership*, 48(4), 79–81.

Iran-Nejad, A. (1990) 'Active and dynamic self-regulation of learning processes', *Review of Educational Research*, 60, 573–602.

Johnson, D. W. and Johnson, R. T. (1993) 'Simulation and gaming: fidelity, feedback and motivation', in J. V. Dempsey and G. C. Sales (eds), *Interactive Instruction and Feedback*, Englewood Cliffs, NJ: Educational Technology.

Johnson, R. T. and Johnson, D. W. (1986) 'Action research: cooperative learning in the science classroom', *Science and Children*, 24, 31–2.

Jonassen, D. H. (1999) 'Designing constructivist learning environments', in C. Reigeluth (ed.), *Instructional-design Theories and Models: A New Paradigm of Instructional Theory*, Mahwah, NJ: Lawrence Erlbaum.

Jonassen, D. H., Tessmer, M. and Hannum, W. H. (1999) *Task Analysis Methods for Instructional Design*, Mahwah, NJ: Lawrence Erlbaum.

Joyce, B., Weil, M. and Showers, B. (1992) *Models of Teaching*, 4th edn, Needham Heights, MA: Allyn and Bacon.

Mason, R. and Kaye, T. (1990) 'Toward a new paradigm for distance education', in L. M. Harasim (ed.), *On-line Education: Perspectives on a New Environment*, New York: Praeger.

Metros, S. and Hedberg, J. (2002) 'More than just a pretty (inter)face: the role of the graphical user interface in engaging online learners', *Quarterly Review of Distance Education*, 3(2), 141–60.

Moore, M. G. (1989) 'Editorial: three types of interaction', *The American Journal of Distance Education*, 3(2), 1–6.

Moore, M. G. (1995) 'The 1995 distance education research symposium: a research agenda', *The American Journal of Distance Education*, 9(2), 1–6.

Neilson, J. (1993) *Usability Engineering*, Boston, MA: AP Professional.

Nelson, L. (1992) 'Collaborative problem-solving', in C. M. Reigeluth (ed.), *Instructional Design Theories and Models: A New Paradigm of Instructional Theory*, Hillsdale, NJ: Lawrence Erlbaum.

Northrup, P. (2001) 'A framework for designing interactivity in Web-based instruction', *Educational Technology*, 41(2), 31–9.

Pfeiffer, J. W. and Jones, J. E. (1975) 'Introduction to the structured experiences section', in J. E. Jones and J. W. Pfeiffer (eds), *The 1975 Annual Handbook for Group Facilitators*, La Jolla, CA: University Associates.

Reigeluth, C. M. and Moore, J. (1999) 'Cognitive education and the cognitive domain', in C. M. Reigeluth (ed.), *Instructional-design Theories and Models: A New Paradigm of Instructional Theory* (Volume II), Mahwah, NJ: Lawrence Erlbaum.

Saba, F. (2000) 'Research in distance education: a status report', *International Review of Research in Open and Distance Learning*, 1(1), 1–9.

Schank, R. C., Berman, T. R. and Macpherson, K. A. (1999) 'Learning by doing', in C. M. Reigeluth (ed.), *Instructional Design Theories and Models: A New Paradigm of Instructional Theory*, Hillsdale, NJ: Lawrence Erlbaum.

Shale, D. and Garrison, D. R. (1990) 'Education and communication', in D. R. Garrison and D. Shale (eds), *Education at a Distance*, Malabar, FL: Robert E. Krieger Publishing.

Simonson, M., Smaldino, S., Albright, M. and Zvacek, S. (2000) *Teaching and Learning at a Distance: Foundations of Distance Education*, Upper Saddle River, NJ: Prentice Hall.

Slavin, R. E. (1987) 'Cooperative learning and the cooperative school', *Educational Leadership*, 47, 14–25.

Slavin, R. E. (1989) 'Research on cooperative learning: an international perspective', *Scandinavian Journal of Educational Research*, 33(4), 231–43.

Souder, W. E. (1993) 'The effectiveness of traditional vs. satellite delivery in three management of technology master's degree programmes', *The American Journal of Distance Education*, 7(1), 37–53.

Thach, E. C. and Murphy, K. L. (1995) 'Competencies for distance education professionals', *Educational Technology Research and Development*, 43(1), 57–79.

Totten, S., Sills, T., Digby, A. and Russ, P. (1991) *Cooperative Learning: A Guide to Research*, New York: Garland.

von Glasersfeld, E. (1989) 'Constructivism in education', in A. Lewy (ed.), *The International Encyclopedia of Curriculum*, Oxford: Pergamon Press.

Vygotsky, L. (1978) *Mind in Society*, Cambridge, MA: Harvard University Press.

Zimmerman, B. J. and Martinez-Pons, M. (1988) 'Construct validation of a strategy model of student self-regulated learning', *Journal of Educational Psychology*, 80, 284–90.

Zimmerman, B. J. and Paulsen, A. S. (1995) 'Self-monitoring during collegiate studying: an invaluable tool for academic self-regulation', in P. R. Pintrich (ed.), *Understanding Self-regulated Learning*, San Francisco, CA: Jossey Bass.

Part II
Design and learning environment

The second section explores the design of learning activities, environments and learning objects as vehicles for practice of skills or processes in a variety of socio-cultural and learning contexts, including the use of games and simulations. These provide a backdrop for the shift in emphasis from the instructivist to more behavioural and motivational approaches that are emerging in this field and how these relate to more socio-cognitive and socio-cultural perspectives on learning and interactions. Within this section, Herrington, Reeves and Oliver present an important model for informing the design, implementation and evaluation of authentic activities in online learning. Also, the section covers the issue of emerging knowledge on learning objects in creating, re-using, sharing and managing learning content. The section also discusses the use of simulation in e-learning based on Min's design theory, the PI theory for learning environments, and how interactions and feedback in simulations contribute to enhancing students' higher order learning.

Chapter 4

Designing interaction as a dialogue game

Linking social and conceptual dimensions of the learning process

Andrew Ravenscroft and Simon McAlister

Designing and supporting learning interactions that are genuinely engaging, meaningful and conceptually stimulating within online learning contexts remains a significant challenge in contemporary education. One currently popular approach which aims to address some key aspects of this problem, and motivational issues in particular, involves articulating interaction as a game. This chapter, whilst in support of this approach, will argue that we need to carefully consider digital gaming approaches in terms of the degree to which they fit with our learning landscape and define how they actually support the development of social or conceptual processes that are involved in learning. We will then describe a 'dialogue game' approach to online dialogue and interaction that integrates with existing, or near-future, pedagogical and technological practices, and explicitly links the social and cognitive dimensions of learning. This is realised through articulating game-playing activity in terms of the development of dialogical and reasoning skills that lead to improved conceptual understanding and collaborative knowledge refinement. This chapter will present: the justification, background and theoretical foundations for this approach; summarise computational and empirical studies that support it; describe a socio-cognitive tool called InterLoc (that mediates, structures and manages educational dialogue games); and provide an exemplar interaction from user trials of this approach. Finally, some key implications this work holds for designing gaming and related types of educational interaction are discussed.

Introduction

Interaction and digital games

Designing and supporting learning interactions that are genuinely engaging, meaningful and conceptually stimulating within online learning contexts remains a significant challenge in contemporary education. One currently popular approach to interaction design, which aims to stimulate meaningful engagement and participation in learning, through fostering the motivation for interaction in particular, suggests articulating interaction as a digital educational game. This approach is attracting increasing attention in the literature (e.g. see Kirriemuir and McFarlane, 2003 for a review) and is inspired by the work of some particularly fierce proponents such as Gee, 2003, 2005; and Prensky, 2001). It is claimed that these approaches, which are typically inspired by or build upon the influences of the digital (or video) gaming industry, can raise the motivation, social and affective engagement, and cultural relevance of learning interactions (e.g. through using the 'kids' technologies or role playing in simulated situations). They also emphasise the role of pleasure, play and 'learning by doing' through collaboration and competition (e.g. see Kirriemuir and McFarlane, 2003, or Facer *et al.*, 2004). But, as Ravenscroft and McAlister (2005, 2006) argue, there is usually a problem with the degree to which these video game inspired approaches fit with our existing or near-future learning landscape. Gee (2003) is quite explicit about this in his support for video game approaches, arguing that digital games, and the learning principles that underlie them, represent a somewhat revolutionary approach to learning and literacy development that cannot be easily accommodated or realised through traditional institutions such as schools or universities. Indeed, he argues that video game approaches actually change the fundamental nature of learning and literacy. Prensky (2001) offers a similar argument, which states that the prevalence of digital game-playing by children actually leads to the development of new types of cognitive skills, and these need to be understood and represented in learning situations in ways that move beyond our traditional ideas about education. Another problem with these (video game) approaches is that they are often weak in linking the game-playing activity to transferable social or conceptual processes and skills that constitute, or are related to, learning. So whilst these digital gaming proponents may offer attractive arguments for 'future' learning, this chapter will argue that we should also adopt a more *problem-focussed, near-future and interaction design approach* to digital games for learning. This position has been elaborated elsewhere by Ravenscroft and McAlister (2006), and will be more concisely stated for the purposes of this chapter. We argue that a more formal and dialogical approach to games (e.g. Vygotsky, 1978; Ravenscroft and Pilkington, 2000) can be used to develop pedagogical innovations that address salient learning problems, such as the development of dialogical and reasoning skills in various types of learners, within the evolving new media landscape. In brief, we argue that carefully designed digital games, such as computer-mediated dialogue games (see Ravenscroft, 2004a for a review), can support engaging, relevant and meaningful learning activities. The following section: make the argument for a dialogical approach to learning and interaction design; demonstrate how this approach can be realised through designing dialogue games; demonstrate current work on a socio-cognitive tool called InterLoc that mediates educational dialogue games; and provide an exemplar interaction from user trials of this approach. Finally, some key implications this work holds for designing gaming and related types of educational interaction are discussed.

Dialogue, developing conceptual skills and interaction as a game

The social constructivism of Vygotsky (1978) emphasises the role of dialogue and organised social activity in the development of higher mental processes and learning. This can provide a foundation and inspiration for approaches to e-learning that emphasise the necessity for collaborative, argumentative and reflective discourses. Vygotsky considered language and dialogue to be the most interesting and powerful semiotic mediators and the primary tools for thinking. He claims that our higher mental functions, such as verbal thought, reasoning, selective attention and reflection, originate in the social. Development proceeds 'from action to thought' and therefore communication and social contact are essential. It is through the communicative process that external signification systems conveying interpersonal communication become internalised to operate as intrapersonal psychological tools that *transform* mental functioning. In other words, internal language and thought are transformed from the 'outside'. This idea is critical to Vygotsky's notions about conceptual development and the evolution of linguistic meaning as we develop our higher level mental processes.

If we accept the social constructivists argued predominance of dialogue as a tool for learning and thinking from a game and interaction perspective, we need to introduce design paradigms that allow us to develop frameworks or tools that support these 'learning dialogues'. This raises important questions such as: how can we apply gaming to socially derived and dialogical processes that constitute meaningful learning interactions? And, how can we use games as a design paradigm for investigating, organising and promoting the sort of dialogue interactions that lead to learning?

A useful starting point for this is to consider Wittgenstein's (1953) notion of a 'language game'. This is a key concept in the later work of Wittgenstein, who argues that in adopting this approach we need to accept that dialogue involves various *sets of rules or conventions*, and these determine what *moves* are permissible or impermissible, successes or failures, with each set of rules identifying a distinct game. A key point is that any given game can be *judged only according to the rules of the game to which it belongs*. Wittgenstein argues that problems result from judging moves in one game by the rules of another. Whilst accepting that many digital games are not primarily dialogical, this latter point deserves some consideration so that we can be aware of cases where we are using the rules of one game (e.g. for 'just' fun) according to the rules of another (e.g. for engaging learning).

If we consider the language game idea in the context of design opportunities offered by digital technologies, it suggests that we can organise, manage and design dialogues for educational purposes. Specifically, we can aim to foster *engaging learning interactions* through designing mediating digital technologies that allow the specification of *rules of interaction* and legitimate *moves* and *features*. In brief, this more formalist and structured approach to games naturally lends itself to the specification of learning interactions and the design of socio-cognitive dialogue tools that support these processes. It then follows that we can develop this formal approach to design digital dialogue games that are not adaptations of existing digital game approaches, but instead are developed through articulating features in terms of generic 'building blocks' of games – such as the goals, roles, tactics and rules of interaction that address particular pedagogical goals, such as supporting and promoting collaborative argumentation (Ravenscroft, 2000; Ravenscroft and Matheson, 2002), critical discussion and reasoning (McAlister *et al.*, 2004a) or more creative and exploratory forms of dialogue along the lines proposed by Wegerif (1996, 2005). In other words, we can develop dialogue games that address particular learning processes and problems. However, to facilitate this leap from the semi-formal and relativist notion of a language game to the design of digital dialogue games, we need a more sophisticated design paradigm, such as the one described below.

Designing digital dialogue games for reasoning and knowledge refinement

Previous research in e-learning dialogue has produced the methodology of *Investigation by Design* (Ravenscroft and Pilkington, 2000) to develop and investigate educational dialogue games. This approach combines discourse analysis and other formal dialogue game techniques to specify models that can be implemented as tools or modelling systems. These game designs and tools are developed through modelling social features of effective dialogical interaction, such as the roles of the interlocutors, the ground rules for commitment and turn-taking, and the type of speech-acts (Searle, 1969) that may be performed. The dialogue games that are developed, whilst sharing the same categories of features (e.g. defined numbers of players, roles, moves and rules), are distinctive in terms of the actual instances and numbers of these features. They are also different in terms of the particular learning problems they address and the learning processes they support whilst retaining certain 'family resemblances' (Wittgenstein, 1953). The approach has been successfully used to design a number of educational dialogue game tools (e.g. DIALAB, CoLLeGE, CLARISSA, AcademicTalk) that are reviewed in Ravenscroft (2004b), and a selection are summarised below.

Dialogue games addressing particular learning problems and processes

Previous research has shown this dialogue game approach to be effective in designing distinctive interaction scenarios addressing particular learning problems and processes. A *facilitating* dialogue game for collaborative argumentation, implemented through the CoLLeGE (Computer Based Lab for Language Games in Education) system (Ravenscroft and Pilkington, 2000), led to conceptual change in science with adults and school children (Ravenscroft, 2000; Ravenscroft and Matheson, 2002). An *inquiry* dialogue game supported improvements in the reflective and diagnostic skills of medical students. And a *critical discussion and reasoning* game, mediated by a tool called AcademicTalk supported deeper and extended argumentation and reasoning in open and distance learning (ODL) students, who showed a more scholarly and dialogical approach to learning and reasoning when compared with a less structured dialogical approach (i.e. synchronous Chat) addressing the same task.

Recent projects funded by the UK JISC (Joint Information Systems Committee) e-learning programme have built upon this previous work. These projects have refined the dialogue game design paradigm and AcademicTalk tool to develop an innovative open source tool called InterLoc that supports the specification, integration and investigation of dialogue games for critical discussion and reasoned dialogue in education. An earlier version of this tool is described in Ravenscroft and McAlister (2005), which, following initial user testing, has been refined into the application described in this article. This tool currently supports three types of dialogue game (see below). One game for critical discussion and reasoning has already been well tested and evaluated (McAlister *et al.*, 2004b). Other games for creative thinking and exploratory dialogue have been specified and are currently being implemented. This tool also links the game interaction to a local activity design and pedagogical context and has the capability to link to other tools developed according to international standards for interoperability and reusability (see Olivier, 2004). The following sections describe in more detail how the dialogue games are developed and specified in terms of the InterLoc approach.

Specifying educational dialogue games

Through applying the *Investigation by Design* methodology described above, the educational dialogue games are specified in terms of the *goals* of the interaction (e.g. critical discussion and reasoning, exploratory dialogue, creative thinking), the *roles* of the participants (e.g. discussant, facilitator), the *intentions/moves* that may be performed (e.g. inform, question, challenge), the *locution openers* that actually express the surface-level realisations of the intentions (e.g. 'My evidence...', 'Is it the case that...', 'I disagree because...') and the *rules of interaction* (e.g. about turn-taking and the legitimate sequencing of moves). These games can be designed 'on paper' using pre-defined templates and realised through instantiating the dialogue tool.

Integrating with the pedagogical and technological landscape

Through using the tool described below, the dialogue games are coordinated within a broader learning activity model of sequenced exercises that integrate with curricula or other educational practices (e.g. preparation, interaction and summary stages linked to a particular course topic). Essentially, the interaction is 'tuned' to the pedagogical context in which it is performed through specifying the nature and ordering of the dialogue game exercises. Additional features allow the production of a personalised and editable summary of the performed dialogues, which provides some 'substance' to the interactions that can be used for other learning activities (e.g. essay plan or personal notes), acting as a resource that can be used for other learning activities. Through creating personalised representations of the collaborative interactions, these activities are given some permanence in terms of the group or individual learning resources and related learning activities.

Developing this tool according to the UK JISC e-learning framework reference model (ELF) for open services, interoperability and standards means that it can link to other applications developed according to the same 'open' framework.

InterLoc: collaborative Interaction through scaffolding Locutions

The tool that is being developed to mediate and manage the educational dialogue games and link these to teaching-learning practices is illustrated in Figure 4.1. This is an improved version of the InterLoc tool that has been described in previous

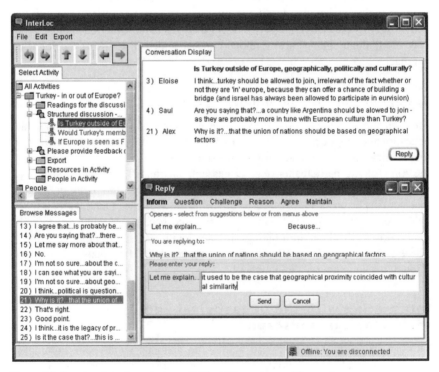

Figure 4.1 InterLoc interface during a Critical Discussion and Reasoning game

work by Ravenscroft and McAlister (2005, 2006). It was also developed through extending the functionality and improving the reusability of a previous tool called AcademicTalk – that supported a Critical Discussion and Reasoning (CDR) dialogue game. This game has been demonstrated and evaluated by McAlister *et al.* (2004a, 2004b), and the current InterLoc tool is available through the Sourceforge Open Source Repository (http://sourceforge.net/). The key features of InterLoc, which has been user tested and pilot tested, will be described below before demonstrating an exemplar interaction taken from a CDR game.

Setting up the dialogue games

To link the game interactions to the pedagogical contexts, InterLoc supports setting up an activity model (McAlister *et al.*, 2004a) that defines and specifies the broader context for the dialogue game exercises and collaborative knowledge building performed by the students. This activity is specified by a tutor or learning manager and centres on stages of preparation, interaction and summary, each of which may contain a number of tasks specialised for the context. These tasks are configured and adjusted to suit a particular learning context and problem, providing the preparatory materials such as pre-readings of source texts, type of dialogue game and sequencing of exercises that suit the particular problem and pedagogical situation. The application comes with a set of editable learning activity templates that allow the learning manager to re-use and adapt existing learning scenarios.

An activity setup tool creates the (XML-based) activity template which supplies the tasks and the instructions related to the group activity. The template includes: the questions (or positions) used to seed discussion; the dialogue game to be used; references to preparatory materials, such as readings, for preparation; and section categories to organise the saving of the dialogues. This latter facility enables the export of the dialogues to a personalised file, allowing the users to create a structured and editable learning resource from their interaction experience. URLs of web-pages may be included in the template to link to online resources, which can be launched and viewed via a browser, or web-pages of instructions to groups, alternatively textual instructions, can be entered directly. This facility to integrate a range of knowledge media formats for preparation is important, as it allows the dialogue game exercises to be focused around various types of 'material', which could be text, video or sound files. The finished activity template is stored in the group discussion room along with all the messages that have been posted, and these are used to update any user joining the room (and therefore keeping the group always up-to-date). Each activity will typically follow the sequence of preparation (supplied readings or multimedia files, and the option to share comments on them), one or more interactions (dialogue game discussions), and then summary (one or more simple discussions as a summing up exercise), with the tasks ordered to follow this scheme.

Mediating the dialogue game interaction

Figure 4.1 shows how the interface manages, scaffolds and structures contributions during the dialogue game exercises. This is arguably the most important interface for supporting the interaction and so is further described below. The dialogue game content is configured by the activity template that can represent Critical Discussion and Reasoning, Creative Thinking and Exploratory Dialogue games. Different sets of openers, rules and preferred next openers are presented during the interaction to represent a particular dialogue game. The examples illustrated represent the Critical Discussion and Reasoning (CDR) game that has been described by McAlister *et al.* (2004a), which builds on extensive previous work into modelling argumentative dialogue conducted by Ravenscroft (2000), Ravenscroft and Pilkington (2000) and Ravenscroft and Matheson (2002). The other games, which are at an earlier stage of development, have been specified through refining the features of the CDR game whilst considering the work on creativity and 'exploratory talk' proposed by Wegerif (1996, 2005).

Managed synchronous dialogue

The InterLoc interface (Figure 4.1), that shows a dialogue during one of the user trials, which was a discussion about Turkey joining the European Union. The interface comprises a navigation pane on the left with a display pane on the right. The navigation pane contains two 'sub' panes, the upper pane (Select Activity) uses a folder metaphor and contains activities, and within them, tasks and threads. The lower pane (Browse Messages) uses a list metaphor and contains a list of the messages sent under a particular (selected) thread. These metaphors represent the essential nature of the items and how they are used, so it was important to make this distinction between the two panes. The extensibility and declarative nature of the folder metaphor for activity structures gives at once a powerful, yet simple approach. The list metaphor for messages is at once recognisable, e.g. to those familiar with chat rooms, as a time-ordered dialogue.

The display pane on the right shows the contents of the selected item in the navigation pane, and the user performs the game by browsing the activity and message panes. For any selected message there is a Conversation Display that becomes the focus of the games and which shows the (unique) sequence of messages in which each message replies to the message above, ending with the selected message. This extracts and unravels a single strand of conversation from all the messages in the thread, and provides a coherent history for the selected message right back to the original thread, allowing the user to see and understand the context of the selected message. In this scheme, the Select Activity pane locates the user in the phase of learning activity, the Browse Messages pane provides an overview of the dialogue and the Conversation Display provides the focus and structuring for the interaction.

When the user wants to reply or respond to a thread or message, they press the 'reply' button on the Conversation Display pane. Figure 4.1 shows the Reply dialog box (lower right) which then appears with a sentence opener, 'Let me explain ...' already chosen and a message being completed. This new message is then added to the end of the current message list and bolded to indicate that it is, as yet, unread. Responses to each user's own contributions are coloured red, to draw a player's attention to the fact that one of their contributions has a response.

Unlike other synchronous approaches, such as Chat where there is pressure to be 'first poster' to keep the new reply next to its antecedent message (Herring, 1999), in InterLoc there is no such necessity, since every reply is placed below its antecedent message when viewed in the Conversation Display. The messages are numbered in the Browse Messages pane and in the Conversation Display pane so that it is easy to match messages between the two windows and therefore select an earlier message in the discussion as appropriate. On posting the new reply, it will become the latest message in the threaded dialogue, but on a 'conversation' which includes the earlier messages. Thus, interesting ideas are less likely to be lost in a muddle of messages and the revisiting of conversations encourages a more reflective, thoughtful and extended consideration of the meaning of the whole conversation.

Locution openers to support critical discussion and reasoned dialogue

InterLoc requires that the learners select a locution opener (e.g. 'I think ...', 'I disagree because ...', 'My evidence ...' etc.) from one of six pre-defined dialogue move categories (e.g. 'Inform', 'Question', 'Challenge', 'Reason', 'Agree', 'Maintain') to perform their contribution and then complete the message in their own words. These locution openers are derived from previous work in speech act theory (Searle, 1969), collaborative working (Soller and Lesgold, 1999) and other empirical research performed by the authors and others (Pilkington, 1999; Ravenscroft and Matheson, 2002; Ravenscroft and McAlister, 2005).

Dialogue rules and guidance on opener selection

Certain openers are highlighted in the move categories when making a selection to suggest them as candidates for making a reply (see Figure 4.1). This 'preferred reply' set of openers is derived from formal dialogue game rules (e.g. Walton, 1984) and corresponds to notions of well-formed and coherent dialogue (for example, 'Can you elaborate? ...' suggests a reply 'Let me elaborate ...'). However, learners are free to choose openers outside this preferred set, so a flexible, non-directive and yet constructive form of guidance is provided.

How the dialogue games and InterLoc work

Before examining an interaction that was performed using InterLoc it is useful to summarise the above to explain concisely how the dialogue games and InterLoc work in practice using a narrative description of events.

A tutor or learning manager, having identified a learning problem that will be addressed by one of the dialogue games, sets up a sequence of exercises that link the game to other educational practices, e.g. discussion groups may be set up to develop their understanding of a particular topic or induct them into academic practices of reasoned debate. The tutor/learning manager then sets up any necessary preparatory material and schedules the dialogue game sessions. When each participant connects to a discussion room with InterLoc they are updated with the related materials (e.g. preparatory readings), the type of dialogue game, and the current state of the activity. So, through 'signing in', each learner instantiates InterLoc according to the game they are performing and their stage in the sequence of learning activities. At any point, learners can create or edit a personalised summary of the dialogue and re-use this as a learning resource. The following section describes in greater detail how dialogical and reasoning processes are supported by InterLoc.

An exemplar dialogue game interaction through InterLoc

The interchange in Table 4.1 demonstrates a Critical Discussion and Reasoning game that was performed during user testing trials at London Metropolitan University (Note: To respect conditions for anonymity the names of the actual players are changed.). The participants in this trial were undergraduate students and games developers. This dialogue was chosen to demonstrate how a dialogue game instantiated through InterLoc mediates and scaffolds reasoned critical discussion. Recent work has pilot tested the tool with varied types of learners and in varied course related contexts.

A interchange involves four players, who engage in constructive conflict to collaboratively justify and clarify their positions related to the question 'Are educational games effective?'. Trisha opens the interchange using *'I think ...'* with an unqualified opinion on the value of learning games (5), and is challenged to justify her statement by Harry using *'Why do you say that? ...'* (6). This stimulates Trisha to explain why learning games are not used by 'media savvy kids' using *'Let me explain ...'* (8). Harry then agrees with her explanation using *'I agree because ...'* and extends her explanation by pointing out that educational developers can't 'keep up' with commercial games developers (14). Note how this interchange has 'unpacked' an informal opinion that 'learning games suck', to develop a more reasoned and coherent argument.

Trisha continues the interchange by backing Harry's analysis of the problem that educational developers cannot compete, using *'I agree because ...'* (15). However,

Table 4.1 A CDR game demonstrating constructive conflict, explanation and partial agreement

If games are effective for education why has there been so little adoption?		
5	Trisha	I think ... alot of learning games suck and that's why they're not used
6	Harry	Why do you say that? ...[1]
8	Trisha	Let me explain ... a large number of games on the market have not caught up with the mainstream video industry with regard to narrative sophistication etc. When they are presented to an already media savvy kid ... they don't play them
14	Harry	I agree because ... I guess as million selling computer games don't even make any money till the third edition, it must be impossible for educational developers to keep up
15	Trisha	I agree because ... the educational industry is outgunned by the "blow 'em up" video game manufacturers. Rather depressing....
19	Craig	I disagree because ... I imagined educational games being played only in educational establishments and shoot em up being played at home. Therefore, the two should not cross.
21	Trisha	Why do you say that? ... if an educational game was seen as fun, wouldn't it stand on equal footing with the shoot em ups?
24	Harry	Let me explain ... the funding for comp games is massive compared to educational games, they make more money now than the film industry, but it's not an immediate turn around. So for an educational game to compete is nigh on impossible.
29	Oliver	Do we all agree? ... That educational games are poorly designed and people are not really interested in them?
33	Harry	I disagree because ... although most are, you can probably learn more about ancient history from playing something like rise of nations than you would remember from a book.
35	Trisha	Good point.

Notes

A conversational interchange consists of messages that reply to a previous message, where messages are numbered in the order they are posted to whole discussion.

1 Identifying phrase removed here.

Craig then rebuts this position using '*I disagree because ...*' (19) to refine the debate, by explaining that 'shoot em up' games and educational games should be thought of differently. Trisha then challenges Craig with '*Why do you say that? ...*' to suggest that these two types of games should not be considered separately (21). Harry then uses '*Let me explain...*' to reiterate the qualification that there is a huge difference in the funding that is put into games for entertainment compared with those for education (24).

Interestingly, Oliver then joins the interchange, using '*Do we all agree? ...*', to test the group opinion and see if they have reached a consensus that 'educational games are poorly designed' (29). But this actually stimulates Harry to disagree with this generalisation about all educational games being poorly designed and lacking interest, and he uses an example of an educational game thought to be good and effective for learning (33). Trisha then agrees with Harry's point using '*Good point*' (35) to end the interchange on a more balanced position (that some games can in fact be better for learning than a book on a similar topic).

This interchange reflects a typical interplay between groups performing this dialogue game, where the approach leads participants from informal and unqualified opinions into a relatively deep collaborative analysis of the issues through offering reasoned arguments and, in turn, critiquing the arguments before developing a more elaborate view. The use of the openers, particularly those that challenge, facilitate dialogical argument with clear, direct responses to the ideas of other players without offending them or discouraging participation. The careful wording of openers facilitates a focus on the ideas rather the personalities of the players. Moreover, the players who have been studied thus far enjoyed the intellectual challenge of these discussions and the constructive argument with their peers (e.g. McAlister *et al.*, 2004b).

Discussion: dialogue games, InterLoc and interaction design

Recent work has supplemented the user testing of InterLoc with a critical analysis of the dialogue game approach to consider how we should further develop this line of work. In particular, we have shifted our emphasis from usability to consider broader dimensions of motivation and pleasure, as they are typically articulated in relation to digital games. Then we have considered these dimensions in the context of approaches that are pedagogically grounded and related to existing learning practices and organisations. The following four points that have already been raised and discussed by Ravenscroft and McAlister (2005) are emphasised and elaborated below to frame our current considerations about interaction design and dialogue games.

First, learners engaging in current educational practices, who may be quite mature and so typically not the focus of most gaming research, will have more extrinsic as well as intrinsic motivation for performing learning interactions when compared to their younger digital gaming counterparts. Learners in existing educational contexts will also be aware of the broader cultural and educational relevance and *value* of certain skills, and this in itself is quite motivating. For example, the need to develop critical thinking and reasoning skills to perform and participate in study, work, debates 'in the pub', or society in general may be more motivating, or as motivating, as any pleasure derived from playful interactions which practise these skills. Also, in these cases a significant amount of pleasure can be experienced through cognitive engagement and satisfaction with performance. We can get excited about ideas and debating them without incorporating highly visual or immersive techniques within the interaction design.

This implies that motivation, pleasure and engagement do not just emerge during (game) interactions in virtual worlds, but these are heavily influenced by what the games 'mean' in the context of cultural expectations and practices in the real world. So we need to be careful when proposing a dimension such as 'fun' as an objective, in ways that are divorced from reflective satisfaction and value.

Second, considering the role of 'meaning', game interaction can be made more relevant (and hence motivating), and more valuable through considering the contextual and environmental factors that influence learning interaction and behaviour. For example, we could increase engagement during the Critical Discussion and Reasoning game through giving greater emphasis to selecting an appropriate *blend* of players, with individual differences in their opinion or backgrounds to seed engaging arguments and discussions. The motivation for game playing will also be improved through having a good *fit* between the game-playing activity and the expectations for learning, e.g. through addressing an important role or niche for developing the practised skills in terms of the curriculum or 'life skills' more generally. It will also be useful to allow players to develop and represent their *actual identities* online, as these are what will matter in their broader educational progression. Practically, players should be given as much control as possible in preparing for a discussion or debate, through offering their 'own' preparatory artefacts where possible. In brief, if the players can take greater ownership of their 'space of debate', then the interactions they pursue are likely to be more meaningful.

Third, central to the approach is the notion that we cannot separate the social and conceptual dimensions of learning (see also Ravenscroft, 2004b) and so must design tools that address their interrelationship. Learning involves processes that are arguably never primarily 'social' or 'cognitive', but are typically both. This has significant implications for interaction design, as we cannot simply 'add in' the social aspects around cognitive representations such as knowledge-based content and vice versa. Instead we need to design with this synthesis in mind. For example, with InterLoc, when the learners perform the dialogical move 'Let me elaborate ...', they are then stimulated to provide a reasoned elaboration. When they perform 'I disagree because ...' they have to think about and express why they disagree, etc.

Finally, it is important to allow seamless *integration* with a learner's personal learning environment or devices and other learning activities. In other words, an educational game that uses ubiquitous technologies and catalyses natural human learning processes will arguably be more 'exploitable' than one that relies on a specialised high memory box and high resolution screen that can only be used in a set number of ways, and typically, in one place (e.g. the bedroom). The work reported by Facer *et al.* (2004) showing how children, using mobile technologies, simulated lion behaviour in a wildlife game ('Savannah') is also an example of how engagement is assisted by the technological fit between the game interaction and the use of ubiquitous technologies familiar to learners.

Conclusion

This chapter has presented an approach to designing and implementing educational interactions as dialogue games that are managed, structured and supported through the design of an innovative open source tool called InterLoc. This tool and approach have culminated from a number of projects that span the past ten years. Central to the approach is the notion that we cannot separate the social and cognitive dimensions of learning and so must design tools that address their interrelationship. This means that there is no quick fix to educational interaction design. Instead it is a sophisticated endeavour that involves pedagogy development, design studies and various types and scales of evaluation that all feed back into one another. And to complicate things further, once new technologies are used to mediate learning interaction and communication they may well change the very nature of the learning processes that occur. Understanding this changing nature of learning and communication that can be brought about by new technologies is not a problem, but is instead both a challenge and opportunity we should welcome as we aim to transform learning for the better.

Acknowledgements

Recent work on the AcademicTalk and InterLoc tools has been carried out with the support of the UK Joint Information Systems Committee (JISC) in the framework of the 'e-tools for teachers and learners' programme. The content of this chapter does not necessarily reflect the position of the JISC, nor does it involve any responsibility on the part of the JISC. We would like to thank all other members of the JISC e-tools AcademicTalk project team who advised about and contributed to the development of the InterLoc application. Specifically, we would like to thank Dr Rupert Wegerif for his contributions to work specifying the particular dialogue games, Professor Eileen Scanlon for advising on the general pedagogical approach and design, and Professor Oleg Liber and Professor Tom Boyle for advising about open source and Standards issues. We are also particularly grateful to Peter Oriogun and Fanee Sazaklidou for their comments on the InterLoc interface and HCI issues and the staff and students of GameLab London for participating in the user trials.

References

Facer, K. (2004) 'Computer games and learning: why do we think it's worth talking about computer games and learning in the same breath?', *Nestafuturelab Discussion Paper*. Online. Available at: http://www.nestafuturelab.org/research/discuss/02discuss01.htm.

Facer, K., Joiner, R., Stanton, D., Reid, J., Hull, R. and Kirk, D. (2004) 'Savannah: mobile gaming and learning?', *Journal of Computer Assisted Learning*, 20/6, 399–409.

Gee, J. P. (2003) *What Video Games Have to Teach us about Learning and Literacy*, Basingstoke: Macmillan.

Gee, J. P. (2005) 'Learning by design: good video games as learning machines', *E-learning*, 2/1, 5–16.

Herring, S. (1999) 'Interactional coherence in CMC', *Journal of Computer Mediated Communication,* 4, 4. Online. Available at: http://www.ascusc.org/jcmc/vol4/issue4/herring.html.

Kirriemur, J. and McFarlane, A. (2003) 'Literature review in games and learning', *NESTA FUTURELAB SERIES*, Report 8, Bristol: NESTA Futurelab.

McAlister, S., Ravenscroft, A and Scanlon, E. (2004a) 'Combining interaction and context design to support collaborative argumentation using a tool for synchronous CMC', *Journal of Computer Assisted Learning: Special Issue: Developing Dialogue for Learning*, 20/3, 194–204.

McAlister, S., Ravenscroft, A. and Scanlon, E. (2004b) 'Designing to promote improved online educational argumentation: an evaluation study', in Banks, S., Goodyear, P., Hodgson, V., Jones, C., Lally, V., McConnell, D. and Steeples, C. (eds) *Networked Learning 2004*, Lancaster and Sheffield Universities. Online. Available at: http://www.shef.ac.uk/nlc2004/Proceedings/Individual_Papers/McAlister_et_ al.htm.

Olivier, B. (2004) 'Application and tool component framework', *JISC Technical Paper.*

Pilkington, R. M. (1999) 'Analysing educational discourse: the DISCOUNT scheme'. Version 3, January 1999, *CBL Technical Report* No. 99/2.

Pilkington, R. and Parker-Jones, C. (1996) 'Interacting with computer-based simulation: the role of dialogue', *Computers and Education*, 27/1, 1–14.

Prensky, M. (2001) *Digital Game-Based Learning*, Columbus, OH: McGraw-Hill Education.

Ravenscroft, A. (2000) 'Designing argumentation for conceptual development', *Computers and Education*, 34, 241–55.

Ravenscroft, A. (2004a) 'From conditioning to learning communities: implications of 50 years of research in eLearning interaction design', *Association for Learning Technology Journal (ALT-J)*, 11(3), 4–18.

Ravenscroft, A. (2004b) 'Towards highly communicative eLearning communities: developing a socio-cultural framework for cognitive change', in R. Land and S. Bayne (eds), *Cyberspace Education*, London: Routledge.

Ravenscroft, A. and McAlister, S. (2005) 'Dialogue games and e-learning: the InterLoc approach', in Looi, C., Jonassen, D. and Ikeda, M. (eds) *Frontiers in Artificial Intelligence and Applications Volume 133, Towards Sustainable and Scaleable Educational Innovations Informed by the Learning Sciences*, Amsterdam: IOS Press, 355–62.

Ravenscroft, A. and McAlister, S. (2006) 'Digital games and learning in cyberspace: a dialogical approach', *E-Learning Journal, Special Issue of Ideas in Cyberspace 2005 Symposium*, 3(1), 38–51.

Ravenscroft, A. and Matheson, M. P. (2002) 'Developing and evaluating dialogue games for collaborative e-learning interaction', *Journal of Computer Assisted Learning Special Issue: Context, Collaboration, Computers and Learning*, 18/1, 93–102.

Ravenscroft, A. and Pilkington, R. M. (2000) 'Investigation by design: developing dialogue models to support reasoning and conceptual change', *International Journal of Artificial Intelligence in Education: Special Issue on Analysing Educational Dialogue Interaction: From Analysis to Models that Support Learning*, 11/1, 273–98.

Searle, J. R. (1969) *Speech Acts: An Essay in the Philosophy of Language*, Cambridge: Cambridge University Press.

Soller, A. and Lesgold, A. (1999) 'Analysing peer dialogue from an active learning perspective', *Proceedings of the AI-ED 99 Workshop: Analysing Educational Dialogue Interaction: Towards Models that Support Learning*. Online. Available at: http://lesgold42.lrdc.pitt.edu/wwwuments/Soller-Lesgold-AI-ED- Workshop.pdf.

Vygotsky, L. (1978) *Mind in Society: The Development of Higher Psychological Processes*, Cambridge, MA: Harvard University Press.

Walton, D. (1984) *Logical Dialogue-Games and Fallacies*, Lanham, MD: University Press America.

Wegerif, R. (1996) 'Using computers to help coach exploratory talk across the curriculum', *Computers and Education*, 26(1–3), 51–60.

Wegerif, R. (2005) 'Reason and creativity in classroom dialogues', *Language and Education*, 19(3), 223–38.

Wittgenstein, L. (1953) *Philosophical Investigations*, translated by G. E. M. Anscombe, Oxford: Blackwell.

Chapter 5

A model of authentic activities for online learning

Jan Herrington, Thomas C. Reeves and Ron Oliver

As online learning opportunities increase, questions must be asked about the quality of teaching and learning that is provided online. Interactivity is a key determinant of the quality of any learning environment, but it is not a well-defined construct. In this chapter, the authors argue that the quality of interactivity is strongly related to the authenticity of the tasks or activities. Further, it is proposed that the more similar learning tasks are to 'real world' tasks, the more likely students are to be engaged in the tasks, and the more likely they are to develop knowledge, skills, and attitudes that will transfer to real contexts. The chapter provides a description of the underlying theory, research, and development initiatives for this design model, including specific case studies. The theory, research and examples cited are integrated into a model for authentic activities in online courses. The chapter concludes with guidelines for the design of complex authentic activities for online learning, and a prescription for a design research agenda to further research and development in this area.

Introduction

Online learning takes many forms in higher education (Pittinsky, 2003). It can, for example, be a component of a traditional face-to-face course whereby enrolled students and their instructor supplement in-class learning activities with an online discussion forum. Alternatively, entire courses may be offered online to provide flexible options for students enrolled in a traditional campus-based degree programme, or to provide higher education access to students located at geographical, temporal, or logistical distances from physical campuses.

Regardless of the form, it is clear that online education is growing. A recent report from the Sloan Consortium (Allen and Seaman, 2004) indicates that enrolment in online courses in the USA is growing by 20 per cent per year with over 2.6 million students enrolled in 2004. These numbers refer to students enrolled in courses that are primarily online; they do encompass the millions of students who experience one or more online components within the structure of a traditional course. Some groups argue that even greater uptake of online learning is occurring. The Online University Consortium, for example, is an organization launched in

2003 to provide online degree programmes from accredited US universities. This organization estimates enrolments in online learning programmes to be growing at the rate of 60 per cent per year (Online University, 2003). In Australia, a number of recent projects have also recognized considerable growth in online learning due to the potential of these technologies as supports for innovation and advancement in teaching and learning (Department of Education, Science and Training, 2003).

As online learning opportunities increase, questions must be asked about the quality of the teaching and learning that is provided online. As described in other chapters in this book, interactivity is a key determinant of the quality of any learning environment, online or otherwise. But interactivity is hardly a well-defined construct (Rose, 1999; Sims, 2000). Multiple definitions are found within the published online learning literature. Some definitions define interactivity in reference to the graphical user interface (GUI) whereas others refer to the interactions that occur from instructor to students, students to students, students to content, and so forth.

In our research and development work (Herrington *et al.*, 2003; Herrington *et al.*, 2004), we have centred our conception of interactivity in reference to the tasks or activities in which students are engaged. We believe that the quality of interactivity is strongly related to the authenticity of the tasks or activities. Further, we propose that the more similar learning tasks are to 'real world' tasks, the more likely students are to be engaged in these tasks and the more likely they are to develop knowledge, skills, and attitudes (KSAs) that will transfer to the eventual contexts for application of those KSAs.

In particular, we have investigated examples of higher education courses that use authentic tasks as a framework for the completion of entire semester courses, or at least very large portions of them. Most online courses are based upon a curriculum-oriented pedagogical model wherein instruction is divided into segments of content, students are assigned readings, and complete weekly tasks that are primarily academic in nature such as viewing online presentations, writing papers, and taking tests. By contrast, our research is focused on courses where the completion of sustained and complex authentic tasks comprises the primary course requirement, thus providing an effective framework for constructing robust mental models related to complex content, developing higher order thinking skills, and nurturing positive affective attitudes and stronger conative tendencies. Most higher education courses should, but fail to, address all three domains of learning: cognitive, affective, and conative (Kolbe, 1997). The differences among these three domains are illustrated in Figure 5.1. We believe that courses based upon authentic tasks and activities have much greater potential to address all three domains whereas those courses that take a primarily academic focus may only attain cognitive outcomes at best.

Cognitive	—	Affective	—	Conative
To know		To feel		To act
Thinking		Feeling		Willing
Thought		Emotion		Volition
Epistemology		Esthetics		Ethics
Knowing		Caring		Doing

Figure 5.1 Comparison of cognitive, affective, and conative learning domains (Kolbe, 1997)

A model of authentic activities

Our research indicates that an innovative approach to online course design requires moving away from traditional academic course activities (lectures, demonstrations, discussions, textbook readings, exams, etc.) to online simulations in which a single authentic task or project becomes the focus of the learning environment. Based on more than a decade of work begun by Herrington and Oliver (1995, 2000), we have defined ten design principles for developing and evaluating authentic online learning tasks or activities:

1 *Authentic activities have real-world relevance:* Activities match as nearly as possible the real-world tasks of professionals in practice rather than decontextualized or classroom-based tasks (e.g. Brown *et al.*, 1989; Cognition and Technology Group at Vanderbilt, 1990a; Cronin, 1993; Jonassen, 1991; Lebow and Wager, 1994; Oliver and Omari, 1999).

2 *Authentic activities are ill-defined, requiring students to define the tasks and sub-tasks needed to complete the activity:* Problems inherent in the activities are ill-defined and open to multiple interpretations rather than easily solved by the application of existing algorithms. Learners must identify their own unique tasks and sub-tasks in order to complete the major task (e.g. Bransford *et al.*, 1990b; Cognition and Technology Group at Vanderbilt, 1990a; Lebow and Wager, 1994; Sternberg *et al.*, 1993).

3 *Authentic activities comprise complex tasks to be investigated by students over a sustained period of time:* Activities are completed in days, weeks and months rather than minutes or hours, requiring significant investment of time and intellectual resources (e.g. Bransford *et al.*, 1990b; Cognition and Technology Group at Vanderbilt, 1990b; Jonassen, 1991; Lebow and Wager, 1994).

4 *Authentic activities provide the opportunity for students to examine the task from different perspectives, using a variety of resources:* The task affords learners the opportunity to examine the problem from a variety of theoretical and practical perspectives, rather than a single perspective that learners must imitate to be successful. The use of a variety of resources rather than a limited

number of pre-selected references requires students to detect relevant from irrelevant information (e.g. Bransford *et al.*, 1990b; Cognition and Technology Group at Vanderbilt, 1990b; Sternberg *et al.*, 1993).

5 *Authentic activities provide the opportunity to collaborate:* Collaboration is integral to the task, both within the course and the real world, rather than it being achievable by an individual learner (e.g. Gordon, 1998; Lebow and Wager, 1994; Young, 1993).

6 *Authentic activities provide the opportunity to reflect:* Activities need to enable learners to make choices and reflect on their learning both individually and socially (e.g. Gordon, 1998; Myers, 1993; Young, 1993).

7 *Authentic activities can be integrated and applied across different subject areas and lead beyond domain-specific outcomes:* Activities encourage interdisciplinary perspectives and enable diverse roles and expertise rather than a single well-defined field or domain (e.g. Bransford *et al.*, 1990a; Bransford *et al.*, 1990b; Jonassen, 1991).

8 *Authentic activities are seamlessly integrated with assessment:* Assessment of activities is seamlessly integrated with the major task in a manner that reflects real-world assessment, rather than separate artificial assessment removed from the nature of the task (e.g. Herrington and Herrington, 1998; Reeves, 2000; Reeves and Okey, 1996; Young, 1995).

9 *Authentic activities create polished products valuable in their own right rather than as preparation for something else:* Activities culminate in the creation of a whole product rather than an exercise or sub-step in preparation for something else (e.g. Barab *et al.*, 2000; Duchastel, 1997; Gordon, 1998).

10 *Authentic activities allow competing solutions and diversity of outcome:* Activities allow a range and diversity of outcomes open to multiple solutions of an original nature, rather than a single correct response obtained by the application of rules and procedures (e.g. Bottge and Hasselbring, 1993; Bransford *et al.*, 1990a; Bransford *et al.*, 1990b; Duchastel, 1997; Young and McNeese, 1993).

Theoretical foundations

The ten design principles listed above are grounded in the philosophy of constructivism, and more specifically situated learning theory (Brown *et al.*, 1989; Lave and Wenger, 1991; McLellan, 1996). The learning principles are based on realistic contexts and active learner involvement rather than the more predominant information-based approaches so frequently encountered in higher education. In 1974, Olson and Bruner contended: 'The acquisition of knowledge as the primary goal of education can be seriously questioned' (Olson and Bruner, 1974, p. 150). Nevertheless, more than three decades later, universities continue to place information-based educational courses on the Internet. According to Postman (1990, para. 26):

[Technology] has amplified the din of information [to] such proportions that for the average person, information no longer has any relation to the solution of problems ... we are glutted with information, drowning in information, have no control over it, don't know what to do with it.

Building on the foundations of research on the characteristics of authentic tasks such as Bransford *et al.* (1990b), Young (1993), and Jonassen (1991), and drawing on other work in case-based learning, anchored instruction, and problem-based learning, it has been possible to produce the provisional framework above for the design and implementation of authentic activities and tasks in learning environments in higher education. The characteristics of the framework were used to select instances of authentic tasks for further investigation.

Case studies

Finding examples of the kinds of higher education courses that exemplify the ten design principles listed above has proven to be more difficult than we originally conceived. Nonetheless, we have found several courses that utilize most of the design principles in our model (see Herrington *et al.*, 2004).

An example of the type of course we have investigated is a postgraduate subject entitled Research Preparation: Research Methods, developed at Edith Cowan University. In this course, students do not learn research methods by studying texts describing research methodologies and appropriate applications. Instead they work virtually in a graduate research centre (Figure 5.2a) where they are given the task of investigating the closure of a rural school. They do this using both qualitative and quantitative methods, and they are assisted by two virtual researchers who have collected data from the community and assembled it in a raw form in the centre. The students can examine school records, population data, interviews with teachers, parents and community members' newspaper reports and other documents (e.g. Figure 5.2b). As the major task, students must

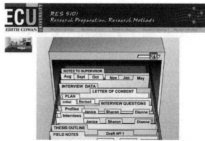

Figure 5.2a The graduate research centre in Research Preparation: Research Methods (Edith Cowan University)

Figure 5.2b Research data accessible via a filing cabinet in Research Preparation: Research Methods

produce a report that analyses the impact of the closure of the school on the rural community.

Searching for an example of a humanities course exemplifying our design principles, we found North American Fiction and Film, developed at Central Queensland University in Australia. As illustrated in Figure 5.3a, students study novels written by North American writers such as Melville, Hemingway, DeLillo, Vonnegut, Atwood, and Esquivel, and they view film versions of the same works (if appropriate). In the course, they are given the role of Editorial Board Members of an online scholarly journal (Figure 5.3b), to which they submit book reviews and articles based on their study of the literature. The students collaboratively design a guide for novice reviewers on how to write a book review. The teacher of the course serves as the journal editor, and an edition of the journal is published online at the end of each semester it is taught.

In the sciences, Coastal and Marine Systems is another postgraduate course developed at Edith Cowan University that used authentic and complex tasks. In this online course, activities are specifically designed to mirror the typical problems that a coastal manager or an environmental consultant might encounter. For example, in one major task (Figure 5.4a), it is proposed that a marina has been developed, and as part of the approval, annual monitoring of water quality is required. The monitoring encompasses water inside the marina as well as a site several hundred metres outside the marina, in well-flushed ocean conditions. The students are provided with a set of real data collected by the course teachers from inside and outside the marina, and they are required to understand, analyse and interpret the data and draw conclusions as to whether the water quality within the marina is different to that outside, and if so explain the possible causes. The evaluation is presented as a report within the context of the renewal of the marina licence. The course is constrained, to a degree, to the requirements of a proprietary course management system (originally the plan included a more realistic interface with clickable visual links and metaphors) (Figure 5.4b), but nevertheless, the task incorporates the characteristics of authentic activities described in our model.

Figure 5.3a North American Fiction and Film (Central Queensland University)

Figure 5.3b Invitation to join Editorial Board in North American Fiction and Film

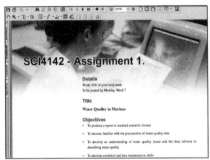

Figure 5.4a Presentation of main activity in Coastal and Marine Systems (Edith Cowan University)

Figure 5.4b BlackBoard interface used in Coastal and Marine Systems

In communication studies, we analysed a web-based course called Writing in Organisations, part of the third-year curriculum for Bachelor of Arts (Communication Studies) at Western Sydney University in Australia. Students in this innovative course learn business communication skills by accepting temporary employment in a virtual recording company (Figure 5.5a). They are given a complex task of preparing a report recommending whether the company would benefit from the introduction of an internal newsletter. In order to complete this activity, they make appointments, keep a diary, 'interview' the director and other employees (Figure 5.5b), and write a range of business letters and memos as required.

A resource developed by the University of Melbourne provides complex and authentic activities for medical students learning a more holistic approach to cervical screening examination techniques. Sensitive Examination Technique uses a case-based approach to allow students to explore the cervical screening process from waiting room, preparation, examination, diagnosis and follow-up. It focuses on exploring the procedure from the woman's perspective, using video and photographs of real people to act as characters. Students examine clinical

Figure 5.5a Writing in Organisations (University of Western Sydney)

Figure 5.5b Simulated interview in Writing in Organisations

information about five women from varied ethnic backgrounds who each have different barriers for completing the cervical examination. The video resources model the processes a good doctor would use with a patient when communicating information about, and completing the procedure. As well as analysing the doctor's techniques, students also engage in the histology of the examination process where they can examine the slides and cells, and provide expert opinion on the case. They then follow through the process by planning how they would contact the woman involved and consider the best way to provide her with the results, and suggest follow-up procedures.

Design guidelines

How is the kind of course described above designed and developed? In addition to adhering to the ten design principles described above, it is also important to create a flexible and adaptive learning environment that uses the affordances of appropriate technologies. For example, when designing a webpage for such a course, it is more appropriate to use a non-linear structure based on the tasks rather than a linear structure based upon weekly content, and if possible to use metaphors for navigation to links and resources, such as a picture of a workplace environment related to the subject area. Ideally, the pace of the course should be determined by the student rather than the teacher, and the teacher's perspective should be one of many, rather than the only one. Resources should be open-ended, with students encouraged to seek out and share new ideas and resources, rather than being provided with specific, bounded resources and reference lists. Assignments as separate questions and answers, essays or projects should no longer exist except as fully integrated assessable products of the tasks themselves. The student's role should not be simply reading, writing and absorbing information, but one of reflecting, analysing, planning, problem-solving, and collaborating. Concomitantly, the teacher's role should no longer be one of presenting information, monitoring progress, or – as is now common with course management systems – checking student access statistics (e.g. number of times pages visited, number of times logged on to site, date of last access, etc.). Instead, the teacher should plan to take a lesser but more significant role, that of providing 'scaffolding', attending to students' inquiries, and stimulating discussion. Consideration of such aspects will help to ensure that potential learning outcomes will not be restricted to memorization of information and factual recall, but expanded to one of understanding, higher order learning, and transfer of skills and knowledge to real problems and situations in appropriate circumstances. Although this remains to be researched, we also predict that desirable affective and conative outcomes are more likely to be attained in authentic learning environments.

Design research

To significantly change the direction of online learning in higher education, we believe that we must adopt new research methods as well as new course designs. To provide refined and improved design guidelines for online learning environments, we encourage what some call development research (van den Akker, 1999) and others refer to as design research (Bannan-Ritland, 2003; Design-Based Research Collective, 2003; Kelly, 2003). Design/development research:

- Focuses on broad-based, complex problems critical to education.
- Involves intensive collaboration among researchers and practitioners.
- Integrates known and hypothetical design principles with technological affordances to render plausible solutions to these complex problems.
- Conducts rigorous and reflective inquiry to test and refine innovative online learning environments as well as to reveal new design principles,.
- Requires long-term engagement that allows for continual refinement of protocols and questions.
- Maintains a commitment to theory construction and explanation while solving real-world problems.

Academic staff in all disciplines can emulate design researchers by engaging in the *scholarship of teaching* intended to optimize the roles of human teachers and digital technologies in higher education (Shulman, 2001). Not enough is known about the demands of online courses on teachers and learners, nor do we understand the most effective alignments of educational objectives, content, subject matter expertise, instructional methods, technological affordances, and assessment strategies for online teaching and learning. Despite a positive future predicted by some (Duderstadt *et al.*, 2002; Pittinsky, 2003), the current state of knowledge in online education is woefully inadequate, and research findings to date are often contradictory. Active participation in design research and the scholarship of teaching across the entire academic spectrum is warranted.

Design research requires that university teachers:

- Define a pedagogical outcome and create learning environments that address it.
- Emphasize content and pedagogy rather than technology.
- Give special attention to supporting human interactions and nurturing learning communities.
- Modify the learning environments until the pedagogical outcome is reached.
- Reflect on the process to reveal design principles that can inform other instructors and researchers, and future development projects.

A survey of college administrators (Allen and Seaman, 2003, p. 3) indicates that:

nearly one-third of ... academic leaders expect that learning outcomes for online education will be superior to face-to-face instruction in three years, and nearly three-quarters of them expect learning outcomes for online education to be equal to or better than face-to-face instruction.

Although these academic leaders confidently predict a rosy future for online learning in higher education, professors and their students seem much less certain of this brave new world of the virtual university (Cuban, 2001; Hara and Kling, 1999; Noble, 2001; Reeves, 2003). Traditional research approaches have failed to provide an adequate foundation for the design of online learning, and thus the need for design research is clear.

Conclusion

A recent survey of student engagement in higher education in the USA (National Survey of Student Engagement, 2004) concluded that students are far less academically engaged than expected by their instructors. The results of this survey involving 163,000 students indicate that only 11 per cent of full-time students spend more than 25 hours a week studying outside their classes – the minimum number of hours academic staff expect students to study to be successful. A disappointing 44 per cent of the students surveyed report studying less than 10 hours per week. Yet over 80 per cent of all students surveyed report 'earning' As and Bs in their courses.

Setting aside problems related to grade inflation and invalid assessment, we think that a major contributor to the lack of engagement exhibited by college students is the focus on academic as opposed to authentic activities and tasks in most university courses. This problem will only be exacerbated by the development of online courses with a decidedly decontextualized academic bent. Fortunately, courses that exemplify the design principles in our model of authentic learning have enormous potential for increasing the engagement of students and helping them to attain higher order outcomes. Authentic activities as the centrepiece of online course design still represent a very small fraction of all online courses, but aided by this and the other chapters in this book, university teachers should feel encouraged to adopt these alternative designs and reap the rewards that will come.

Acknowledgements

Our research collaboration has been partially funded by the Australian Research Council, the Australian-American Fulbright Commission, and our respective universities. With thanks to the dedicated and talented teachers and instructional designers and their teams who have shared their work with us: Max Angus, Trevor Bennett, Clare Brook, Marsha Durham, John Fitzsimmons, Jan Gray, Mike Keppell, Annette Koenders, Paul Lavery, Maria Northcote, Russ Pennell, Heather

Sparrow; and the University of Western Sydney, Central Queensland University, the University of Melbourne and Edith Cowan University.

References

Alessi, S. (1988) 'Fidelity in the design of instructional simulations', *Journal of Computer-Based Instruction*, 15(2), 40–7.

Allen, I. E. and Seaman, J. (2003) *Sizing the Opportunity: The Quality and Extent of Online Education in the United States, 2002 and 2003*, Needham, MA: The Sloan Consortium. Report. Online. Available at: http://www.aln.org/resources/sizing_opportunity.pdf (Accessed 12 December 2003).

Allen, I. E., and Seaman, J. (2004) *Entering the Mainstream: The Quality and Extent of Online Education in the United States, 2003 and 2004*, Needham, MA: The Sloan Consortium. Report. Online. Available at: http://www.sloan-c.org/resources/survey.asp (Accessed 24 November 2004).

Bannan-Ritland, B. (2003) 'The role of design in research: the integrative learning design framework', *Educational Researcher*, 32(1), 21–4.

Barab, S.A., Squire, K.D. and Dueber, W. (2000) 'A co-evolutionary model for supporting the emergence of authenticity', *Educational Technology Research and Development*, 48(2), 37–62.

Bottge, B. A. and Hasselbring, T. S. (1993) 'Taking word problems off the page', *Educational Leadership*, 50(7), 36–8.

Bransford, J. D., Sherwood, R. D., Hasselbring, T. S., Kinzer, C. K. and Williams, S. M. (1990a) 'Anchored instruction: why we need it and how technology can help', in D. Nix and R. Spiro (eds), *Cognition, Education and Multimedia: Exploring Ideas in High Technology*, Hillsdale, NJ: Lawrence Erlbaum.

Bransford, J. D., Vye, N., Kinzer, C. and Risko, V. (1990b) 'Teaching thinking and content knowledge: toward an integrated approach', in B. F. Jones and L. Idol (eds), *Dimensions of Thinking and Cognitive Instruction*, Hillsdale, NJ: Lawrence Erlbaum.

Brown, J. S., Collins, A. and Duguid, P. (1989) 'Situated cognition and the culture of learning', *Educational Researcher*, 18(1), 32–42.

Cognition and Technology Group at Vanderbilt (1990a) 'Anchored instruction and its relationship to situated cognition', *Educational Researcher*, 19(6), 2–10.

Cognition and Technology Group at Vanderbilt (1990b) 'Technology and the design of generative learning environments', *Educational Technology*, 31(5), 34–40.

Cronin, J. C. (1993) 'Four misconceptions about authentic learning', *Educational Leadership*, 50(7), 78–80.

Cuban, L. (2001) *Oversold and Underused: Computers in the Classroom*, Cambridge, MA: Harvard University Press.

Department of Education, Science and Training (DEST) (2003) *Australia's Teachers, Australia's Future: Advancing Innovation, Science, Technology and Mathematics. Agenda for Action*. Retrieved 19 November, 2004, from www.dest.gov.au/schools/teachingreview/ documents/Agenda_for_Action.pdf.

Design-Based Research Collective (2003) 'Design-based research: an emerging paradigm for educational inquiry', *Educational Researcher*, 32(1), 5–8.

Duchastel, P. C. (1997) 'A Web-based model for university instruction', *Journal of Educational Technology Systems*, 25(3), 221–8.

Duderstadt, J. J., Atkins, D. E. and Van Houweling, D. (2002) *Higher Education in the Digital Age: Technology Issues and Strategies for American Colleges and Universities*, Westport, CT: American Council on Education and Praeger.

Gordon, R. (1998) 'Balancing real-world problems with real-world results', *Phi Delta Kappan*, 79, 390–3.

Hara, N. and Kling, R. (1999) 'Students' frustrations with a web-based distance education course', *First Monday*, 4(12). Online. Available at: http://www.firstmonday.dk/issues/issue4_12/hara/ (Accessed 10 October, 2003).

Herrington, J. and Herrington, A. (1998) 'Authentic assessment and multimedia: how university students respond to a model of authentic assessment', *Higher Education Research and Development*, 17(3), 305–22.

Herrington, J. and Oliver, R. (1995) 'Critical characteristics of situated learning: implications for the instructional design of multimedia', in J. Pearce and A. Ellis (eds), *Learning with Technology*, Parkville, Vic: University of Melbourne. Online. Available at: http://www.ascilite.org.au/conferences/melbourne95/smtu/papers/herrington.pdf (Accessed 24 November 2004).

Herrington, J. and Oliver, R. (2000) 'An instructional design framework for authentic learning environments', *Educational Technology Research and Development*, 48(3), 23–48.

Herrington, J., Oliver, R. and Reeves, T. C. (2003) 'Patterns of engagement in authentic online learning environments', *Australian Journal of Educational Technology*, 19(1), 59–71.

Herrington, J., Reeves, T. C., Oliver, R. and Woo, Y. (2004) 'Designing authentic activities in web-based courses', *Journal of Computing in Higher Education*, 16(1), 3–29.

Jonassen, D. (1991) 'Evaluating constructivistic learning', *Educational Technology*, 31(9), 28–33.

Kelly, A. E. (2003) 'Research as design', *Educational Researcher*, 32(1), 3–4.

Kolbe, K. (1997) *The Conative Connection: Acting on Instinct*, Boston, MA: Addison-Wesley.

Lave, J. and Wenger, E. (1991) *Situated Learning: Legitimate Peripheral Participation*, Cambridge: Cambridge University Press.

Lebow, D. and Wager, W. W. (1994) 'Authentic activity as a model for appropriate learning activity: implications for emerging instructional technologies', *Canadian Journal of Educational Communication*, 23(3), 231–44.

McLellan, H. (ed.) (1996) *Situated Learning Perspectives*, Englewood Cliffs, NJ: Educational Technology Publications.

Myers, S. (1993) 'A trial for Dmitri Karamazov', *Educational Leadership*, 50(7), 71–2.

National Survey of Student Engagement (2004) *Student Engagement: Pathways to Collegiate Success*, Bloomington, IN: Indiana University Center for Postsecondary Research.

Noble, D. F. (2001) *Digital Diploma Mills: The Automation of Higher Education*, New York: Monthly Review Press.

Oliver, R. and Omari, A. (1999) 'Using online technologies to support problem based learning: learners responses and perceptions', *Australian Journal of Educational Technology*, 15, 158–79.

Olson, D. R. and Bruner, J. S. (1974) 'Learning through experience and learning through media', in D. R. Olson (ed.), *Media and Symbols: The Forms of Expression,*

Communication, and Education, Chicago, IL: National Society for the Study of Education.

Online University (2003) *Press release*. Online. Available at: http://www.onlineuc.net/ may21pr.html (Accessed 9 November 2004).

Pittinsky, M. S. (ed.) (2003) *The Wired Tower: Perspectives on the Impact of the Internet on Higher Education*, Upper Saddle River, NJ: Prentice Hall.

Postman, N. (1990) *Informing Ourselves to Death*. Presentation to a Meeting of the German Informatics Society, 11 October 1990, Stuttgart, Germany. Online. Available at: http:// www.preservenet.com/theory/Postman.html (Accessed 13 September 2004).

Reeves, T. C. (2000) 'Alternative assessment approaches for online learning environments in higher education', *Journal of Educational Computing Research*, 23(1), 101–11.

Reeves, T. C. (2003) 'Storm clouds on the digital education horizon', *Journal of Computing in Higher Education*, 15(1), 3–26.

Reeves, T. C. and Okey, J. R. (1996) 'Alternative assessment for constructivist learning environments', in B. G. Wilson (ed.), *Constructivist Learning Environments: Case Studies in Instructional Design*, Englewood Cliffs, NJ: Educational Technology Publications.

Rose, E. (1999) 'Deconstructing interactivity in educational computing', *Educational Technology*, 39(1), 43–9.

Shulman, L. (2001) 'Inventing the future', in P. Hutchings (ed.), *Opening Lines: Approaches to the Scholarship of Teaching and Learning*, Menlo Park, CA: Carnegie Publications.

Sims, R. (2000) 'An interactive conundrum: constructs of interactivity and learning theory', *Australian Journal of Educational Technology*, 16(1), 45–57.

Sternberg, R. J., Wagner, R. K. and Okagaki, L. (1993) 'Practical intelligence: the nature and role of tacit knowledge in work and at school', in J. M. Puckett and H. W. Reese (eds), *Mechanisms of Everyday Cognition*, Hillsdale, NJ: Lawrence Erlbaum.

Van den Akker, J. (1999) 'Principles and methods of development research', in J. van den Akker, N. Nieveen, R. M. Branch, K. L. Gustafson and T. Plomp, (eds), *Design Methodology and Developmental Research in Education and Training*, Dordrecht: Kluwer Academic Publishers.

Young, M. F. (1993) 'Instructional design for situated learning', *Educational Technology Research and Development*, 41(1), 43–58.

Young, M. F. (1995) 'Assessment of situated learning using computer environments', *Journal of Science Education and Technology*, 4(1), 89–96.

Young, M. F. and McNeese, M. (1993) 'A situated cognition approach to problem solving with implications for computer-based learning and assessment', in G. Salvendy and M. J. Smith (eds), *Human–Computer Interaction: Software and Hardware Interfaces*, New York: Elsevier Science Publishers.

Chapter 6

Learning designs, learner interactions and learning objects

Sue Bennett, Lori Lockyer and Barry Harper

Introduction

Until recently, the drive for reusability and interoperability in implementing online educational settings has been considered mainly from a technical perspective, with the introduction of a broad range of standards and tools. These technical prescriptions have underpinned much of the learning object research and development work to date. However, emerging knowledge about the implementation of pedagogical principles and new theoretical understanding that exposes the inadequacy of instructional design strategies for online learning (Oliver *et al.*, 2003) are now driving significant investigation into the reusability of learning designs and the application of learning objects within these.

The idea of reusability within a learning context is not new, in that teachers and instructors have always made use of prepared resources, but what is strongly pushing the agenda currently is the global potential for reusability via the Internet. The concept of learning object use and reuse is based on three assumptions:

- The first is that a person (being a teacher, instructional designer, or even a student) will want to and will be able to find appropriate learning materials to reuse within their own learning setting. For this to be facilitated by the Internet, a learning object must exist in an appropriate form to allow it to be shared easily (e.g. in digital form).
- The second assumption is that learning objects will reside in places from which they can be retrieved easily (e.g. a learning object repository) and they must be accompanied by an appropriate annotation to facilitate their identification and retrieval (metadata).
- Third, it is assumed that teachers and instructors will be able to create and implement learning experiences that can be supported by learning objects.

Although these ideas seem relatively straightforward, they also assume that the definition of learning objects is firmly established, that there is a standard annotation methodology, and that teachers and designers know how to incorporate learning objects into their instructional contexts. These issues, however, are yet to be fully explored (Anderson, 2003; Bush, 2002; Collis and Strijker, 2001; Hodgins, 2002; Agostinho *et al.*, 2004), but must be investigated as a crucial research agenda if reusability in an educational sense is be to achieved on anything greater than an individual scale. This chapter explores the emergence of generic learning designs as a framework for supporting the design of pedagogically sound learner interactions within the context of reusability and learning object technologies.

Learning objects and reusability

There is significant debate over how learning objects should be defined (Sosteric and Hesemeier, 2004). The Learning Technology Standards Committee (LTSC) within the Institute of Electrical and Electronics Engineers (IEEE) offered a broad definition, proposing that a learning object is 'any entity, digital or non-digital, that may be used for learning, education or training' (IEEE, 2002, p. 3). However, definitions that exclude non-digital format have become more popular, for example a learning object is 'any digital resource that can be reused to support learning' (Wiley, 2002, p. 6). There has also been discussion about the granularity of a learning object, given that a digital resource can range from small resources, such as digital images or excerpts of text, to larger resources, such as 'Web pages that combine text, images, and other media or applications to deliver complete experiences (a complete instructional event)' (Wiley, 2002, p. 6).

Uncertainty about how large or small a learning object should be has led others to focus more on explicating the 'learning' aspect of the digital resource. Downes (2003) argued that to be classed as a learning object, a digital resource must be inherently instructional: 'A mere picture is not a learning object because there is no instruction inherent in the picture. The context would describe what is to be learned from the picture' (p. 1). This helps to distinguish a 'learning object' from a mere 'content object'. The Learning Federation schools online curriculum content initiative (2003) takes a similar stance stating that learning objects must have educational integrity, that is, they can be 'identified, tracked, referenced, used and reused for a variety of learning purposes' (p. 1). As do Mohan and Greer (2003), who argue that a learning object 'facilitates a single learning objective' and 'may be reused in a different context' (p. 258).

This notion of 'reusability' emerges as a key concept in the learning object literature, leading to further refinements in definition such as the proposal by Hummel *et al.* (2004) that a learning object must be reproducible, addressable (i.e. connected with a URL and accompanied by metadata), used to perform learning or support activities, and made available for others to use.

From this brief survey of learning object definitions it is evident that an agreed definition of a learning object is still under development, however the effort to determine just what a learning object is has drawn out some of the essential characteristics. It may be that a more specific definition is not feasible as yet because reusability is not well understood. It may be that what makes a learning object reusable in a primary school classroom is not what makes a learning object reusable for training purposes. Thus, it may be necessary to adopt different learning object definitions to best suit different communities of users. This offers flexibility in applying the learning object approaches, but provides challenges to developing standards designed to promote interoperability.

Metadata standards and interoperability

The last decade has seen considerable effort devoted to the development of learning object metadata standards for the purpose of achieving interoperability, so that learning objects using the same metadata schema can be used by any tool or system that complies with that schema. The assumption that learning objects must be identifiable and retrievable requires that learning objects are interoperable and can be easily identified as meeting a particular learning need.

Learning Object Metadata (LOM) developed by IEEE (2002) is a standard that has been widely used in learning object initiatives. Recent applications and critiques of LOM have revealed several limitations of the metadata educational descriptors (Allert et al., 2002; Friesen et al., 2002b; Suthers, 2001, Agostinho et al., 2004), with the two most significant issues for interoperability being: the lack of fully explicated definitions of the educational category; and the development of a variety of metadata application profiles for different communities of users. Calls have also been made for additional sets of descriptors to be developed, such as those describing 'educational rationale' as proposed by Carey et al. (2002). This situation has led to significant variations in the way that LOM has been applied.

Some initiatives have used a subset of LOM. CanCore (Friesen et al., 2002b) has adopted a streamlined approach by recommending the use of 60 of the 77 LOM elements. This is a pragmatic approach, offering a compromise between the complexity of the full LOM set and the minimalism of the Dublin Core approach (Friesen et al., 2003). Provision is also made within the LOM standard for extension and additions, allowing communities to define their own vocabularies. For example, Agostinho et al. (2004) have described an analysis of a series of learning objects from higher education and drawn from this a framework and vocabulary for developing an application profile for this sector of education (which is published at http://www.digitalmedia.uow.edu.au/sldf.html). Other initiatives, such as The Learning Federation (TLF), have developed customised metadata schemata. The TLF approach incorporates elements from LOM, Dublin Core and the Education Network Australia (EdNA), in addition to defining some new elements (The Learning Federation, 2003).

These activities exemplify the trend for particular educational communities to adapt existing metadata standards to suit their own needs (Friesen et al., 2002a). The implications for reuse of learning objects coded under such customised schemes are yet to be fully explored, but will test assumptions about how easily users will be able to identify, retrieve and reuse objects. In addition to efforts such as these that focus on the learning object level, there is also research underway into how learning objects will be integrated into the design of engaging learning experiences.

Learning designs

A myriad of learning objects are now being created and collected through initiatives around the world such as The Cooperative Learning Object Exchange of Ontario (http://cloe.on.ca), The Learning Federation (http://www.thelearningfederation. edu.au), Multimedia Education Resource for Learning and Online Teaching (http://www.merlot.org), and a raft of digital libraries (see Marlino and Sumner, 2002). Despite these activities, there is still a significant divide between those researchers working on standards for describing learning objects, and those interested in the learning settings in which these objects will need to be integrated into learning experiences.

However, the support needed by teachers and instructors to integrate learning objects is now becoming a major research focus through the investigation of pedagogically sound learning designs. A realisation is emerging that the creation of a learning design that incorporates learning objects is not merely a matter of sequencing those learning objects, but requires a coherent and well-founded pedagogical approach. The concept of a learning design applied within an Internet-mediated context that is cognisant of reusability has now been well established, but is being interpreted and implemented in a number of ways.

One well-known approach has evolved from information systems and is characterised by the current research in learning objects through learning technology standards, such as the IMS Learning Design (IMS LD) standard. IMS LD attempts to specify a particular 'unit of learning' using a pedagogical meta-language. Another approach has focused on the development of learning designs based on knowledge of best practice, presenting these designs as specific cases or reducing them to a generic design template and description, and attaching appropriate learning objects. Two linked projects, The Learning Designs Project, funded by the Australian University Teaching Committee (Harper *et al.*, 2001), and The Smart Learning Design Framework (SLDF) project (Agostinho *et al.*, 2003), have developed this conceptualisation of the application of learning designs. The two approaches are described in detail below.

Learning design implementation: standard pedagogical 'language'

Standardisation is a means to ensure interoperability between systems and this has been approached both through learning management systems and learning environments standardisation initiatives. These initiatives, such as IEEE Learning Technology Standards Committee (LTSC), the IMS Global Consortium (IMS), or the Advanced Distributed Learning Network (ADLNET) have developed a broad range of standards, from high-level specifications for architectures to bindings for certain components.

The development of standards

As learning object standards developed, Koper (2001) and Pawlowski (2001) argued that the representation of metadata did not provide an adequate representation of pedagogical concepts for the linking of learning objects. Additionally, there was no adequate mapping of the content-oriented representation to a pedagogy-oriented representation. A variety of models were developed to close the gap, for example a Tutorial Markup Language (TML) for development of tutorial systems (Netquest, 2000). A more promising approach for the representation of pedagogical concepts at the time was the Educational Modelling Language (EML), based on a meta-model for pedagogical modelling (Koper, 2001).

EML is a notational system, implemented through XML coding and displayed through an EML-aware player. It was developed by a team at the Open University of the Netherlands (OUNL) and designed to describe a variety of instructional models as learning designs. The conceptualisation of the design was driven by a view that the prevailing content-centric view of e-learning should evolve to an activity-centric view. The development and implementation of EML has been extensively described by the OUNL team (see Koper, 2001; Koper and Olivier, 2004; Hummel *et al.*, 2004). In essence it provides a formal XML-based meta-language for describing learning interactions. The language has been developed from analysis of pedagogical approaches, through a methodology that described learning designs in terms of the person, role, method, activity and environment constructs. The schema incorporates a description of the method of instruction, components of the resulting learning environment, the activities, the learner, and the role they take in the learning interaction.

Learning design in the context of IMS

In February 2003, the IMS Learning Design 1.0 (IMS Global Learning Consortium, 2003) was approved as a specification. The specification incorporates EML as the learning design schema, defined by Koper and Olivier (2004) as 'an application of a pedagogical model for a specific learning objective, target group and specific context or knowledge domain' (p. 98). In this context the term 'learning design' has two meanings – the set of machine-readable instructions that describe the design, and the pedagogical underpinning of the design when implemented. The tools for the implementation of the IMS LD are now being developed, with runtime and authoring architectures being investigated by a variety of research and development teams, with recent developments summarised in Olivier (2004).

However, in order for the IMS Learning Design specifications to be widely used by educators and instructional designers, effective mechanisms for users to access, interact with and contribute to designs will be needed. Buzza *et al.* (2005) suggest that repositories of learning designs will need to be developed, and that collections of best practice designs, such as The Learning Designs Project, offer an excellent start by providing designs that have been proven through research and evaluation and that are described in practical and purposeful terms.

Learning design implementation: best practice

The collection and analysis of best practice examples is a time consuming process and requires access to high quality exemplars. Significant advances have been made in this area through initiatives such as the SoURCE project (http://www.source.ac.uk/) which has developed a library of case studies of educational software reuse (Laurillard and McAndrew, 2003), and The Learning Designs Project which has provided a collection of case studies and generic learning designs (see Agostinho *et al.*, 2002; Harper *et al.*, 2001).

Developing a description of best practice learning designs

The Learning Designs Project defined a learning design to be a planned learning experience and developed a formal representation based on an analysis of over 50 technology-supported learning experiences in higher education. The analysis was based on work by Oliver and Herrington (2001), who identified three critical elements of learning designs: learning tasks, learning resources and learning supports. The analysis was implemented through use of the Evaluation and Redevelopment Framework (ERF), which has been fully described in Agostinho *et al.* (2002). The framework was based on the work of Boud and Prosser (2002), who argued that a high quality learning design must:

- Engage learners by considering their prior knowledge and desires, and build on their expectations;
- Acknowledge the learning context by considering how the implementation of the learning design is located within the broader program of study;
- Challenge learners through active participation, encouraging them to be self-critical and to go beyond what is provided; and
- Provide practice by encouraging learners to articulate and demonstrate to themselves and their peers what they are learning.

(See also Chapter 5 by Herrington, Reeves and Oliver, and Chapter 8 by Anderson.)

The evaluation instrument was used to facilitate two objectives:

- To identify learning designs implemented with ICT that had potential to foster high quality learning experiences; and
- To determine whether such learning designs had the potential for redevelopment in a generic form.

The analysis of the learning designs submitted to the project resulted in the construction of a simple taxonomy of learning designs (Oliver *et al.*, 2002) and a formalism that allowed the design to be graphically represented in terms of sequence and resources. The project Web site (http://www.learningdesigns. uow.edu.au) includes a collection of 32 learning designs cases, which are fully documented. Five generic learning designs are also provided, each of which includes instructions for implementation in another learning setting. Figure 6.1 shows an example of a generic learning design represented through the formalism developed in the project.

The formal descriptions developed by The Learning Designs Project offer guidance through the instructional design process for a university teacher wishing to adapt one of the learning designs to his or her own context, and are a means by which institutions might provide supports and structures to assist the process.

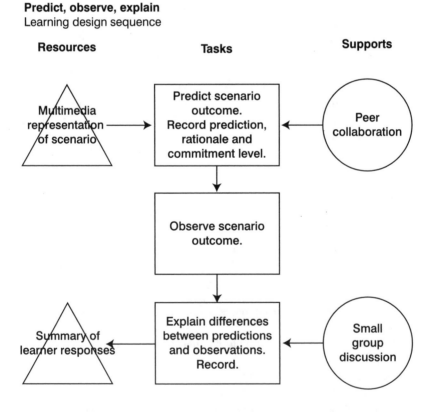

Figure 6.1 One of the generic designs formalised in The Learning Designs Project

However, it was beyond the scope of this project to specifically investigate the reuse or management of resources, such as learning objects, in relation to a learning design. This work was undertaken in a subsequent project.

Combining best practice learning designs and learning objects

The Smart Learning Design Framework (SLDF) project progressed this work further to incorporate learning objects and learning designs derived from best practice together with an authoring support, and explored some of the fundamental assumptions about reusability. The project aimed to draw together learning objects and learning designs by defining a process that would assist teachers and instructional designers to create an online 'unit of study', which might consist of a single activity, a module or whole subject.

The project operationalised the designs from The Learning Designs Project by developing a prototype tool that would support university teachers or instructional designers to:

- Search or browse a collection of generic learning designs and select one appropriate to a particular educational setting;
- Adapt the learning design to the educational setting according to the guidance offered within the system;
- Access existing learning object repositories to search and retrieve suitable learning objects to be used within the adapted learning design, and/or add learning objects that they had created or located themselves; and
- Package the completed design into a 'unit of study' for delivery via the available hardware devices and/or networks.

The innovation in this work centred on the use of generic learning designs to facilitate the design and development process, and the use of MPEG-21 as a platform-independent framework for packaging and delivery. The end product of the process, the unit of study, was packaged as an MPEG-21 'digital item'. A digital item is a structured digital object that provides a hierarchy for a compilation of resources. In essence, a digital item comprises three elements (Rump, 2002):

- Reference to resources (resources, such as images, audio tracks and text, are external to the digital item, and so defined by a reference);
- Metadata (data about the resource reference); and
- Structure (description of the relationship between resources).

The use of MPEG-21 was consistent with the reusability and interoperability requirements of learning designs and learning objects, offering the following advantages:

- Use of this international standard ensured that units of study produced using the SLDF would be made interoperable with the broad range of infrastructure being developed for industries such as music and broadcasting;
- MPEG-21 digital items can be configured for the usage environment, which can include such things as user capabilities and preferences (Vetro *et al.*, 2002), and different terminal and network requirements;
- Digital items can be accessed over a network, from broadcast content or on local storage and removable media;
- Digital items can contain resources of any type (Iverson, 2002), including those specified by the content types commonly used in learning objects;
- Resources included in a digital item can have their intellectual property rights protected, and access and usage can be monitored (Bormans and Hill, 2002); and
- Using digital items to deliver learning objects allows sequencing and decision making to be made during multimedia content delivery (Bormans and Hill, 2002), allowing tailoring to users' requirements, thus ensuring an appropriate and contextualised educational experience.

Digital items can be structured with learning designs to form larger digital items the size of units of study or courses. This structure presents a seamless mechanism to allow various learning objects to be grouped, while still retaining the rights, description and adaptability of the individual learning objects. An illustration of the SLDF hierarchical structure is provided in Figure 6.2. The learning designs are incorporated as flexible templates with guidance to support teachers and designers in making decisions about the pedagogical principles being used in the unit of study.

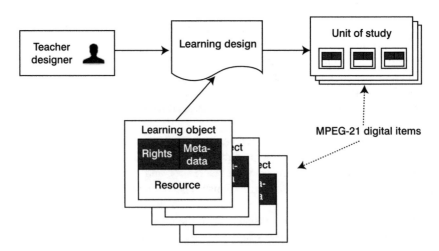

Figure 6.2 Representation of the Smart Learning Design Framework

At the lowest level, learning objects in this project are considered to be the smallest coherent pedagogical unit that cannot be broken into smaller units (for example, a quiz, an audio track, an image accompanied with explanatory text) and are represented as individual MPEG-21 digital items. This structure allows each learning object to have individual metadata and rights protection and enables the sharing and storage of the learning objects in large educational repositories that support the broader MPEG-21 format. A detailed description of the system can be found in Lukasiak *et al.* (2005).

Conclusion

Both approaches to the integration of pedagogical principles in the form of learning designs with reusable digital resources in the form of learning objects have strengths and weaknesses. The IMS LD model is based strongly on standards and a common pedagogical mark-up language that can be examined and interpreted. However, it is an approach that will require either skilled personnel who can code in the pedagogical language or the development of appropriate authoring tools to enable teachers and instructional designers to construct learning designs. The best practice approach adopted by the SLDF project draws on successful and well tested learning designs and provides descriptions and guidance that can be understood by a teacher or instructional designer, but requires the development of full-scale construction tools and mapping to fully support a standard. Both approaches offer ways ahead to explore the assumptions being made about reuse and interoperability in educational settings, and may prove to complement each other well.

Acknowledgements

Aspects of the work reported here form part of two research projects: 'A Smart Learning Design Framework' (Barry Harper, Ian Burnett, Jason Lukasiak, Lori Lockyer, Sue Bennett and Shirley Agostinho), funded by the Smart Internet Technology Cooperative Research Centre (http://www.smartinternet.com.au); and the 2000–2 Australian Universities Teaching Committee project entitled 'Information and Communication Technologies and Their Role in Flexible Learning', funded through the Higher Education Innovation Programme (HEIP) via the Commonwealth Department of Education, Science and Training. Consortium: Project Team – Professor Barry Harper (University of Wollongong), Professor Ron Oliver (Edith Cowan University), Professor John Hedberg (University of Wollongong), Professor Sandra Wills (University of Wollongong); Research Team – Dr Jan Herrington (Edith Cowan University), Dr Garry Hoban (University of Wollongong), Dr Lori Lockyer (University of Wollongong), Associate Professor Catherine McLoughlin (Australian Catholic University). For information about this project visit the project Web site: http://www.learningdesigns.uow.edu.au or contact: Project Manager, Dr Shirley Agostinho (University of Wollongong).

References

Agostinho, S., Bennett, S., Lockyer, L. and Harper, B. (2003) 'Integrating learning objects with learning designs', in G. Crisp, D. Thiele, I. Scholten, S. Barker and J. Baron (eds), *Interact, Integrate, Impact: Proceedings of the 20th Annual Conference of the Australasian Society for Computers in Learning in Tertiary Education*, Adelaide: University of Adelaide.

Agostinho, S., Bennett, S., Lockyer, L. and Harper, B. (2004) 'Developing a learning object metadata application profile based on LOM suitable for the Australian higher education context', *Australian Journal of Educational Technology*, 20(2), 191–208.

Agostinho, S., Oliver, R., Harper, B., Hedberg, H. and Wills, S. (2002) 'A tool to evaluate the potential for an ICT-based learning design to foster "high-quality learning"', in A. Williamson, C. Gunn, A. Young and T. Clear (eds), *Winds of change in the sea of learning: Proceedings of the 19th Annual Conference of the Australasian Society for Computers in Learning in Tertiary Education*, Auckland, New Zealand: UNITEC Institute of Technology.

Allert, H., Dhraief, H. and Nejdl, W. (2002) 'Meta-level category "Role" in Metadata standards for learning: instructional roles and instructional qualities of learning objects', Paper presented at COSIGN-2002: The 2nd International Conference on Computational Semiotics for Games and New Media, University of Augsburg, Germany, 2–4 September. Online. Retrieved 9 May, 2003 from http://www.kinonet.com/conferences/cosign2002/.

Anderson, T. A. (2003) 'I object! Moving beyond learning objects to learning components, *Educational Technology*, July–August, 19–24.

Bormans, J. and Hill, K. (eds) (2002) MPEG-21 Overview v.5, International Organisation for Standardisation, Organisation Internationale De Normalisation ISO/IEC JTC1/SC29/WG11 Coding of Moving Pictures and Audio. Online. Retrieved 22 May, 2003, from http://www.chiariglione.org/mpeg/standards/mpeg-21/mpeg-21.htm.

Boud, D. and Prosser, M. (2002) 'Appraising new technologies for learning: a framework for development', *Educational Media International*, 39(3–4), 237–45.

Bush, M. D. (2002) 'Connecting instructional design to international standards for content reusability', *Educational Technology*, 42(6), 5–13.

Buzza, D. C., Bean, D., Harrigan, K. and Carey, T. T. (2005) 'Learning design repositories: adapting learning design specifications for shared instructional knowledge', *Canadian Journal of Learning and Technology*, 30(3) Online. Retrieved 29 March, 2005 from http://www.cjlt.ca/content/vol30.3/buzza.html.

Carey, T., Swallow, J. and Oldfield, W. (2002) 'Educational rationale metadata for learning objects', *Canadian Journal of Learning and Technology*, 28(3) Online. Retrieved 2 April 2003 from http://www.cjlt.ca/content/vol28.3/.

Collis, B. and Strijker, A. (2001) 'New pedagogies and re-usable learning objects: toward a new economy in education', *Journal of Educational Technology Systems*, 30(2), 137–57.

Downes, S. (2003) *Design, Standards and Reusability*. Online. Retrieved 31 March 2005 from http://www.downes.ca/cgi-bin/website/view.cgi?dbs=Articleandkey=1059622263.

Friesen, N., Mason, J. and Ward, N. (2002a) 'Building educational metadata application profiles', *Proceedings of DC-2002: Metadata for E-Communities: Supporting Diversity and Convergence*, Florence, Italy, 13–17 October, pp. 63–9. Frienze University Press.

Friesen, N., Roberts, A. and Fisher, S. (2002b) 'CanCore: Metadata for Learning Objects', *Canadian Journal of Learning and Technology*, 28(3) Online. Retrieved March 2003, from http://www/cjlt.ca/content/vol28.3/.

Friesen, N., Fisher, S. and Roberts, A. (10 September 2003) *CanCore Learning Resource Metadata Application Profile: CanCore Guidelines for the implementation of Learning Object Metadata Version 1.9*. Athabasca University. Online. Retrieved October 2003, from http://www.cancore.ca/.

Harper, B., Oliver, R. and Agostinho, S. (2001) 'Developing generic tools for use in flexible learning: a preliminary progress report', in G. Kennedy, M. Keppell, C. McNaught and T. Petrovic (eds), *Meeting at the Crossroads: Proceedings of the 18th Annual Conference of the Australian Society for Computers in Learning in Tertiary Education*, Melbourne: Biomedical Multimedia Unit, The University of Melbourne.

Hodgins, H. W. (2002) 'The future of learning objects', in D. A. Wiley (ed.), *The Instructional Use of Learning Objects*, Bloomington, IN: AIT/AECT.

Hummel, H., Manderveld, J., Tattersall, C. and Koper, R. (2004) 'Educational modelling language and learning design: new opportunities for instructional reusability and personalised learning', *International Journal of Learning Technology*, 1(1), 111–26.

IEEE (2002, 15 July 2002) Draft Standard for Learning Objects Metadata. Learning Technology Standards Committee of the IEEE. Retrieved 13 March, 2003, from http://ltsc.ieee.org/doc/wg12/LOM_1484_12_1_v1_Final_Draft.pdf.

IMS Global Learning Consortium (2003) IMS Learning Design. Information Model, Best Practice and Implementation Guide, Binding document, Schemas, Retrieved July 19, 2004 from http://www.imsglobal.org/learningdesign/index.cfm.

Iverson, V. (2002) MPEG-21 Digital Item Declaration FDIS, ISO/IEC JTC1/SC29/ WG11/ N4831, International Organisation for Standardization, Fairfax.

Koper, E. J. R. (2001) 'Modelling units of study from a pedagogical perspective: the pedagogical metamodel behind EML', Heerlen: Open Universiteit Nederland, Retrieved July 19, 2004 from http://eml.ou.nl/introduction/docs/ped-metamodel.pdf.

Koper, R. and Olivier, B. (2004) 'Representing the learning design of units of learning', *Educational Technology and Society*, 7(3), 97–111.

Laurillard, D. and McAndrew, P. (2003) 'Reusable educational software: a basis for generic learning activities', in A. Littlejohn (ed.), *Reusing Online Resources: A Sustainable Approach to E-learning*, London: Kogan Page.

Lukasiak, J., Agostinho, S., Bennett, S., Harper, B., Lockyer, L. and Powley, B. (2005) 'Learning objects and learning designs: an integrated system for reusable, adaptive and shareable learning content', *ALT-J, Research in Learning Technology*, 13(2), June, 151–69.

Marlino, M. and Sumner, T. (2002) 'Educational digital libraries; building community; building libraries', in P. Barker and S. Rebelsky (eds), *Proceedings of ED-MEDIA 2002 World Conference on Educational Multimedia, Hypermedia and Telecommunications*, Denver, CO: Association for the Advancement of Computing in Education.

Mohan, P. and Greer, J. (2003) 'Reusable learning objects: current status and future directions', in D. Lassner and C. McNaught (eds), *Proceedings of ED-MEDIA 2003 World Conference on Educational Multimedia, Hypermedia and Telecommunication*, Honolulu, HI: AACE.

Netquest (2000) Tutorial Markup Language (TML) [WWW Document] URL http://www.ilrt.bris.ac.uk/ netquest/liveserver/TML_INSTALL/doc/tml.html, last access 25 September 2000.

Oliver, R. and Herrington, J. (2001) *Teaching and Learning Online: A Beginner's Guide to e-Learning and e-Teaching in Higher Education*, Western Australia: Edith Cowan University.

Oliver, R., O'Donoghue, J. and Harper, B. (2003) 'Institutional implementation of ICT in higher education: an Australian perspective', in J. Seale (ed.), *Learning Technology in Transition: From Individual Enthusiasm to Institutional Implementation*, Meppel: Swets and Zeitlinger.

Oliver, R., Harper, B., Hedberg, J., Wills, S. and Agostinho, S. (2002) 'Formalising the description of learning designs', in A. Goody, J. Herrington and M. Northcote (eds), *Quality Conversations: Research and Development in Higher Education*, Volume 25, Jamison, ACT: HERDSA.

Olivier, B. (2004) Learning Design Update. Online. Retrieved 31 March 2005 from http://www.jisc.ac.uk/uploaded_documents/Learning_Design_State_of_Play.pdf.

Owston, R. D. (1997) 'The World Wide Web: a technology to enhance teaching and learning?', *Educational Researcher*, 26(2), 27–33.

Pawlowski, J. M. (2001) 'Das Essener-Lern-Modell (ELM): Ein Vorgehensmodell zur Entwicklung computerunterstützter Lernumgebungen' (The Essen-Learning Model (ELM): A Development Model for the Development of Computer-Supported Learning Environments). Dissertation. University of Essen, Germany.

Rump, N. (October, 2002) MPEG-21 FDS – Frequently Asked Questions (FAQ) v5.0, ISO/IEC JTC1/SC29/WG11/N5187, International Organisation for Standardization, Shanghai.

Sosteric, M. and Hesemeier, S. (2004) 'A first step towards a theory of learning objects', in R. McGreal (ed.), *Online Education Using Learning Objects*, London: RoutledgeFalmer.

Suthers, D. D. (2001) 'Evaluating the learning object metadata for K-12 educational resources', in J. R. Hartley, T. Okamoto, Kinshuk and J. P. Klus (eds), *Proceedings of the Second IEEE International Conference on Advanced Learning Technologies*, Madison, WI: IEEE.

The Learning Federation schools online curriculum content initiative (15 June 2003) Metadata Application Profile: Version 1.3. Report produced by Curriculum Corporation and education.au limited. Online. Retrieved March 2004, from http://www.thelearningfederation.edu.au/.

Vetro, A., Perkis, A. and Devillers, S. (eds) (2002) MPEG-21 Digital Item Adaptation WD (v2.0), ISO/IEC JTC1/SC29/WG11/N4944, Klagenfurt, July 2002.

Wiley, D. A. (2002) 'Connecting learning objects to instructional design theory: a definition, a metaphor, and a taxonomy', in D. A. Wiley (ed.), *The Instructional Use of Learning Objects*, Bloomington, IN: AIT/AECT.

Chapter 7

Methods of learning in simulation environments

Rik Min

Simulation is a real container concept: consisting of various methods of learning. These include: role plays, group discussions, games, war training simulators, model driven simulation, virtual reality, etc. Simulation for learning on the World Wide Web (WWW) is part of the age long tradition in discovery learning. With computer-based learning environments, simulations can be used in education and training based on six different 'learning models'. This chapter describes the use of simulation in e-learning based on Min's design theory, the PI theory for learning environments based on problem solving on a screen, and how interactions and feedback in simulations have contributed in enhancing students' higher order learning.

Introduction

Discovery learning

Discovery learning is one of the common forms of learning. Individuals acquire knowledge through this form of learning without being consciously aware of it. Children discover words and their meanings by chance. They become aware of relationships between words and physical quantities, and between cause and effect. The acquisition of knowledge by children and young adults from the '*worlds*' round about them occurs somewhat effortlessly (Papert, 1980). The last two decades witnessed an increased focus on discovery learning by the International Simulation and Gaming Association (ISAGA) through the promotion of games, simulation and role plays (Greenblatt, 1979). The use of games, simulation and role plays in learning has created scientific interest groups around micro-worlds, constructivism and concept mapping (Vygotsky, 1981; Dicheva and Kommers, 1999).

Simulations

Certain interesting activities and situations in the real world can be 'replicated' on computers by means of simulation and micro-worlds. Through this approach, children and students can learn, gain knowledge and acquire skills and abilities with the help of technological tools or with a simulated reality. However, experience and evidence from research suggest that for individuals to achieve the intended learning or skills, 'coaching' is essential. Discovery learning on one's own effort is very inefficient as this may involve a waste of time. If a teacher wants his pupils to achieve a target, s/he will have to provide some guidance and scaffolding in the form of: assignments, cases, manuals and/or instruction, parallel to (computer-based) learning environments – either paper-based, computer-based or Web-based (Min, 1999).

The Web

During the last 20 years, we have experienced a revolution in learning technologies and a huge evolutionary development in the field of computing and computer technology. There is no aspect of education or educational science that has not been influenced by the computer and the WWW (Web). Many people watch the television daily and engage in some form of learning. A lot of the content that is broadcast is digital. In the course of the broadcast many activities and events (we may refer to as interactions) occur at the same time and may be at different geographic locations around the world. The content being transmitted is 'teacher-free'. In the future, learning will become increasingly common, and can be acquired via screens (e.g. television screens) and online (see Collis, 1998). This mode of learning is possible as a result of:

- the contents being digital;
- the software for delivery of content being relatively small and compact (e.g. java-applets for simulations); and
- the instructions for learning being delivered via canned streaming video (Min, 1999).

Learning and working (in digital learning environments)

In the last five years, about half of the working and learning population in Holland spend a few hours daily in front of a computer or screen. Many of the screens are: computer-based work-environments; instruction-environments; do-environments and complete study-environments. These technologies and environments all have digital contents: digital instruction-texts, interactive digital video and virtual reality (VR) and are connected to the Web.

The World Wide Web (Web)

No one in the academic world can escape the powerful influence of the Web. The Web will be increasingly used for course material, texts, e-books and as a source for moving image material. Students will have to find their own way in 'study landscapes' and 'study homes'. On browsing through the Web, one can come across something that one likes and in an instant download it completely onto one's own personal computer (PC) or learning tool. This analogy corresponds perfectly with the perception that children have of their environment. They are daily engaged in searching worldwide for all kinds of wonderful stuff. They zap from one television programme to the next. They live and operate in a world completely different to the one their parents used to know. The Web is ideally suited to the children's lifestyle. To the children and youth, the Web is one huge hard disk with all kinds of files: text, images, sound, video and even complete learning tools in the form of applets. In other words, it is a multimedia library par excellence ('e-learning'). Everything is easily accessible and in the eyes of children either for free or cheap. The Web offers the opportunity of searching for, retrieving and re-using materials many times over. Teachers can either see the Web as a multimedia broadcasting station that is on air 24 hours a day or as an enormous fast duplicator that includes envelopes and stamps: email functionality. In essence, the Web offers a lot of potential and dare I say 'plenty of tricks' for both teachers and pupils.

Contrary to the common belief, the Web is of course not better, cheaper or more effective than other media such as books, television or video. However, it is convenient, faster and offers, relatively speaking, easier access to other sources of information and resources than other media. In other words, it is more efficient under certain conditions. The provision on the Web of dynamic items such as 'simulations' and intelligent 'agents' will add an important new functionality to already existing educational tools. With such developments, it is my belief that within the next ten to 20 years, online learning, work and do-environments with all kinds of digital contents will become a common commodity and available at prices that everyone can afford.

Micro-worlds

At a school or university, most (if not all) of the pupils/students will come into contact and engage with new digital learning tools or discovery environments such as simulation and other micro-worlds. Individuals differ in how they learn. Hence, designers, teachers or researchers who wish to use new learning technologies in their teaching with a group of learners (e.g. children, pupils, students, adults, etc.) must ensure that the teaching and learning approach adopted for the target group is fit for the purpose intended. However, there are some rules which apply across all the groups as a general principle. For example, no individual, be they children or an adult, wants to listen to and/or watch 'a long boring speech' as a form of instruction or learning. Today's children are 'digital natives': they can engage in a variety of digital tasks at any one time, for example, they can 'zap from' one digital television station to another whilst listening to music, browsing through their course work or lesson notes and at the same time sending text messages on a mobile phone (Juwah, 2005, personal communication). This situation illustrates a phenomenon of 'multi-tasking' in which youngsters can work, play, learn, cut, paste and communicate all at once.

Types of digital learning environments (on the Web)

The Web consists of many types of digital learning environments. These include:

- ordinary texts for reading;
- simple data files;
- more or less simple or complex and/or relational data banks;
- many types of canned lessons: from plain text about a certain subject with pictures to teachers on video files, 'talking heads' or college sheets with parallel linked audio-visual explanation with the voice and moving picture of the teacher in question;
- discovery environments, games, learning texts, drills and practise-like programmes;
- coarse digital learning tools in the form of 'applets' (small applications), such as simulations, the subject of this article.

From an educational perspective, the concept of simulation covers many types of learning methods and very concrete multimedia products.

Simulation in general

Simulation is a real container concept: it is multi-explicable. Simulation as a method of teaching and learning can be used in many forms: role plays, group discussions, management games, war games, training simulators, model driven simulation etc. Recently, virtual reality has been added to the list. The list below describes the various types of simulation used in education (please note that the list is not exhaustive):

- not dependent on computers:
  - role plays
  - group discussions
  - business games
  - simulated discussions
  - games;
- dependent on computers:
  - simulated discussions (patient simulations) (computer-based)
  - computer games
  - computer simulation based on mathematical models of phenomena
  - intelligent computer simulation (ICS)
  - training simulators (e.g. ship simulators).

In this chapter, simulation is explored from the perspective of individual learning (i.e. self learning or self teaching) using a simulation programme as a learning tool. It is intended to limit this discourse to computer-based simulations. Virtual reality (VR) will not be discussed, except as an open, rich learning or discovery environment, and training simulators are merely mentioned in passing. VR and large mechanic training simulators for aviation and shipping are important subjects that deserve a separate focus and the limited space of this chapter will not enable us to cover the topics accordingly. However, it is important to point out that VR and training simulators are expensive to construct or purchase and are complicated to implement in education. This chapter will focus more on ordinary, 'model-driven computer simulation': computer simulation based on mathematical models of phenomena that we consider very important to introduce into educational lessons as worthwhile learning experiences via the Web and computers (see Figure 7.1).

Computer simulation: model-driven simulations

Ordinary model-driven computer simulations can be used as a learning tool. They are valuable multimedia products which can bring phenomena from the 'real world' to both the classroom and the home. Examples of model-driven

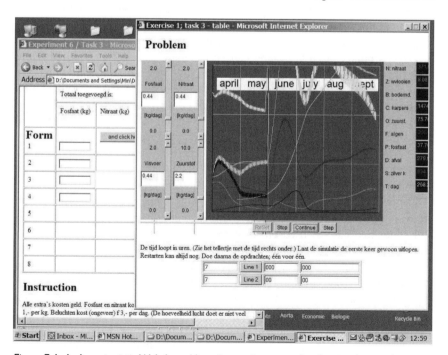

Figure 7.1 A characteristic Web-based learning environment for the simulation of phenomena from reality: here a very complex fish pond.

computer simulations include: the growth of crops in the tropics, epidemiology of and cure of diseases, oil exploration in the North Sea, economic forecast for the Dutch economy, etc. All the above complex sequences of events are instantly made available to the learner through digital communication and at a fraction of the cost and in quick time. Because of their versatility and the potential they offer, teachers and educationalists like and do use such learning tools in schools, colleges and universities, for in-company training or extra mural training in general at institutions such as the Open University, Dutch Training College Leiden (LOI) or at home. The potential for simulations is greatly enhanced as graphics, animations, movement, video and other dynamic forms of representation become even more affordable. Simulations cannot run without mathematical models (i.e. 'model-driven') to describe the relative phenomena or, if knowledge-based, to give intelligent feedback. However, simulations depend on the power of the computer for the digitisation of all kinds of information and feedback.

Simulations can be produced on interactive CD (CD-I) or random access memory CD-ROM, or downloaded from the electronic highway (Web).

Methods of learning

The works of Piaget, Papert and Vygotsky on discovery learning and constructivism are of great importance in helping us understand the pedagogy of simulations for learning in open, powerful, digital, online learning environments. The following paragraphs provide brief summaries of the overlap in their work.

Piaget's philosophy of learning can be summarised as follows: possibly the most important role for the teacher is to provide an environment in which the child can experience spontaneous research (active and personal experimentation and observation). The classroom should be filled with authentic opportunities to challenge the students. The students should be given the freedom to understand and construct meaning at their own pace through personal experiences as they develop through individual developmental processes. Learning is an active process in which errors will be made and solutions will be found. These are important to assimilation and accommodation to achieve equilibrium (Piaget, 1977, p. 6–9).

Piaget's and Papert's philosophies of learning have made a huge impact on the way we see the functionality of learning tools. The future of learning tools will undoubtedly be focused on 'discovery learning'. However, there are other forms of instruction than most practitioners realise exist or care to explore and to implement. Children and young adults apply constructivist learning methods when the 'novelty' of what is being learned is close enough to their present world of experience. Vygotsky (1981) makes the point that constructivism is an important method of learning in open learning environments and when using simulations.

Constructivism is a method of learning which involves active participation of the learner. This in some instance will involve 'hands-on' activities to make learning realistic.

Constructivism can be used or applied very well as a *leitmotif* for every designer of online learning environments. Vygotsky's theory on constructivism is an important directive for online learning environments and for simulation, as it emphasises cultural and social contexts in learning and supports a discovery model of learning. This approach to learning places the teacher in an active role of a guide (and co-learner) while the students' mental abilities develop naturally through various paths of discovery.

Vygotsky's three key principles are:

1   Making Meaning: the people around the student greatly affect the way he or she sees the world;
2   Tools for Cognitive Development: the type and quality of these tools determine the pattern and rate of development;
3   The Zone of Proximal Development (ZPD) (see Chapter 1).

Cause and result

Simulations can consist of various interactions; they are intended to:

* link up things and help students to make connections between issues, causes and effects;
* engage and motivate the students;
* help improve the students' understanding of the phenomenon being studied.

Simulation is similar to an individually carried out practical that is aimed to mobilise knowledge that is already present and is usually derived from earlier, often classical lessons. Consequently, this educational aim demands design and architecture. Design and user interface of a stand-alone simulation of this type are completely different from an instruction programme or tutorial courseware which usually leaves little to the imagination of the student. There are open learning environments for insight training or exercising, with little or no instruction. There are also learning environments where everything is (or has to be) stored in large complicated data files. Here, intelligence and sometimes visual dynamic feedback play a major part. This complex, dynamic, intelligent feedback is very important to keep the learning processes going. Sometimes this feedback is wordless, sometimes graphic, sometimes with all kinds of animations and/or animation-objects, and also in the form of intelligently generated video-fragments. These simulations are called 'intelligent computer simulations' (ICS). (See Figure 7.2 and the associated text about ICS.)

How to apply simulations? How should a curriculum be structured?

Learning tools of the type described here are almost always intended as part of a series of lessons in a random curriculum. These learning tools contribute in

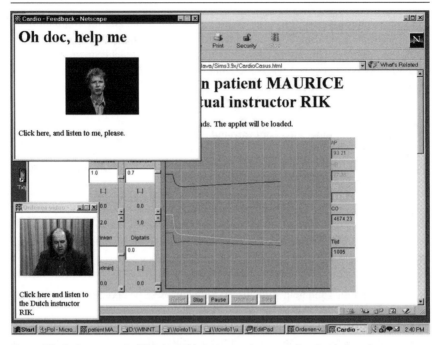

Figure 7.2 A characteristic Web-based learning environment for simulating phenomena from reality

motivating students to further learn about the topic or activity or subject being studied.

With increased knowledge and research, more effort is geared towards designing complete electronic teaching packages which can be downloaded from the Web, thus enabling online learning – preferably 'teacher-free'. However, one should be aware of the setbacks and impact that poorly designed, integrated digital learning environments can have both on the learning process and the learner. We will discuss that briefly further down, with practical concepts and a design theory which was developed for this purpose.

Computer simulation as a learning tool is one of the main subjects in educational instrumentation technology. Instrumentation technology is the latest branch of applied educational science. Computer simulation is 'ordinary' simulation, using a computer, usually an ordinary (standard) desktop computer: a Macintosh, Sun or Windows computer. Another characteristic is that there is almost always output on a monitor; sometimes on several and also on large monitors. Simulations require that many things can be seen and lots of tools are on standby or in view (or intervention possibilities or different types of instruction), and preferably remain so, while the user is working. The aim is not to get all asynchronous parts into the computer. It is often not necessary at all. Just imagine an instruction manual or a big wall board. A piece of paper or something in a folder is usually more practical and cheaper. The consideration to put everything digitally in an embedded application originates from the desire to have the latest version or gadgets (of something that belongs together) and can be viewed at a glance or that can be downloaded easily. Yet printing something out may still prove the easiest method if you want to use that information.

Methods

To make optimal use of expensive, powerful environments that are rich in feedback, you can apply model-driven simulations of phenomena for the following:

- to demonstrate or explain something (in front of the class);
- to make it possible for a student to practise (individually or in pairs):
  - with assignments (let them do something)
  - with cases (problem solving)
  - with proper instructions;
- to test a student;
- to help understand theoretical problems or at least being able to visualise them;
- to assess a student and 'measure' if s/he has understood something of the theory and whether s/he can apply it in practice.

Imitations of 'reality' or simulations of phenomena ('model-driven simulation') can be used to explain something in class, but can also be used to test someone on insight or skill. Simulations cannot merely be used functionally, but can also be used for individual learning. An individual can learn something on his own through discovery or via being coached in an environment rich in feedback. These two situations are the extremes. The application of educational methods is called 'methods of learning' or 'learning models'.

Methods of learning and instruction – learning models

Coaching or a method of learning is necessary in all online environment, but also in an open work environment and in virtual realities (VR). The facilitator of learning has to offer the user/learner something, e.g. 'an instruction', even if it is only a hint. Simulations based on mathematical models – both those on the Web and on CD-ROM– can be applied in six different ways. In our approach there are six different methods of learning; also called 'learning models'. Every learning model has its particular pros and cons. For the purpose of this chapter, this is how we define 'learning models':

Learning models are acting patterns of students, who use a computer simulation programme in a certain way that was previously determined by the designer.

The aim is to record the general patterns of an average student in such a learning situation, and not individual behaviour. Both the designer and teacher using simulations should be aware of the objective behaviour elicited by the method of instruction. Apart from student characteristics, every method of learning has its particular, specific, objective (dynamic) characteristics (Min, 1992). Dynamic behaviour of learning models is characterised most by the different methods of instruction. These instructions which are used to facilitate learning can be computer-based – adaptive – or artificial intelligence based (as in ITS or ICS), delivered at the appropriate time of need either as single or multiple messages. In one of the learning models there is no instruction whatsoever. We highlight six different methods of learning, namely:

- Free discovery learning;
- Learning by doing assignments;
- Guided or coached learning:
    - with a help-system (passive or intelligent)
    - with a complete instruction programme (sequential or parallel)
    - with a more or less intelligent system for generating test questions
    - with an 'intelligent tutor' (ITS systems);
- Problem oriented learning, based on a problem or case;
- Learning by carrying out 'real' scientific experiments;
- Learning with 'intelligent' computer simulation models (ICS programmes).

Of the six methods highlighted, only the first five are discussed. Most methods have different variations which are not discussed in detail. With the third method, we have mentioned the different approaches because they cause essential differences in the learning process. Min (1992) calls these methods of learning 'qualitative learning models'.

Free discovery learning

The intention of 'free discovery learning' is to allow the student to work on his/her own. S/he can do things that they like and believe are useful. In this learning situation, s/he can mediate in a model or in a micro-world and try to discover relations between actors and variables. One student will do something to teach himself a certain skill, the other to create a certain game effect. In general, a learner will soon be bored with a computer simulation programme using this method. It is usually a system with a certain simplicity. In order to make proper use of simulations, background knowledge is needed and a plan of approach. Free discovery learning – with little or no instruction – should not be recommended. A learner who simply tries something out and does not know how things work or cannot engage with the tool will never make the most of simulation learning.

It is essential to provide some form of coaching or instruction. This will guarantee the teacher that all possible outcomes of the programme will actually appear. Reality, even when simulated, is so complicated that a user without preparation or coaching will not see or discover anything worth learning. Thus, it is important that the user of free delivery learning should have good domain knowledge. That is why the method of 'free discovery learning' is never used on its own in practice. Coaching should be provided in a realistic learning environment either in the form of an assignment, a case, an instruction programme or an oral task given by a teacher.

Learning with the help of assignments

Learning by doing assignments is often applied, in particular to discovery simulations. The learner is asked to carry out assignments and see what happens. Before a learner engages with the assignment s/he is asked to write down what s/he thinks is going to happen. Thus, the learner learns to formulate a hypothesis before embarking on the task. That hypothesis is then tested immediately in a simulated reality. The tasks in this method of learning can be simple at first, but progress with an increasing complexity. At the same time, certain technical actions, such as operating a scroll bar, are learned almost automatically. The student learns to operate a computer simulation programme and to see all possible outcomes within a certain timeframe. Although the student does not have to solve problems on his own with this method or have to understand the model completely, this activity involves the development of higher order skills such as critical thinking, problem framing, analysis, synthesis, evaluation and reflection.

In general, the assignments are supplied in writing (parallel to the PC) or digitally (usually also parallel) (the notion 'parallel' or 'parallel instruction' is discussed below). These assignments may be a couple of loose worksheets or bundled together in a workbook. Worksheets or workbook have been designed in such a way that there is ample space for notes and questions. Questions and answers can be taken home at the end of a session or given to the teacher, for his/her assessment.

Coached learning

Coached or guided learning requires a differently designed simulation environment which does not involve the learner in self learning. Whilst the computer simulation programmes may look identical, guided learning environments contain a variety of functionalities and tools to enable the delivery of appropriate scaffolding, coaching and/or guidance. Here, we attempt to distinguish between the four kinds of 'coaching' or 'guidance'. These are:

- a help system with relatively passive, extra information which can be supplied when the learner asks for it;
- a complete piece of tutorial courseware or a simple piece of instruction used as a 'coach'. This can be done in two different ways: it can be embedded in the instruction or by 'running' the instruction beside the simulation on a 'multi-tasking' operating system;

- a more or less intelligent system for generating test questions. This coaching method can be particularly useful for simulations involving lots of dialogues. Such systems give the students feedback by setting them certain test questions at specific moments. The feedback will depend on the performance of the individual learner. An example of this coaching method is used in Min and Ephraim's anamnesis training programme. This simulation programme generates multiple choice questions on the screen, at unpredictable moments, depending on how the learner passed through the programme (Min and Ephraim, 1979);
- an 'intelligent tutor'. Simulations which can be supplied with an 'ITS system' ('intelligent tutoring system') are still being developed. The potential of an 'intelligent tutor' has so far not been fully realised. This is because it is really difficult to create an intelligent tutor that will think up several options like a human can. The present systems which have been described in literature – usually made with Prolog or Lisp – rarely achieve the level that could be achieved with simple, tutorial COO.

The 'intelligent tutoring systems' (ITS) should not be confused with 'intelligent computer simulations' (ICS). According to Min's (1987) definition, intelligent computer simulation programmes (ICS-programmes) are computer simulations which are based on an expert system instead of a mathematical model. Such an ICS-programme may contain one or more mathematical models or an intelligent tutor as well (see Figure 7.2).

Coaching or guidance methods can be used separately and/or as a combination of two or more methods.

Learning based on cases

Case based learning is 'problem oriented learning'. Here learners work with written materials in which a 'case' is described in detail. Learners should follow the steps of such a case in sequence. The case is produced as a computer simulation programme with one or two gaps or omissions. The phenomenon that belongs to the case is shown on the screen, but not in the instruction. This can be found on some loose or bundled worksheets in a workbook. The phenomena on the screen are presented dynamically. They are determined by the setup of the underlying model as intended by the designer of the programme or the teacher. While 'running' the case, certain variables exhibit 'abnormal' operations or 'characteristics'. The learner's first action when solving the case, is to analyse the phenomena. The conclusion of that analysis will be to propose a hypothesis. Next, that hypothesis has to be tested. Testing is done by changing one or more parameters in such a way that the model behaves 'normally' again. Then, that parameter setup can be seen as the cause for the 'abnormality'.

However, the phenomenon can also be compensated for, instead of being solved. This is called 'treatment of symptoms'. If all the symptoms are correctly treated following a series of logically sequenced interventions, a 'normal', seemingly healthy situation occurs.

In this brief illustration of case based learning, the following interactions are observed: 'analysing the phenomenon' (the problem); 'making a diagnosis'; 'solving the problem' or 'taking (therapeutic) action' (which involves responding to feedback); and reflection on performance and practice. Obviously, this mode of learning is far more interesting, engaging and challenging to the learner than discovery learning. This demonstrates that careful thought and variation in pedagogy can involve series of interactions that are used to promote effective higher order learning.

Learning by scientific experimentation

This mode of learning involves 'learning by doing', however, the activities are simulated and not real. This mode of learning is suitable for use in 'alternative practicals' in higher vocational or university education as a means of enabling the learners to gain insight into a variety of processes, procedures, systems, etc. For example, if the experiment involves some form of measurement to enable the generation of data (i.e. relative numerical values of variables in relation to that model parameter), simulation can be used to give the learners insight into a particular phenomenon being studied. The students may be asked to write down the numerical values on paper or a worksheet, or electronically or on a scratch pad (which can be an input field on a Web page) and thereafter the data is transformed into graphical format (similar to results generated from real experiments), thereby allowing the students to see certain relationships between the variable being studied based on the graphical representation.

This mode of learning prepares the students for 'real' practicals enabling them to concentrate on the primary learning targets (e.g. feeling living tissue, seeing real blood, recognising emotions, etc.). But most importantly, this mode of teaching and learning is essential so as not to make any mistakes in the secondary aspects of learning and performance, for example, in aspects involving the risk of 'life and limb'.

The iterations and re-iterations (interactions) are so diverse and range from the simple manipulation and responding to feedback through to complex aspects of analysing, negotiating, decision making, reflection, etc.

These simulation methods are quick to run, save resources and can be repeated several times to help consolidate learning.

As earlier stated, the sixth method – learning with intelligent computer simulations – is beyond the scope of this chapter.

It is the intention of the group of researchers that I work with to schematise each of the methods of learning described above. The schemas will be some form of flowcharts. These charts we wish to refer to as 'learning models'. A learning model in this case should not be confused with a model that is used in computer simulation programmes. A learning model is (for the time being) a concept in the form of a flowchart which depicts how long an (average) user spends in a computer simulation programme. It shows what the learner does (qualitatively) and what s/he may have learned. Once we have more data we intend to describe these learning models also quantitatively in terms of time, number of failures and so on.

Instruction tools versus learning tools

There are often misunderstandings about concepts and definitions in research. These are fairly frequent within 'instruction technology'. Many 'instruction technologists' systematically fail to distinguish between instruction tools and learning tools. In our view, instruction tools are a 'one-way medium', like for instance a PowerPoint presentation – even when it contains all kinds of animation effects – or an instruction film about the tunnel effect in diodes. Whereas a learning tool is an entirely different entity. A (real) learning tool is a 'two-way medium' which always has 'two-way traffic' – for example, an ordinary box of building blocks or Meccano set, without a manual, or a micro-world environment without proper tools like a coach or a paper manual. In order to short-circuit the discussion between scientists and worlds of thinking, we have developed a fairly simple, general, conceptual, dynamic thinking model to show the difference between 'learning' and 'instruction' (in learning situations): an analogon (Min *et al.*, 1999). It is an effort to make certain definitions unambiguous, to depict a proper relation scheme and a model. Finally, it is intended to catch the dynamics of learning in a few modern concepts, such as motivation of the user and their ability to learn a curriculum.

Learning

For years, my colleagues and I have tried to fathom the process of learning within educational science. We know much about instruction but little about learning or acquiring knowledge and insight. A lot of research is done in educational science into methods of instruction, but relatively little into learning with learning tools. This chapter tries to make a start with that. What we should focus on is having discussions about how to create a model of the process of learning. How can learning be modelled? To start with, we would need a model with the basic quantities and the relations between them, to provide scientists with a stepping stone for their discussions. In 1997, the Dutch minister for education launched the concept 'study ability'. The points of action for this concept should be recorded in a larger entity – conceptually – in an understandable model. Then, we should know at least what we are talking about: for example, where does a concept find a 'point of action' in the overall learning process? In 1999, we constructed an unambiguous and irrefutable thinking model, an analogon, to describe the phenomenon of learning. This may, in the long run, help us to fathom the process of learning (with learning and instruction tools) and associated conditions. In the article on the model of simulation which is available on the Web, we were able to demonstrate the relationship between the most relevant concepts and other variables in learning (Min *et al.*, 2000).

A wide range of educational supply types

In general one should offer students or pupils a widely differentiated range of learning tools in a learning situation. Simulations have always been a welcome break within boring sections of a difficult learning activity. Simulations compliment huge volumes of text, they create insight and therefore offer clarity of understanding of the subject matter. Learning designers are well aware of these facts, first as writers of simulation programmes, and second as teachers when developing interesting learning tasks and assignments.

Learning tools and curricula

Learning tools are critical in underpinning learning and as such should always be embedded within a good curriculum. The penalty of not embedding learning tools in the curriculum is poor quality learning and may result in the learning not achieving the intended learning outcomes. Good learning tools should be appropriately designed, diverse and wide ranging and produced for different purposes.

In order to create a good curriculum with simulations, one should know the target group and its exact characteristics. Learning designers should have an understanding of the target group/students they are dealing with, their previous or prior knowledge and relevant information about other entry behaviour.

To ensure variety in teaching and learning processes and to meet learners' needs, simulations can be used at any stage of the curriculum provided the learners have been given adequate grounding in the subject/topic being studied. As in all forms of learning, the quality of learning can be assessed using appropriate methods and practices.

However, some minimum requirements have to be met to ensure an effective computer simulation programme. These are:

- the simulation programme itself should be unambiguous and clear;
- there should be at least three kinds of good manuals:
  - for the student
  - for the teacher
  - for the technical/maintenance staff (or in combination);
- there should be proper instruction, at least three kinds, namely:
  - generic instructions (explanations, scaffolds, etc.)
  - authentic assignments
  - authentic cases and case descriptions;
- there should be a fit-for-purpose learning environment based on sound pedagogical design and should incorporate as a minimum the following components for an online environment:

- good communication and learning tools relevant to the form of learning
- a shared/collaborative space
- resource facility
- monitoring and learning management system
- recording facility;
- there should be adequate feedback, diverse and preferably multi-dimensional.

The provision of the above minimum requirements will ensure that the learning environment is fit for the purpose intended and that the students will benefit from a quality learning experience.

Different individuals engage with learning in different ways. Whilst some students want structured lessons, others may prefer engaging with unstructured material. Regardless of the students' learning styles, authentic (i.e. relevant and contextualised) activities and tasks are essential requirements in the process of learning.

In creating a curriculum, it is important that learning designers/teachers seek appropriate feedback. For new curricula, this feedback may be in the form of the learners' entry behaviours – prior knowledge, level of skills, abilities, etc. For existing curricula, feedback may be gained from students' performance in learning tasks, activities and assessments. The feedback gained from the students should be used to inform and shape the curriculum. In simulation learning, such feedback is vital in design cases, programmes and assignments to reflect effectively the phenomena being presented as learning activities to the students. Good feedback promotes effective learning. Lack of or inadequate feedback can ruin a valuable educational experience and the cost involved in producing ineffective simulations is quite high.

In learning, practice they say makes perfect and is the key to success. However, blind practice should be avoided. The learning designer or teacher should endeavour to prevent the blind practice approach to learning. If a student has the wrong knowledge, practice may yield the wrong results (see De Jong, 1999).

Variety they say is the spice of life. Good education should provide the learners with different forms of learning, instructional methods and learning tools. Learning tools such as simulations can be organised and used by the teacher to meet different teaching and learning needs. An essential characteristic of a good learning tool is that it should be adaptable to different contexts and situations and MacTHESIS-based simulations have proved that they are good simulations.

Designing model-driven simulations

Simulation programmes have always been supplied with paper tutoring or instruction materials. Simulations with this type of coaching proved most successful in practice. Simulations that were supplied without instructions or coaching often 'disappeared' into the ether, even if they were well designed or programmed. Research has shown that the success of simulations is largely determined by the presence of carefully composed work sheets or booklets with assignments and/or loose case descriptions. However, in this age of zapping and searching we should also consider electronic forms of coaching (teacher-free). This is obvious because everything already takes place 'at a distance' in 'studiehuizen' (study homes) or at home.

Electronic coaching

Many researchers have tried to provide coaching electronically. This often failed. Examples have been described in which one half of the monitor contained instruction and the other an open learning environment for simulation. These 'view port like' solutions indicate that the designer realises the user's need to have information side by side. S/he wants to be able to compare things, which is very easy to do with paper instruction materials, whereas a designer of educational online learning and instruction environments only has a limited area available (that of the screen). The main bottle-neck proves to be the abundance of information which the designer believes necessary and the lack of space on the PC's monitor. In a sense, the monitor is the most imperfect part of today's computers. Many people are not aware of this because a monitor also has many advantages.

Linearity

Monitors were designed and made for linear programmes. Images appear and at the same time others disappear. Designers of interactive programmes want to achieve completely different things with their products than film and video designers. TV is a 'one-way medium'. In a film or a conversation on TV, the continuous disappearance of images is no problem. There is sufficient redundancy in information to get the message across. With teaching programmes on a computer, courseware and educational software in general, the implicit limitations of the monitor proved to play a major part, and in particular in simulation learning environments. People are not always aware that many problems with simulations are related to this limitation. In a teaching programme, certain information (available for instance on part of the screen) should be consulted (continually) during a different part of the lesson. If this was not anticipated by the designer, his/her product will soon become redundant. Teaching programmes and teaching environments in general imply two-way traffic. The monitor itself cannot be manipulated, but it can be done indirectly with a mouse.

Retrieving earlier presented information is still a problem. It is often more practical to print information from the screen and consult it, rather than trying to find it again and again. Many solutions have been invented for this problem: for example, scrolling information; fast responsive but expensive computers; hypertext-like structures and so on. Yet few solutions really work, because a user should have a certain level of skill. Windowing techniques, if properly applied, are excellent.

Parallelism (as a concept)

Designers have found many solutions for these 'space' problems. For instance, by filling the screen with all kinds of information, i.e. presenting information in parallel, but this approach has many ergonomic disadvantages. These are: crammed text; poor sentence structure; too much visual and textual information which becomes too small for transmission via the screen, etc. The arrival of windowing techniques and the desktop philosophy was not only a technical breakthrough, but proved to be a big step forward in particular for a beginner, who does not want to see anything but his own application. At the beginning, professional makers of software and in particular computer scientists, often did not realise the use of loose, movable windows on the screen. Using Windows also had its disadvantages, its complexity and the irritating way of programming.

Especially for individuals who hate to remember useless things (like a command), they were quick to foresee the revolutionary aspect of the Windows technology for education. This was particularly true for people with poor short-term memory or people who do not want to be bothered by unnecessary details (Min, 1994).

The parallel instruction theory: a design theory

At first, electronic methods for instruction and help systems were not as easy to use as paper instruction materials. The first impulse of designers and informaticians was to solve everything electronically, but this failed to work in practice. In simulation, the best ergonomical presentation for instructions proved to be a loose, movable, parallel window. This was possible provided that the instruction programme could be used independently from both the main programme and the status of the mathematical model ('asynchronous'). We called the method of using these two separate programmes, the simulation and the instruction programme, the 'asynchronous method of use' in our research. This word indicates that the concept 'open learning environment' does not merely concern the simulation environment, but another component, namely, an instruction programme that can be used free of obligations and separate from the simulator. With the 'asynchronous method of use' one can decide whether to use the second component or not and to what extent. Instruction should only be given if the student asks for it or if there is an obvious need for it. A good interactive learning tool should be a 'two-way medium' and not a 'one-way medium', like ordinary 'courseware', a simple (digital) 'learning text' or 'programmed instructions'.

It became clear from our experiments that in interactive open learning environments, the user often feels the need to see or put things side by side (often unconsciously). If necessary, s/he wants to be able to move things (temporarily), in order to be able to study the underlying information. In short, parallelism in the user interface of educational programmes plays an important part in the solution of problems that designers have to face. Apparently, traditional (serial) user interfaces, in which something that appears on the screen will disappear in the next step, often makes too strong a demand on one's memory (Claessens *et al.*, 1999). More details on parallelism and the underlying theories are further described in a paper by Min *et al.* (2004).

Conclusion

The future

I was and still am in a sense an advocate of paper materials, paper instructions or even wall boards. At the back of the hall where I work, where the series Internet computers are, is a wall board – a kind of haven, a sort of 'organiser' in the chaos of the hyper world. From an educational point of view, certain things can be guaranteed with traditional means, but not with digital means. The advantages of digital means and contents are evident, but in an open discovery environment, the ordinary PC monitor simply does not have enough space to enable us to see everything and keep it there. We need better founded design theories which can address the questions – why does it not work and under what condition can you make it work?

The combination of a monitor with a PC is a unique one for simulation. Simulation immediately shows the surplus value of computers. There is no other method with which you can change complex, fuzzy, model-driven simulations into a modern interactive and powerful learning tool. This can be with or without a complex two- or three-dimensional animation appearance. The problem is that the learning environment has to be organised in such a way that real learning can take place. In a simulation session the teacher should be able to predict the learning effects. The user of a case should benefit from using the programme and the effects should be easy to demonstrate and measure. A computer is a good and unique medium for calculations, predictions and making decisions through expert systems via rule bases. It is also good for doing all kinds of other digital, dynamic things. Thus, you can try and create all kinds of beautiful, effective simulations, although they are expensive to produce. The concept of parallelism is a breakthrough. The parallel instruction theory for simulation and other open online learning, and/or work environments provides a cognitive framework for further study and for the development of better products to support a diverse range of interactions for effective online or e-learning. I am convinced of that.

Min's parallel instruction theory for simulations is in keeping with the view as it occurs in the cognitive load theory of Sweller *et al.*, as recently highlighted at the Education Research Days 2000 in Leiden by Kirschner (Kirschner, 2000).

It is very practical to use instructions and simulations in a learning situation. Both instructions and simulations can be downloaded via a network. In essence, a network is an excellent carrier for both: 'simulation on demand' and 'instruction on demand', as it is more practical than using CD-ROMs or CDs. E-learning as a method of learning has potential the future. But how can an open, online learning environment be combined with a less informal adaptive instruction environment that is rich in feedback. In other words, how can the advantages of constructivism be combined with the advantages of the classical instruction theory? This should be done in such a way that all those components which are critical in forming an optimal curriculum are captured in a 'place or location', in a manageable and effective manner and at the right moment.

What has been extensively described in this chapter is a combination of my insights gained from research in educational sciences, the experiences of children and (young) adults in a world of zapping and the products of searching (with search engines or clever 'agents'). I am of the belief that the methods of learning and learning tools described here can make a positive contribution in providing useful insight into the learning process, and to help make e-learning more dynamic, because ordinary education is much too often very static.

Note

Part of this chapter has been published in 'Simulation and discovery learning in an age of zapping and searching: learning models (a treatise about the educational strength and availability of digital learning tools and simulation on the world wide web)' in *Turkish Online Journal of Distance Education* – TOJDE, April 2003. ISSN 1302-6488, Volume 4, Number 2. Online. Available at: http://tojde.anadolu. edu.tr/tojde10/articles/rikmin.htm.

References

Claessens, M., Min, M. B. F. and Moonen, J. (1999) 'The effect of different ICT-designs on learning specific tasks', first year report of PhD study, University of Twente, Enschede.

Collis, B. (1998) 'Teleware: instrumentation for tele-learning', inaugural speech at Enschede 1 October 1998. Enschede: University of Twente.

de Jong, A. J. M. (1999) 'De proef op de som', inaugural speech at Enschede, 30 September 1999, Enschede: University of Twente.

Dicheva, D. and Kommers, P. (eds) (1999) 'Microworlds for education and continuous learning', *International Journal of Continuing Engineering Education and Life-long Learning*, special issue, 9(2/3/4,) 177–328.

Greenblatt, C. (1979) 'How to build a simulation/game', *Proceedings of the 10th Conference of the International Simulation and Gaming Association*: ISAGA (ed. K. Bruin), Leeuwarden. Vol. I and II. Groningen: Rijksuniversiteit Groningen.

Juwah, C. (2005) 'Digital natives and multi-skilling'. Personal communication – telephone discussion of 21 March 2005.

Kirschner, P. (2000) Symposium over de Cognitieve Belasting Theorie en het ontwerpen van instructie, *Proceedings van de ORD 2000* (with. J. Merriënboer, P. van Gerven, F. Paas, H. Schmidt, H. Tabbers and R. Martens) Leiden: ICLON/University Leiden.

Min, F. B. M. (1987) *Computersimulatie als leermiddel: een inleiding in methoden en technieken*, Schoonhoven: Academic Service.

Min, F. B. M. (1992) 'Parallel instruction, a theory for educational computer simulation', *Interactive Learning International*, 8(3), 177–83.

Min, F. B. M. (1994) 'Parallelism in open learning and working environments', *Britsh Journal of Educational Technology*, 25(2), 108–12.

Min, F. B. M. (1999) Interactive micro-worlds on the World Wide Web. *International Journal of Continuing Engineering, Education and Long-life Learning,* 9(2/3/4), 302–14. Online. Available at: http://projects.edte.utwente.nl/pi/papers/JavaWeb.html.

Min, F. B. M. and Ephraim, K. H. (1979) 'Computer assisted instruction voor het leren overzien van de anamnese', *Proccedings Medisch Informatica Congress '79* (ed. J. L. Willems), Antwerp: Acco Leuven.

Min, F. B. M., Vos, H., Kommers, P. and van Dijkum, C. (1999) 'Een algemeen dynamisch denk-model voor leren: een analogon; een poging om te komen tot een eenduidige vorm van bepaalde begripsomschrijvingen; een goed relatieschema; een model; en tenslotte om de dynamiek van het leren in relatie tot enkele moderne begrippen vast te leggen'. Online. Available at: http://projects.edte.utwente.nl/pi/Papers/LerenModel.html.

Min, F. B. M., Vos, H., Kommers, P. and van Dijkum, C. (2000) 'A concept model for learning: an attempt to define a proper relations scheme between instruction, learning and to establish the dynamics of learning in relation to modern political and educational concepts'. Online. Available at: http://projects.edte.utwente.nl/pi.papers/Learning.htm.

Min, R., Yu, T., Penkelink, G. and Vos, H. (2004) 'A comparison of parallelism in interface designs for computer-based learning environments', *Journal of Computer Assisted Learning*, 20, 360.

Papert, S. (1980) *Mindstorms: Children, Computers and Powerful Ideas*, New York: Basic Books.

Piaget, J. (1977) *The Development of Thought: Equilibration of Cognitive Structures*, New York: Viking.

Vygotsky, L. (1981) 'The instrumental method in psychology', in J. Wertsch (ed.), *The Concept of Activity in Soviet Psychology*, Armonk, NY: Sharpe.

Part III

Practice

This section details the various types of educational interactions and how each interaction is associated with different temporal and space-based constraints on participants and the impact different interactions have on learning. It also highlights how some media effects distinguish one type of mediated interaction over another for achievement of particular learning outcomes. Particular attention is paid to the existing and emerging educational interactions involving learners and focuses on those enhanced by the emergence of the Educational Semantic Web.

The section explores the concept of 'talk' in synchronous discussion/chat and asynchronous sessions (including web conferencing) and its role in enhancing interactions in online learning. Also, the section discusses interactions in online peer learning and the role of technology in promoting peer to peer learning through permitting interactions via shared spaces (data and resource sharing). The section concludes with a description of interactivity and interactions in videoconference teaching within a distributed network of learning institutions.

Chapter 8

Interaction in learning and teaching on the Educational Semantic Web

Terry Anderson

Interaction as a critical component of the educational process has long been recognized as a critical variable in achievement, persistence, enjoyment and approach to learning in formal educational contexts. However, there are many definitions of interaction and types of educational interaction (Anderson, 2003b). Each is associated with different temporal and space-based constraints on participants. Further, there is likely some media effect (Kozma, 1994) (especially in distance education applications) that distinguishes one type of mediated interaction over another for achievement of particular learning outcomes. Finally, the cost of interaction varies considerably not only depending upon the quantity and quality of that interaction, but also upon the perceived value of the role of the interactive participants. For example, direct interaction with teachers is perceived as more valuable and thus demands more return than interaction time among and between students or content.

In earlier works I have built upon the work of Moore (1989), Fulford and Zhang (1993), Wagner (1994), and others to describe the three major types of interaction in education directly involving students. These being student–teacher; student –student and student–content interactions. I have postulated that there exists a general equivalency amongst the types such that high levels of interaction in any one form allows for reduced interaction in the other two forms, with little loss in education effectiveness and considerable gain in cost effectiveness (Anderson, 2003a). As an example, a learning sequence with high levels of student–student interaction (such as a collaborative learning project) could likely be effective with lower degrees of student–teacher interaction (perhaps just setting the problem and tasks, and assessing the final product) and lower levels of student–content interaction (knowledge that is built into the final product is elicited or created by the group as it constructs the project).

In this chapter, I explore the types of existing and emerging educational interactions involving learners and focus on those enhanced by the emergence of the Educational Semantic Web (ESW). I will speculate as to their capacity to support substitution so as to create effective and efficient distance education courses. I conclude with a presentation of a model designed for learner-paced study at Athabasca University, Canada's Open University, and a proposal to apply these interaction theories to learner-paced study.

The context of the Educational Semantic Web

The Educational Semantic Web is the application of advanced web tools and web organization to education applications. It builds upon three building blocks or affordances (Anderson and Whitelock, 2004; Anderson, 2004a). First is the capacity of the semantic web to support effective retrieval of vast amounts of content. This educational content – often referred to as 'learning objects' – is available in multiple formats from text, to video, to computer animation. This content is packaged for educational use in an equally broad set of learning activities from independent study tutorials, to collaborative work projects, to virtual labs. The content of the ESW also includes reference and archive data not necessarily packaged originally for educational use – but capable of being re-purposed for such use. It also contains real-time data generated continuously by sensors and tracking tools that are becoming common as computers are deployed to capture, tabulate and store data gathered from sensors in a variety of contexts from animal and climatic observations to monitoring of markets. Though still in nascent state, the vision imprinted on many of us by the producers of Star Trek television series is being realized. This affordance was illustrated in almost every episode when a crew member queried the computer about any possible topic and received an instant response. Of course, this is not a reality yet, but continuously improving search engines, voice input and output and our understanding of how to organize content for diverse forms of retrieval is giving us more than just a glimpse of this vision.

The second affordance is that of supporting and enhancing human communication. Recently, this capacity has been referred to as '*social computing*'. It refers to the ESW's capacity to facilitate humans finding each other, building communities, collaborating in both virtual and real space, learning collaboratively and in many other ways enjoying and learning from each other's company (Davies, 2003; Musser *et al.*, 2003; Jordan *et al.*, 2003; Shirkey, 2003). These human communications are ubiquitous – taking advantage of the surging interest in mobile communications technologies. They are also multi-formatted, moving between asynchronous and synchronous forms of text, audio and video to meet needs, preferences and bandwidth availability of learners and teachers.

The third affordance is the capacity of the ESW to support autonomous agents. Autonomous agents are computer code that is capable of acting with relative autonomy on the ESW to accomplish tasks on behalf of learners, teachers and educational administrators and support staff (Baylor and Kim, 2003). Agents function by reading and processing the structured metadata associated with content and humans. Using the computing power of their host computers they are capable of inferencing, categorizing, prioritizing and otherwise manipulating and displaying data in support of educational activities. Like the futuristic vision from

Star Trek, educational agents are as yet not fully or completely functional. Yet we see early examples (Chen and Wasson, 2005; Beer and Whately, 2002; Lieberman, 2002; Thomas and Watt, 2002) and a great deal of work being done with commercial applications. Agent development is the focus of significant computer science research (see for example the proceedings from eight annual conferences at http://www.autonomousagents.org/). I am convinced that a personal agent will soon be helping me to teach my classes and assisting both myself and my students in a variety of educational tasks common to networked education systems and practices.

In the next section, I overview how these three affordances of the Educational Semantic Web and especially the interactions between learners and teachers, learners and learners and learners and content are enhanced when the affordances of the Educational Semantic Web are utilized to support learner interactions.

Teacher–student interaction

A traditional concept of teacher–student interaction has been elucidated by the American President James Garfield who was reported to have defined the ideal university as 'Mark Hopkins (then President of William's College) at one end of a log and a student on the other'. Since then the 'log' has expanded into cyberspace and the conversation has expended into multiple audio, text and visually enhanced formats. Yet there remains a sense that personal identification and other aspects of 'teacher presence' (Brady and Bedient, 2003) are important, if not critical, components of the educational process. The problem with teacher–student interaction is that there is only a limited amount of 'room on the log'. Further, the teacher often is not sitting on her 'end of the log' when their intervention is most advantageous for the learner. Simply put, student–teacher interaction is not scaleable. Student–teacher interaction may be critically important for certain personalized learning outcomes and it is a valuable addition to many interactions on the Educational Semantic Web. However, it must be used judiciously so as to not constrain access to formal learning through high cost. Our global educational goal must be set broad enough to accommodate the millions of learners currently denied educational opportunity and the even larger number who will need lifelong learning opportunities that are low cost, accessible, effective and fun. For these reasons I see a migration (but not elimination) of direct student–teacher interaction to student–student and student–content learning designs.

The most obvious and traditional way to transfer student–teacher to student–content interaction is by mediating the interaction and capturing it as 'canned' content transcribed in textbooks, videos, audio recordings and various combinations of mediated interactions. These types of substitutions are easily accommodated on the ESW. An example is the edited text book *Theory and Practice of Online Learning* (Anderson and Elloumni, 2004) that we produced at Athabasca University and distribute free of charge under a Creative Commons Licence. This book is available in hard copy and we have sold 300 copies. More importantly over 65,000 individuals have downloaded (and perhaps many have printed) the online version of the book during the two years since its publication. This open distribution of content is not restricted to text. The ubiquity of digital video cameras and web streaming technologies allows individual teachers to create low cost videos of themselves lecturing, discussing, personalizing and in other ways humanizing their teaching without forcing them to 'sit on the log'.

More interactive sequences are also commonplace in web-based courses that use asynchronous text conferencing. These interactions are time shifted to allow participants 'anytime/anywhere' access. Importantly, since they are automatically captured in machine readable formats, they may be used (with permission of the participants, of course), and re-used in frequently asked question files, exemplar illustrations, e-portfolios and other data management applications. As importantly, they can be used as models and reference sources for learners working at times long removed from the original interaction. Some have argued that the contextualization in a local scene of these types of recordings diminishes their efficacy. But in a globally conscious world, the expression and contextualization of the messages themselves creates a learning opportunity as learners are challenged to make sense of ideas, comments and critiques of those from a different culture and context.

We are also learning that student–teacher interactions are very diverse but that most can be categorized into content areas and types. In an interesting study of tutor interaction with students through comments and annotations to essay-type assignments, Moreale and her colleagues at the Open University found that there are positive correlations between the mark received and the number and type of tutor comments (Moreale *et al.*, 2002). Underlying this work is an attempt to understand and push the limits of learning by substituting teacher–student with other forms of interaction.

Another example of this type of substitution is the construction of response and conversational systems. We have had fun and seen examples and interesting student perceptions of dialogue with simple types of Eliza-like response systems built using Artificial Intelligent Markup Language (AIML) (Wallace, n.d.). Our Freudbot is designed to engage, in response to student prompts, in a conversation about Freud's theories of personality. Early results of study of the logs of these interactions show that Fruedbot is rather didactic and tends to want to steer the conversation towards opportunities to move into a lecture-like mode of discourse. As an academic myself, I was not surprised with this apparent quirk of an academic personality since I know many colleagues with similar conversation styles. Freudbot illustrates the tendency for humans to treat their machines like living beings (Reeves and Nass, 1996). I am not arguing that conversations with human beings are equivalent to those with machines. Each serves unique functions but they can also be substituted for each other in many educational contexts. For example, I never go to a human bank teller unless there is a fault in the automated teller. Thus, valuable human time is reserved for exceptional and very special types of interaction.

Many such interactions can effectively be replaced by interaction with less scarce human and machine resources. For example, the student support call centre in the School of Business at Athabasca currently handles over 80 per cent of student inquiries (Woudstra *et al.*, 2004) that arise as they pursue independent undergraduate study. Only 20 per cent of the questions are passed on to academic experts for response. These queries are monitored, the time for resolution tabulated, and the answers are made available for both tutors and call centre advisors in computerized FAQ (frequently asked question) files. As technologies improve and learner networking efficacy and access increases we are likely to see continuing substitution, for routine questions, transactions and other student support concerns using friendly, database-driven inquiry systems (Anderson, 2004b).

Teachers' agents will undertake a variety of tasks designed to reduce repetitive and time-consuming administrative functions associated with teaching; helping teachers remain current as to discipline and pedagogical developments in their fields and in creating and monitoring student learning activities. Many will remember the still futuristic 'Knowledge Navigator' promotional video created by Apple in the late 1980s. In this video, an attractive, voice activated, personal agent acted as research assistant, secretary and confidant to a busy university lecturer. Some researchers have argued (Nowak, 2004; Dowling, 2002) that such anthropomorphic representation of agents increases their efficacy, but doubtless different description and functionality yet needs to be evolved and tested with users to confirm what form(s) these teachers' agents will take. They will evolve to respond to both voice and text input and output as dictated by the circumstances and preference of the users. For example, I look forward to the day when my teacher agent notifies me that three students have not accessed the learning management system for the past four days and asks politely if I wish to send my usual 'we are missing your participation' letter. Completing such a routine task with current tools is time consuming and not personally rewarding to busy teachers.

Student–student interaction

Much has been learned about the efficacy of increasing student–student content over the past three decades. This type of interaction takes many forms including peer tutoring (Rourke and Anderson, 2002; Damon, 1984), collaborative (Springer *et al.*, 1999) and cooperative learning (Slavin, 1995), and informal study groups (Robertshaw, 2000). This literature argues that collaborative learning increases learner control and motivation, enhances learning outcomes and creates opportunities to increase social connectedness and networking among learners. These in turn lead to higher satisfaction and lower attrition rates. As they migrate to networked learning, the challenges and increased opportunities of these forms of intense student–student interactions are being recognized and most cases resolved (Fung, 2004; Harasim, 2002).

Recently, a new genre of networking applications has appeared on the Net. These applications are often referred to as 'social computing' or 'presence' applications. In an interesting overview of this software, Davies (2003) argues that social computing serves not to create a parallel universe of cyber relationships, but rather works to integrate online and face-to-face life. Other researchers argue that social software not only supports, documents, charts and archives social interaction, but also provides for critical social feedback (Shirkey, 2003; Kaplan-Leiserson, 2003). An example of this type of feedback and reputation development is exemplified by the trust ratings on systems such as E-Bay.

These social software tools will be used on the ESW to enhance and support student–student interaction thereby creating and sustaining formal and informal learning communities. For example 'introducer systems' (MeetUp, Udate, Ryze, Tribe) are currently in use to connect general web users – often for business or dating goals. They could easily be adapted to focus on common learning goals, interests and concerns. These are all first generation systems and as they evolve and mature to the state where they allow students to connect to each other, without invading their privacy, they will increase in value to the education community. WIKIs and systems such as LiveJournal allow the creation and ongoing development of group diaries, commentaries and other documentation of individual and group concerns. Such tools make it much easier for groups of learners to manage collaboration on documents and learning artifact products. Chatrooms have been in educational use for at least 15 years, but more elaborate text (MOOs and MUDs) and graphic virtual worlds (2ndlife.com) can also be usefully employed to facilitate real-time student–student interaction (Shih *et al.*, 2005). Instant text messaging has become ubiquitous in many developing and developed countries. The incapacity for learners to discover and communicate with each other in real-time and to be able to determine when learners are available for communication has often been a major constraint for collaboration in distance education contexts. Blogs (web-based logs) are being used in a whole host of ways by teachers, individuals and groups of learners (Downes, 2004) to publicly develop and share their communication skills. Often this content is distributed using Rich Site Syndication (RSS) to support public review, argument and resolution of topic issues by students globally – in the process creating outstanding international learning opportunities. Although mobile or m-learning using technologies and applications seems as yet restrictive due to small screen sizes and restrictions on network availability, the recent mobile learning conferences (see http://www.mobilearn.org/) and books (Kukulska-Hulme and Traxler, 2005) are reporting very interesting educational applications of these technologies. M-Learning situates learning and training in the context of use (Nyiri, 2002; Brown *et al.*, 1989) thereby increasing its usefulness and relevance. Proponents of social software argue that these tools enhance social relationships by illuminating, codifying and tracking communication for good effect (Davies, 2003). Many of the software solutions for effective online learning communities are still in developmental stages and many learners have not had experience with any of these tools. Thus, a sustained developmental research programme is required in which we test evolving tools in the real communities of learning that are created. Learner agents will be used by learners to overcome some of the logistical aspects of creating and maintaining effective interactions. In my own online teaching I have noticed group interactions seem to take at least twice as long when they occur online as compared to face-to-face. This is largely due to the challenges of synchronizing activities, and the challenges of supporting and documenting dialogue and decision making. The richness of face-to-face interaction, with the implicit advantages of body language and shared context will likely not be totally replicated at a distance, nonetheless use of agents that can find, organize and schedule access to both material and human resources will significantly enhance this capacity. The I-Help system developed by the University of Saskatchewan (Greer *et al.*, 2001) is an interesting example of a student agent system that facilitates and encourages students to help each other. I-Help works by allowing each enrolled student to create an agent that is aware of the student's areas and levels of expertise, their interest and availability in providing help, and the cost of that service. When a student desires peer help, they can instruct their agent to find the agent of a likely helper, negotiate a fee for service, monitor the resulting email exchanges of help given and keep track of the quality of that help for future requests for help. The I-Help is like other agent systems still under development, but it provides a useful working prototype of the way in which learner agents will be used on the ESW to connect students, thus enhancing student–student interaction.

Student–content interaction

Students have since the earliest medieval universities gathered at places where there is access to content as well as other learners and teachers. The development of the web has nearly made obsolete this dependency on place-based access to content, since much is available anywhere/anytime. However, it is useful to look at the pedagogical benefits that are made possible by use of the web to deliver, annotate and support student–content interaction. First is the general level of access and the resulting capacity for specialization. With whole libraries online, it is not necessary to assign only a single set of content resources for student–content interaction. This results in increases in choice and variety not only in content but in the means by which the content and learner can interact (the instructional design). Net-based content is also highly accessible in that it can be displayed in formats appropriate to learners and can adapt to many physical challenges they face such as deafness or visual impairment.

Net-based content is also capable of providing interactive feedback. Butler and Winne (1995) point out that feedback can be both internal (derived by the student themselves) or external (generated by persons or machines other than the student). They go on to argue that there must exist a congruency between the feedback and the student's capacity to act upon that feedback to change their behaviour. Feedback that is ignored or delivered in a language or condition that is not comprehensible or motivating to the student does not result in the changes to student thought or behaviour that are necessary to demonstrate effective learning. Customizing feedback and student–content interaction to create personalized learning sequences has been the Holy Grail of artificial intelligence research in education for over 30 years. Although the challenges of building truly adaptive systems are legion, progress is being made in systems that build and maintain learning profiles that can be used to customize feedback, sequence and learning activities. An example of this type of feedback and reputation development is exemplified by the trust ratings on systems such as E-Bay.

However, interacting with content first requires that the teacher and the learner be able to find and acquire that content. For the past five years we have been working to develop learning objective repositories that provide a systematic way for creators to distribute and consumers retrieve a wide variety of such learning objects (see www.careo.ca). Moving from the early efforts to create accessible databases, to more sophisticated means to catalogue or tag these objects (Friesen *et al.*, 2002), to creating systems that support and distribute metadata among repositories (McGreal *et al.*, 2004), we have been able to build the technical capacity to create, catalogue and retrieve these objects. However, we see as yet unresolved problems relating to the actual use (or more accurately non-use) of the metatag fields (Friesen, 2004), challenges of defining and acknowledging ownership, difficulties in maintaining identification through various versions and adaptations of objects, and perhaps most critically the challenges of developing an active community of both contributors and users of these repositories. The efforts of the CLOE (www.cloe.ca) group in supporting communities, developing a reciprocal use agreement for extraction and submission of objects, and in tracking object use are the first efforts at tackling these community issues within established universities. The dialogue (and construction of operating systems) around educational objects and their use and re-use illustrates the need for large quantities of content to be made available and accessible. However, we are just at the beginning of finding ways that these objects can be sued to customize learning to maximize learner–content interaction.

But how is all this potential of the ESW to be instantiated in real-life educational programming? I now turn to a short case study examining my own university and present a model for enhancing interaction in a cost effective way for our learner-paced programming.

Case study

Towards the ESW at Athabasca University

Athabasca University – Canada's Open University – has an uncommon delivery model in that its undergraduate programme (25,000 enrolments) allows for continuous intake and learner pacing of their study. Athabasca University is dedicated to the removal of barriers that restrict access to, and success in, university-level studies and to increasing equality of educational opportunity for adult learners worldwide (Athabasca University Mission Statement, 2002). Many of our students are attracted to the flexible delivery model that allows them to commence studies when they are available and more importantly to work at a pace that meets their time constraints. In the past the delivery model relied on print-based packages and tutorial support provided via telephone by academic tutors. Only in very exceptional contexts was face-to-face tutorial support provided and all of Athabasca's 600 courses in 51 degree programmes are delivered at a distance (see www.athabascau.ca for more details).

Independent or student-paced learning models create administrative and pedagogical challenges. As a single mode distance delivery institution, we have built our admissions, student support and tuition systems around continuous intake and so are able to meet the administrative challenges with purpose built policy and practice. However, the explosion of interest in collaborative and cooperative learning pedagogy, including a focus on learning communities, has caused us to reappraise our delivery model, with a view to determining if it is possible to maintain our niche market of learner-paced delivery and at the same time allow for increased student–student interaction. The problem is challenging not only in that students begin their course study during any month of the year, but even those that start near the same time often have different expectations and plans for the length of time they will take to complete the course. Finally, through surveys we know that many of our students choose our independent study mode precisely so that they are not forced to work collaboratively with peers.

In 2004 we developed a research plan to investigate this issue and hopefully develop a model for resolving this dilemma. The research methodology consisted of telephone interviews with distance educators globally who confront the same or similar challenges, interviews with our current faculty to learn of their efforts to provide student–student interaction support (most commonly through optional computer conferencing forums), and a survey of students enrolled in courses in which such support had been enabled. Space precludes a discussion of the findings, but I would like to share the model that we have developed as a result of this work.

The goal of the model is to help us create a system that provides high quality, scaleable education that is learner-paced and still meets the social needs of active students. Figure 8.1 illustrates this model.

The model illustrates three critical components of the learning system. The content and student support services are familiar components of Athabasca's current delivery model, however, each needs to be under continuous revision to insure that they are exploiting the emerging capacity of the ESW. The major innovation described in the model is the enhancement of learner–learner interaction to create and sustain learning communities. This component has been supported informally in the past, but we argue that much more can and should be done to augment and support this critical component of lifelong learning.

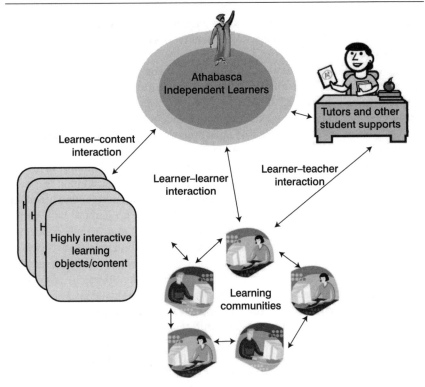

Figure 8.1 A proposed model of student-paced learning at Athabasca University

Interactive learning objects

High quality learning content has always been a defining characteristic of Athabasca and other single mode distance delivery institutions. However, in the past most of this content has been text-based, linear and often didactic in nature. Developments in media technology coupled with greater understanding of pedagogical theory allow us to create more sophisticated modes of student–content interaction (as described previously) to engage, motivate and stimulate students using a variety of media and instructional designs. This of course does not preclude text content, but neither does it rely on textbooks and study guides for nearly all content. Second, new forms of knowledge management and re-use, often referred to as learning objects, are creating an opportunity for much greater sharing, re-using, and effectively managing learning content. Athabasca University must quickly move to integrate its valuable content resources into a content management system or learning object repository to develop a systematic means to store, search and catalogue its considerable intellectual resources. Third, means to systematically combine, sequence and package these resources must be developed so that objects can be amalgamated into effective learning sequences and designs. The development of systems based upon emerging standards (such as SCORM and IMS Learning Design) provides early examples of systems designed to undertake this task in ways that allow the final product to be further adapted in response to unique student needs (Koper, 2001). Finally, ways must be developed that allow faculty members and subject matter experts to easily revise content so that it remains 'evergreen'. The demands of a continuous enrolment system are challenges to regular updating of content, but systems need to be developed that allow versions of the course to be revised and enhanced, while the course is being offered in real time.

Learning community

The Athabasca learning community has always existed informally within the undergraduate system. It is time for this system to be recognized and supported so that it can play an increased and pivotal role in provision of quality, cost effective education. The learning community is made up not only of other students registered in the course, but also of professionals, former students, supporters, family members, informal lifelong learners, mentors and others interested in the content and in each other. The learning community is supported through resources (such as collaborative learning objects) and through environments that allow for exchange, acquaintance, encouragement and query. A variety of social software is used to create this environment. Tutors and other student support services are welcomed into the learning community but they do not control or orchestrate this community. Rather, they participate in ways that help students reach their own learning goals, meet the staff's own learning needs and support the community at minimal costs. Within the community, students locate partners for work on collaborative learning objects and participate in a variety of formal and informal discussion groups, some of which will be directly related to course content, others to more general socializing, and informal learning.

The community also provides referral and 'meet-me' services to its members for those seeking peer support, study groups, employment, advice, leads, personal support and related resources.

Tutors and other student support

This student–teacher interaction component of the model provides personalized service when needed, but it also provides a range of automated services such as frequently asked questions, library tutorials and call centre question response. The critical student assessment function is located in this component to ensure quality of student outcomes and subsequent academic credit and award. This includes the current invigilation services but also grows into machine generated and marketed assignments as used in the Athabasca School of Business (Annand and Huber, 2002). Much of the literature in educational use of online community assumes the active participation and organization of a teacher within a cohort of paced learners (see for example Harasim *et al.*, 1995 or Salmon, 2000). As this model is designed for a cohort of students working in synchronized pace through a course, it is not appropriate for Athabasca's student-paced delivery model. Rather, the tutor role within the community should be one of learning activity designer, professional advisor, learning trouble-shooter, co-investigator and assessor. Our experience of attempting to facilitate similar groups has shown that participation is very limited due primarily to lack of critical mass and sustained interest by both learners and tutors. Thus, we look to create more self-sufficient learning communities.

Management, research and evaluation

The outer circle surrounding the learner in Figure 8.1 represents the interface between these three learning components and the student. This interface is part portal serving as a door to resources and part a monitoring and tracking tool that guides, documents and assists the learner in their interactions with other independent students, content, community and Athabasca staff. The tracking component of the interface helps us understand and assess the use and efficacy of these three sets of resources and is critical to our continuous evolution of our learning environment. Through continuous design and re-design coupled with multifaceted research and evaluation, we ensure that the learning environment continues to grow and take advantage of technical and pedagogical opportunities.

Conclusion

The discussion above and the example from Athabasca University illustrate that interaction plays a primary role in successful online learning. However, the ESW opens the door for much more extensive use of student–content and student–student interaction and allows us to begin building systems that actively use learner-managed communities to enhance learner–learner interaction and autonomous agents to alleviate administrative, scheduling and other bottlenecks that arise. The ESW is still more of a dream than a reality, yet there is growing evidence that it will be built and it will create many more diverse forms and models of lifelong education. Our challenge is to ensure that these models do not increase the cost of education, but indeed, make substantial progress towards creating high quality educational opportunies that are accessible and affordable by all citizens of the planet.

References

Anderson, T. (2003a) 'Getting the mix right: an updated and theoretical rational for interaction', *International Review of Research in Open and Distance learning*, 4(2) Online. Available at: http://www.irrodl.org/content/v4.2/anderson.html (Accessed 30 October 2003).

Anderson, T. (2003b) 'Modes of interaction in distance education: recent developments and research questions', in M. Moore (ed.), *Handbook of Distance Education*, Mahwah, NJ: Lawrence Erlbaum.

Anderson, T. (2004a) 'The Educational Semantic Web: a vision for the next phase of educational computing', *Educational Technology*, 44(5), 5–9.

Anderson, T. (2004b) 'Student services in a networked world', in J. Brindley, C. Walti, and O. Zawacki-Richter (eds), *Learner Support in Open, Distance and Online Learning Environments*, Oldenburg: Bibliotheks- und Informationssystem der Universität Oldenburg.

Anderson, T. and Elloumni, F. (2004) *Theory and Practice of Online Learning*, Athabasca AB Canada: Athabasca University. Retrieved 5 September 2004 from http://cde. athabascau.ca/online_book.

Anderson, T. and Whitelock, D. (2004) 'The Educational Semantic Web: visioning and practicing the future of education', *Journal of Interactive Media in Education*, 1. Online. Available at: http://www-jime.open.ac.uk/2004/1 (Accessed 24 April 2004).

Annand, D. and Huber, C. (2002) 'Development of an automated exam marking system at Athabasca University', *Proceedings of the ICDE/Canadian Association of Distance Educators Conference*. Canadian Association for Distance Education. Online. Available at: www.cade-aced.ca/icdepapers/annandhuber.htm (Accessed 10 September 2004).

Baylor, A. and Kim, Y. (2003) 'Validating pedagogical agent roles: expert, motivator, and mentor', *World Conference on Educational Multimedia, Hypermedia and Telecommunications*, 1. Online. Available at: http://dl.aace.org/12794 (Accessed 15 June 2004).

Beer, M. and Whately, J. (2002) 'A multi-agent architecture to support synchronous collaborative learning in an international environment', *International Conference on Autonomous Agents*. ACM. Online. Available at: http://delivery.acm.org/10.1145/550 000/544860/p505-beer.pdf?key1=544860andkey2=3756400701andcoll=GUIDEand dl=GUIDEandCFID=14459982andCFTOKEN=17157121 (Accessed 28 November 2003).

Brady, E. and Bedient, D. (2003) 'The effects of teacher presence on student performance and attitudes', WebCT Impact 2003, 5th Annual WebCT User Conference, San Diego, California, July.

Brown, J. S., Collins, A. and Duguid, P. (1989) 'Situated cognition and the culture of learning', *Educational Researcher*, 18(1), 32–42.

Butler, D. and Winne, P. (1995) 'Feedback and self-regulated learning: a theoretical synthesis', *Review of Educational Research*, 65(3), 245–81.

Chen, W. and Wasson, B. (2005) 'Intelligent agents supporting distributed collaborative learning', in F. O. Lin (ed.), *Designing Distributed Learning Environments with Intelligent Software Agents*, Hershey: Information Science Publishing.

Damon, W. (1984) 'Peer interaction: the untapped potential', *Journal of Applied Developmental Psychology*, 5, 331–43.

Davies, W. (2003) *You Don't Know Me, but... Social Capital and Social Software*, London: Work Foundation. Online. Available at: http://theworkfoundation.com/research/ isociety/social_capital_main.jsp (Accessed 10 September 2004).

Dowling, C. (2002) 'Software agents and the human factor in the electronic classroom', *Untangling the Web: Establishing Learning Links Conference*. ASET. Online. Available at: http://www.aset.org.au/confs/2002/dowling.html (Accessed 28 November 2003).

Downes, S. (2004) 'Educational blogging', *Educause Review*, 39(5). Online. Available at: http://www.educause.edu/pub/er/erm04/erm0450.asp?bhcp=1 (Accessed 10 September 2004).

Friesen, N. (2004) 'A report on the international learning object metadata survey', *International Review of Research in Open and Distance Learning*, 5(3). Online. Available at: http://www.irrodl.org/index.php/irrodl/article/view/195/277(Accessed June 2006).

Friesen, N., Roberts, A. and Fisher, S. (2002) 'CanCore: learning object metadata', *Canadian Journal of Learning and Technology*, 28(3). Online. Available at: http://www.cjlt.ca/content/vol28.3/friesen_etal.html (Accessed 10 September 2004).

Fulford, C. P. and Zhang, S. (1993) 'Perceptions of interaction: the critical predictor in distance education', *American Journal of Distance Education*, 7(3), 8–21.

Fung, Y. (2004) 'Collaborative online learning: interaction patterns and limiting factors', *Open Learning*, 19(2), 135–50.

Greer, J., McCalla, G., Vassileva, J., Deters, R., Bull, S. and Kettel, L. (2001) 'Lessons learned in deploying a multi-agent learning support system: the I-Help experience', AIED. Online. Available at: http://julita.usask.ca/Texte/Aied01-camera.pdf (Accessed 2 April 2003).

Harasim, L. (2002) 'What makes online learning communities successful? The role of collaborative learning in social and intellectual development', in C. Vrasidas and G. Glass (eds), *Distance education and distributed learning*, Greenwich, CO: Information Age Publishing.

Harasim, L., Hiltz, S., Teles, L. and Turoff, M. (1995) *Learning Networks: A Field Guide to Teaching and Learning Online*, London: MIT Press.

Jordan, K., Hauser, J. and Foster, S. (2003) 'The augmented social network: building identity and trust into the next-generation Internet', *First Monday*, 8(8). Online. Available at: http://firstmonday.org/issues/current_issue/jordan/index.html (Accessed 12 August 2004).

Kaplan-Leiserson, A. (2003) 'We learning: social software and e-learning', *Learning Curcuits* (December). Online. Available at: http://www.learningcircuits.org/2003/dec2003/kaplan.htm (Accessed 20 December 2003).

Koper, R. (2001) *Modeling Units of Study from a Pedagogical Perspective: The Pedagogical Meta-model Behind EML*, Heerlen: Open University of the Netherlands. Online. Available at: http://eml.ou.nl/introduction/docs/ped-metamodel.pdf (Accessed 28 June 2002).

Kozma, R. (1994) 'Will media influence learning? Reframing the debate', *Educational Technology Research and Development*, 42(2), 7–19.

Kukulska-Hulme, A. and Traxler, J. (2005) *Mobile Learning: A Handbook for Educators and Trainers*, London: RoutledgeFalmer.

Lieberman, H. (2002) 'Interfaces that give and take advice', in J. Carroll (ed.), *Human Computer Interaction in the New Millennium*, New York: Addison-Wesley.

McGreal, R., Anderson, T., Babin, G., Downes, S. and Friesen, N. (2004) 'EduSource: Canada's learning object repository network', *International Journal of Instructional Technology and Distance Learning*. Online. Available at: http://www.itdl.org/Journal/Mar_04/article01.htm (Accessed 10 September 2004).

Moore, M. (1989) 'Three types of interaction', *American Journal of Distance Education*, 3(2), 1–6.

Moreale E., Whitelock D., Raw, Y. and Watt, S. (2002) 'What measures do we need to build an electronic monitoring tool for postgraduate tutor marked assignments?', *Proccedings of the 6th Computer Assisted Assessment Conference.* Loughborough University. Online. Available at: http://www.lboro.ac.uk/service/ltd/flicaa/conf2002/pdfs/moreale_e1.pdf (Accessed 10 September 2004).

Musser, D., Wedman, J. and Laffey, J. (2003) 'Social computing and collaborative learning environments', *The 3rd IEEE International Conference on Advanced Learning Technologies.* IEEE Computer Society. http://csdl.computer.org/comp/proceedings/icalt/2003/1967/00/19670520.pdf (Accessed 14 January 2004).

Nowak, K. (2004) 'The influence of anthropomorphism and agency on social judgement in virtual environments', *Journal of Computer Mediated Communications*, 9(2). Online. Available at: http://www.ascusc.org/jcmc/vol9/issue2/nowak.html#abstract (Accessed 1 February 2004).

Nyiri, K. (2002) 'Towards a philosophy of M-learning', *IEEE International Workshop on Wireless and Mobile Technologies in Education.* IEEE. Online. Available at: http://21st. century.phil-inst.hu/eng/m-learning/nyiri_m-learn_philos.htm (Accessed 25 April 2004).

Reeves, B. and Nass, C. (1996) *The Media Equation: How People Treat Computers, Television, and New Media Like Real People and Places*, Stanford, CA: CSLI Publications.

Robertshaw, R. (2000) *Support Groups in Distance Education*, Vancouver: Commonwealth of Learning. Online. Available at: http://www.col.org/Knowledge/pdf/KSsupportgroups. pdf (Accessed 10 September 2004).

Rourke, L. and Anderson, T. (2002) 'Using peer teams to lead online discussions', *Journal of Interactive Media in Education*, 2(1). Online. Available at: http://www-jime.open. ac.uk/2002/1 (Retrieved May 2006).

Salmon, G. (2000) *E-moderating: The Key to Teaching and Learning Online*, London: Kogan Page.

Shih, T., Wang, Y. and Chen, Y. (2005) 'A VR-based virtual agent system', in F. O. Lin (ed.), *Designing Distributed Learning Environments with Intelligent Software Agents*, Hershey: Information Science Publishing.

Shirkey, C. (2003) *Social Software and the Politics of Groups.* Online. Available at: http:// shirky.com/writings/group_politics.html (Accessed 24 April 2003).

Slavin, R. (1995) *Cooperative Learning Theory, Research, and Practice*, 2nd edn, Boston, MA: Allyn and Bacon.

Springer, L., Stanne, M. and Donovan, S. (1999) 'Effects of small-group learning on undergraduates in science, mathematics, engineering and technology: a meta-analysis', *Review of Educational Research*, 16(1), 21–51.

Thomas, M. and Watt, S. (2002) 'Intelligent instant messaging agents to support collaborative learning', *Proceedings of the 16 British Human Computer Interface Conference*, London: Springer Verlag.

Wagner, E. D. (1994) 'In support of a functional definition of interaction', *The American Journal of Distance Education*, 8(2), 6–26.

Wallace, R.S. (n.d.) Anatomy of A.L.I.C.E. (Artificial Linguistic Internet Computer Entity) A.L.I.C.E. Artificial Intelligence Foundation, Inc. Online. Available at: http://www. alicebot.org/anatomy.html.

Woudstra, A., Huber, C. and Michalczuk, K. (2004) 'Call centres in distance education', in T. Anderson and F. Elloumni (eds), *Theory and Practice of Online Learning*, Athabasca: Athabasca University.

Chapter 9

Interactions in online discussions

A pedagogical perspective

Sanjaya Mishra and Charles Juwah

Introduction

Education is a kind of communication process (Tiffin and Rajasingham, 1995). This educational communication process has four components – the learner, the teacher, some problem in a particular context, and knowledge to solve the problem (Vygotsky, 1978). These components interact among each other, at different levels, to enable the learner to apply knowledge to the problems. As it is with any communication process, a feedback loop maintains the continuity of the process, and thereby, helps in the process of learning. Interaction is inherent in learning, since it is the outcome of an educational communication process. Most theories of learning suggest that to be effective, learning needs to be active (Khan and McWilliam, 1998). Laurillard (1993) provides a social, communicative and conversational model of teaching and learning in which knowledge is a negotiated commodity. Vygotsky (1978) stated that learning is culturally influenced, and talking and interaction are essential for learning (McLaughlin and Oliver, 1997).

Previous research indicates that interaction is the key in the classroom (Flanders, 1970); a higher level of interaction results in more positive attitudes (Garrison, 1990); and interaction leads to a high level of achievement (McCrosky and Anderson, 1976). Flottemesch (2000), after a review of literature on interaction in distance education, concludes that 'Interaction in the classroom (traditional or distance learning) plays a key role in a student's learning, retention and overall perceptions of the course/instructor effectiveness' (p. 49). Similarly Wallace (2003), having reviewed the research literature on interaction in the online higher education context says:

> Substantial evidence exists to support the importance of social presence, student interaction, and teacher presence in online learning environments. Settings in which students and teachers establish social presence, in which teachers interact with students and support them in a variety of ways, and in which student participation is high, are likely site for student learning, and student satisfaction.
>
> (p. 271)

The concept of interaction

Wagner (1989) has suggested that 'interaction' functions as an attribute of effective instruction, where as 'interactivity' functions as an attribute of contemporary instructional delivery systems. Interaction is 'sustained, two-way communication among two or more persons for purposes of explaining and challenging perspectives' (Garrison, 1993, p. 16), whereas choice, non-sequential access to choice, responsiveness to learner, monitoring information use, personal choice helper, adaptability, playfulness, facilitation of interpersonal communication, and ease of adding information are dimensions of interactivity (Chou, 2003) that today's instructional systems display. According to Wagner (1994, p. 8), 'interactions are reciprocal events that requires at least two objects and two actions' and instructional interaction takes place between a learner and his/her environment. Instructional interactions are intended to change the behaviour of learners towards an educational goal. Moore (1989) suggested three types of interaction in the context of open and distance education – learner–content interaction, learner–instructor interaction, and learner–learner interaction. Bates (1991) pointed out that there are two types of interaction – social and individual. He emphasized that social interaction between learners and teachers need to be balanced *vis-à-vis* the learners' interaction with learning resources. Hillman *et al.* (1994) added a fourth kind of interaction to Moore's categories, as learner–interface interaction. They emphasize that increasing use of technology as the means of communication forces the emergence of learner–interface interaction. According to them, the inability to achieve learner–interface interaction successfully can result in distorted learning. Paulsen (1997), in the context of computer mediated communication describes four possibilities of interaction. These four paradigms of interaction are:

- the one-alone method or the World Wide Web paradigm, where the learner interacts with the teaching software (database, expert system, electronic book, Computer Aided Instruction (CAI), hypertext, etc.);
- the one-to-one method or e-mail paradigm, where the learner interacts with his/her teacher or peer(s);
- the one-to-many method or the bulletin board paradigm, where a teacher or student addresses a large number of students; and
- the many-to-many method or the conferencing paradigm, where a group of people teach and learn at the same time through discussion, group projects, forum, etc.

Berg (1999) categorized interaction into intrapersonal and interpersonal. According to him, intrapersonal interaction is a reflective process through which a learner processes information/content of a course in his/her mind in order to internalize, assimilate and make sense of it to construct his/her own knowledge. In other words intrapersonal interaction is a must for learning to happen, while interpersonal interaction occurs when learners interact with one another and/or their instructors about the content to make sense of what they are learning. As such, in this chapter we are concerned with the interpersonal interaction (instructional and social) that has influence on the learning process. Instructional interaction are constructed of four components – context of the interaction; challenge of a stimulus to exhibit effective behaviour; learner activity as a response to the context and challenge; and feedback on the process (Allen, 2003). Figure 9.1 depicts the types of interaction in the technology-mediated learning context, and as mentioned earlier, it can take place in any of the four paradigms identified by Paulsen (1997).

Theoretical underpinnings

Parer (1994), in his paper 'Towards a theory of open and distance learning', emphasized that 'structure' and 'dialogue' are essential foundations to create learning environments. We can trace the theoretical underpinnings of interaction to the concept of transactional distance, which is a function of the two variables – 'dialogue' and 'structure'. Dialogue is 'the extent to which, in any educational programme, learner and educator are able to respond to each other'; structure is 'a measure of an educational programme's responsiveness to a learner's individual

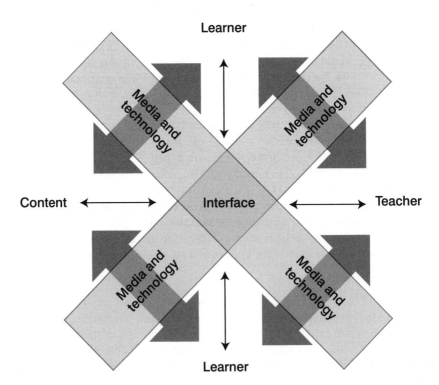

Figure 9.1 Interactions in technology mediated teaching-learning

needs' (Moore, 1983, p. 171). Fulford (1993) uses the theory of cognitive speed to explain the need for interaction. According to this theory, people speak at the rate of 125–50 words per minute (wpm), though the mind can comprehend information delivered twice the rate of ordinary speech. If learners are not engaged in intrapersonal interaction, their attention gets diverted due to the partial use of the cognitive capacity. Thus interaction makes use of the full cognitive capacity, and learning remains focused. Fulford and Zhang (1993) found that learners' perception of overall interaction is a critical factor of learner satisfaction. Ragan (1998) describes five principles of interaction as a means to create 'learning communities'. These principles are:

- Effective learning environments should involve frequent and meaningful interactions among the learners, with the instructional materials, and between the learner and the instructor. When instructional technologies are employed as a part of the educational programme, the interface between the learner and technology should also be considered.
- Social interaction between the learners enriches the learning community and should be encouraged and supported throughout the instructional design of educational programmes.
- The use of electronic communication technologies should be considered as a tool for creating and maintaining the learning communities for learners at a distance. These technologies may also support active and collaborative learning activities.
- Distance education programmes should employ creative solutions to fulfil the objectives traditionally achieved via residency requirements: interaction among faculty, students, and peers beyond direct instruction; access to advising and academic support services and resources; and socialization in the field of study.
- To help reduce barriers to establishing social relationships, participants should be given the opportunity to build confidence and competence with the distance education paradigm and supporting technologies.

Media and technologies for interaction

Bates (1995) makes a distinction between media and technology. According to him, television as a medium could be delivered through various technologies such as satellite, cable, videocassettes, etc. He has identified the five most important media in education as direct human contact (face-to-face), text (including still graphics), audio, television, and computing. Similarly he also categorizes technology into two groups – one-way technologies and two-way technologies, the distinction being that the former does not allow interpersonal communication, whereas the latter does. Interpersonal communication is of two types – synchronous and asynchronous (Berg, 1999; Liaw and Haung, 2000), which can be facilitated through two-way technologies. Based on Moore's typology of interaction, and

Table 9.1 Interaction technologies/media

Interaction	Two-way technologies	
	Synchronous	Asynchronous
Learner–Content	Teleconference • Audio • Video • Computer Interactive radio	Interactive multimedia Web-based instruction Facsimile
Learner–Instructor	Face-to-face counselling Telephone Chat (one-to-one/conference) Audiographics Teleconference Interactive radio	E-mail Mailing lists, discussion boards Facsimile
Learner–Learner	Self help groups Chat groups (one-to-one conference) Teleconference Interactive radio	E-mail Mailing list, discussion board Facsimile

the nature of interpersonal communication through two-way technologies, the different kinds of technologies used for interaction are depicted in Table 9.1.

Learner–content interaction

Holmberg (1986) calls it 'internal didactic conversation' when the learner interacts with the information and ideas they encounter in a text. Learners interact with the content available in a medium through intrapersonal interaction and comprehend the content. Today, technology can facilitate learner–content interaction through teleconference and the interactive features of the World Wide Web (Chou, 2003).

Learner–instructor interaction

As the name suggests, it is the interaction between the learner and the instructor/ tutor. The purpose of interaction here could be both social and instructional in nature. As a part of social interaction, the instructor provides counselling support, encourages learners, and motivates them. As for instructional interaction, the instructor clarifies doubts, elaborates difficult points, explains concepts, demonstrates processes etc.

Learner–learner interaction

The peer group interaction can be facilitated through two-way technologies. The learner–learner interaction builds the confidence of the learner, encourages a spirit of competition and, most importantly, facilitates cooperative and collaborative learning.

Concept of discussion

Discussion (conversation or talk) is a social activity in which individuals engage with each other to explore and negotiate options. It also provides the opportunity:

- in which our knowledge and ideas are challenged;
- for individuals to listen to alternative perspectives, to affirm, revise and/or reject our earlier views or hypotheses.

Discussion can be held on a one-to-one or one-to-many basis. In online education, discussions are mediated by technology and can be asynchronous or synchronous.

Interactions in Web-based learning

The World Wide Web, being a medium capable of interaction functions (Chou, 2003), it provides all the three kinds of interactions mentioned in Table 9.1. According to Gunawardena *et al.* (1998), the web provides online interaction for knowledge construction, which can be categorized into five phases:

- sharing/comparing of information;
- discovery and exploration of dissonance or inconsistency among ideas, concepts, or statements;
- negotiation of meaning/co-construction of knowledge;
- testing and modification of proposed synthesis or co-construction; and
- agreement statement(s)/applications of newly constructed meaning.

Salmon (2000) developed a five stage model to depict the process of student engagement in online classes:

- access and motivation;
- online socialization;
- information exchange;
- knowledge construction; and
- development.

Salmon refers to the online teacher as an e-moderator, who facilitates these five stages of student engagement online. Though e-mail is the most used technology on the Web, online interactions for teaching/learning are facilitated by mailing lists, discussion groups (asynchronous conference) and chat (one-to-one and conference). Integrated web based learning systems more popularly known as Learning Management Systems (e.g. WebCT, Blackboard, Centra, etc.) provide all these facilities from scratch. E-mail provides an easy and cost-effective form of asynchronous communication to inform as well as clarify doubts of the learners.

E-mail is also used for collaborative group work at a distance. Mailing lists are many-to-many channels of communication on the Internet, managed using specialized software such as Listserv, Majordomo, and Listproc (Mishra, 2001). Mailing lists can be moderated or un-moderated, and can be used to collaboratively discuss and debate issues in learning community. Discussion boards are similar to mailing lists, but are available on the World Wide Web as a series of threaded discussions. Internet Relay Chat (IRC) is the standard for synchronous, text-based chat on the Internet. Chat can be one-to-one, or can operate in a group conferencing mode. Today chat software can use voice as well as Web cameras to facilitate real-time virtual classrooms. In the next sub-sections, we discuss the methods and techniques of using threaded discussions and chat sessions for teaching and learning.

Using threaded discussion boards

Discussion boards are tools which provide facilities for a diverse range of uses in online classroom situations. Some of the uses include:

- a communication tool which provides space for discussion and dialogue on a topic/subject matter being considered between learner–learner on a one-to-one basis and between learner–tutor on one-to-many basis. Such discussion can be asynchronous or synchronous;
- a forum for interaction and networking amongst learners/users;
- a repository of learning materials and artefacts;
- serve as learning histories to which learners can refer in the future because of the permanent nature of the record of contributions.

As the name suggests, the messages are displayed on the Web as they are received and appended to the original message, showing hierarchical relationships of messages. Use of the interactive database technology allows these messages to be sorted by dates and topics as well. However, using the threaded discussion for teaching and learning is a difficult task and requires planning for any teaching activity to be successful. The following guidelines, prepared based on a review of literature (Kelly, 2004; Mishra and Jain, 2002; Piskurich, 2001; Flottemesch, 2000; Berge and Muilenberg, 2000; Feenberg, 1989; Eisley, 1992), may be useful for organizing effective threaded discussion:

- integrate discussion questions throughout the course that contribute to the learning objectives and are not just add-on assignments;
- make student participation expectations clear, and assign grading value;

- keep the class size reasonable, say between 12–18 participants, but this depends on the number of postings expected from the learners;
- send a personal and welcoming message to each learner well before the discussion begins;
- use open-ended questions to promote divergent thoughts;
- identify main points of discussion early to focus it around them;
- use different formats for discussion (e.g. debate [for and against], critique, etc.) to avoid monotony;
- provide reasonable time to study and participate in discussion; stagger assignment due dates;
- ensure that learners treat each other respectfully;
- respond to learners posting within 24 hours;
- provide individualized and frequent feedback to learners;
- guide discussion; direct less and suggest more;
- encourage learners to assess each other's work; use peer assessment as part of the evaluation strategy;
- summarize discussions periodically;
- invite participation from browsers (lurkers) and missing members without offending them (some believe 'lurkers' is both an offensive word and a pejorative term).;
- provide separate discussion space for socialization so that non-academic matters are discussed separately.

Using chat sessions

Chat can be used in one-to-one situation or in small group tutorials. For effective use of chat in teaching, the following experiential guidelines are useful:

- keep the group size small with about four to five learners;
- prepare an agenda for discussion with definite starting and ending times;
- give pre-reading materials, Web links, etc. in advance before the synchronous discussion;
- communicate about the agenda and time in advance; and confirm learner participation;
- schedule the time in consultation with the learners, especially if they are in a different time zone;
- identify a moderator out of the learners and leave the discussion to them; just observe the discussion, guide and summarize the main points from time to time;
- allow time for social interactions before and after the academic discussion (e.g. Hello, How are you?, Goodbye);
- continue discussion as per the agenda items;
- use different formats, such as quiz or brainstorming, apart from regular discussion;

- keep a permanent record of all discussions;
- use humour, anecdotes, etc.

Pedagogical implications for online discussion

Whilst discussion boards and chat facilities have great potential in enhancing learning via dialogue, the authors' experience is that less effective use is made of this versatile tool. Also, it is important to note that not all students/learners are comfortable with using these facilities. Some of the reasons may be cultural, linguistic or simply fear – fear of inadequacy in the language of discourse or effective use of the technology (in terms of speed of typing for synchronous chat) and of being publicly ridiculed by peers, etc. See Cameo below for an abridged response from a participant (Alex – name disguised for confidentiality) on a group discussion list. The feeling expressed by Alex is not too dissimilar from those expressed by some of our students.

Some members of the group have expressed lack of confidence in posting to a discussion group. The problem for this lack of confidence is not entirely limited to the difference in one's native language. Other factors which contributed to this lack of confidence included:

- Self consciousness that one's language is not academic enough;
- Being intimidated by polished grammar, sentence structure and syntax;
- Fear of communicating in the written word because of the permanence of the written posts;
- Inability to type at a moderately fast pace resulting in the fact that most of my ideas are lost before I complete composing my thoughts in the written words.

However, my resolve has been that of 'do it'. So, my advice to others is that you have great ideas, questions and contributions to make. Go for it.

Alex

In many instances, posts in discussion forums are irrelevant and sometimes very unwieldy due to sheer volume of posts, thus causing the students to lose sight of the essence of the discussion. These situations in our view usually arise as a result of inappropriate use or improper use of discussions. This scenario raises the question – should online discussions be assessed. If so, what would the criteria be?

Key points to consider

What can tutors/facilitators of online learning do to ensure that learners are helped to cope effectively with issues that may impact on the quality of their learning experience in online discussions and chats?

From our experience as online facilitators we proffer the following:

- establish a purpose and context for the discussion and the intended outcomes;
- establish the relevance of the discussion in the student's learning by making links to the intended learning outcomes;
- provide learners with much needed training in IT skills as well as socialize them to enable effective use of the discussion board;
- tutors and learners need to be culturally aware and to provide adequate support and encouragement to enable their fellow learners to participate effectively online and to meet their learning needs (or refer the learner to an appropriate source of help);
- tutor/facilitator/moderator needs to frequently summarize the posts to help focus learning; where discussions are beginning to stall or to be diverted from the central theme to issues not relevant to learning, the facilitator should end the thread of discussion and begin a new one or provide guidance to help steer the discussion in the right direction.

If the discussions are to be assessed (we are of the view that they should be), appropriate assessment guidelines, criteria and rubrics should be devised. Where appropriate, learners can be involved in devising the assessment criteria. Such criteria should specify the following:

- the nature of the assessment and how the assessment is to be graded (see Table 9.2, exemplar rubric for assessing discussions);
- quality and quantity of posts;
- deadline for posts. (Do ensure that learners do not have assessment deadlines bunched up together as this may lead to assessment overload, resulting in some students not being able to cope. Such a situation may inadvertently lead to students dropping out of the course.)

Online teacher professional development

... a real expectation for the use of the Internet in course delivery is that, contrary to an expectation that the role of the teacher will diminish with Internet or Computer-based delivery, the demands on the teacher's time remain the same and may increase. However, the types of demand change. This is where the teacher must change in order to provide a service for learners.

(Forsyth, 1996, p. 33)

Table 9.2 Rubric for assessing online discussions and interactions

		Description
Level 1	No interactions	Students download material from the Web, read notes and send assignment to tutor. Does not initiate any interactions with peers. Level of synthesis, analysis and integration of theory to practice is very limited and superficial. Submitted work lacks critical reflection on own learning and/or practice. Attainment of the intended learning outcomes is very patchy.
Level 2	Low level interactions	Limited use of communications facilities (e.g. mailing list, e-mail), initiates few interactions and dialogues with peers and tutors, and does so only when required and with significant guidance; argument presented is ineffective and lacks synthesis and coherence; very limited evidence of integration of theory to practice. Other people's posts are sometimes acknowledged. Reflection on own learning and/or practice is very limited, discursive and lacks critical analysis; achieves one or two of the intended learning outcomes. Number of posts is sufficient and met the given deadline.
Level 3	Moderate level interactions	Makes good use of diverse range of two-way communication tools; with guidance initiates and facilitates some interactions and dialogues with peers and tutor/facilitator; limited evidence of synthesis in argument presented; some gaps in the linking theory to practice; integrates ideas from own learning and others' posts (with due acknowledgement); critically reflects on own learning and/or practice and achieves some of the intended learning outcomes. Number of posts is sufficient and met the given deadline.
Level 4	High level interactions	Makes very good use of a diverse range of two-way communication tools and multiple media; facilitates and initiates many interactions and dialogues with peers and tutor/facilitator with minimum or no guidance; good evidence of synthesis and coherence in argument presented; good linking of theory to practice; good integration of ideas from own learning and others' posts (with due acknowledgement); critically reflects on own learning and/or practice; achieves most of the intended learning outcomes. Number of posts is sufficient and met the given deadline.
Level 5	Outstanding level interactions	Makes effective and efficient use of a diverse range of two way communication tools and multiple media; facilitates and initiates several interactions and dialogues with peers and tutor/facilitator autonomously; exemplary range and depth of attainment of all intended learning outcomes underscored by plentiful evidence of linking theory to practice; very good synthesis and coherence in argument presented; excellent integration of ideas from own learning and others' posts (with due acknowledgement); critically reflects on own learning and/or practice. Number of posts is sufficient and met the given deadline.

Source: Juwah, C. (2003) Rubric for assessing interactions.

The changes brought about by online teaching and learning have created considerable new demands for teachers. Some teachers feel that their roles have been subverted by the designs and functions of the new technologies (Brennan *et al.*, 2001). However, teachers are using more and more interactive and learner-centred approaches, especially the Web, e-mail, chat and discussion forums. Their role shifts from 'sage on the stage' to 'guide on the side'. Alongside this change, teachers need to improve their ability to manage time and improve skills to facilitate online discussions. Even the best classroom facilitator will need some orientation and practice if they are going to function effectively online (Piskurich, 2001).

According to Inglis *et al.* (1999), staff development initiatives for online learning will be successful if all those who are involved in the group are committed to change and have a common understanding of the directions of the change. Pulist (2001, p. 66) suggests the following to ensure the effectiveness of staff development in an online learning environment:

- staff should have ample opportunities to reflect on the benefits and limitations of technology;
- staff development should be ongoing and systematic for lasting impact;
- in order to enable the teachers to benefit from each other's experiences, training and workshops should be supplemented by peer coaching and modelling (mentoring);
- the training should be based on actual activities to be undertaken by the teachers;
- hands-on exploratory experiences with technology should be provided to the participants.

Booker (2000, p. 36) provides the following strategies to support teachers in online teaching and learning:

- training in using the technology and teaching in the online environment;
- receiving support and feedback through mentor or buddy systems with more experienced online teachers available for advice to novices;
- ensuring technical help is available when required;
- providing links to other staff developers and IT staff as part of a team of online facilitators;
- managerial support for initiatives;
- teacher chat room and/or discussion lists;
- checklist of tasks, action, etc.;
- newsletters …

Conclusion

In this chapter, we have discussed the concept of interaction and its role in learning. We have traced the theoretical roots of the role of interaction in learning to the cognitive speed theory and Moore's theory of transactional distance. We have also identified the synchronous and asynchronous two-way technologies useful for learner–content, learner–instructor and learner–learner interactions, with a focus on Web-based learning, where effective uses of threaded discussion forums and chat have been discussed. At the end, a case has been made for appropriate staff development strategies for online teachers. It is suggested that professional development for online teachers should be inclusive and take into account training on technology apart from the skills of effective facilitation of synchronous and asynchronous discussions through practical hands-on training.

References

Allen, M. W. (2003) 'I had no idea: how to build creative e-learning experiences', *Educational Technology*, 43(6), 15–20.

Bates, A.W. (1991) 'Interactivity as a criterion for media selection in distance education', *Never Too Far*, 16, 5–6.

Bates, A. W. (1995) *Technology, Open Learning and Distance Education*, London: Routledge.

Berg, Z. L. (1999) 'Interaction in post-secondary Web-based learning', *Educational Technology*, 39(1), 5–11.

Berge, Z. L. and Muilenberg, L. (2000) 'Designing discussion question for online, adult learning', *Educational Technology*, 40(5), 53–6.

Booker, D. (2000) *Getting to Grips with Online Delivery*, Kensington Park: NCVER.

Brennan, R., McFadden, M. and Law, E. (2001) *All that Glitters is not Gold: Online Delivery of Education and Training*, Kensington Park: NCVER.

Chou, Chien (2003) 'Interactivity and interactive functions in web-based learning systems: a technical framework for designers', *British Journal of Educational Technology*, 34(3), 265–79.

Eisley, M. E. (1992) 'Guidelines for conducting instructional discussion on a computer conference', *DEOS News*, 2(1). Online. Available at: http://www.ed.psu.edu/atsde/deos/deosnews/deosnews2_1.asp (Accessed 3 November 2004).

Feenberg, A (1989) 'The written world: on the theory and practice of computer conferencing', in R. Mason and A. Kaye (eds), *Mindwave: Communication, Computers, and Distance Education*, Oxford: Pergamon Press.

Flanders, N. A. (1970) *Analysing Teaching Behaviour*, Reading: Addison-Wesley.

Flottemesch, K. (2000) 'Building effective interaction in distance education: a review of the literature', *Educational Technology*, 40(3), 46–51.

Forsyth, I. (1996) *Teaching and Learning Materials and the Internet*, London: Kogan Page.

Fulford, C. P. (1993) 'Can learning be more efficient? Using compressed speech audio tapes to enhance systematically designed text', *Educational Technology*, 33(2), 51–9.

Fulford, C. P. and Zhang S. (1993) 'Perceptions of interaction: the critical predictor in distance education', *American Journal of Distance Education*, 7(3), 8–21.

Garrison, D. R. (1990) 'An analysis and evaluation of audio teleconferencing to facilitate education at a distance', *American Journal of Distance Education*, 4(3), 13–24.

Garrison, D. R. (1993) 'Quality and theory in distance education: theoretical consideration', in D. Keegan (ed.), *Theoretical Principles of Distance Education*, New York: Routledge.

Gunawardena, C. N., Lowe, C. A. and Anderson, T. (1998) 'Transcript analysis of computer mediated conferences as a tool for testing constructivist and social-constructivist learning theories', Paper presented at the Annual Conference on Distance Teaching and Learning, Madison, WI, 5–7 August.

Hillman, D. C. A., Willis, D. J. and Gunawardena, C. N. (1994) 'Learner–Interface interaction in distance education: an extension of contemporary models and strategies for practitioners', *American Journal of Distance Education*, 8(2), 30–42.

Holmberg, B. (1986) *Growth and Structure of Distance Education*, London: Croom Helm.

Inglis, A., Ling, P. and Joosten, V. (1999) *Delivering Digitally: Managing the Transition to the Knowledge,* London: Kogan Page.

Juwah, C. (2003) 'Rubric for assessing interactions'. Postgraduate Certificate in Higher Education Learning and Teaching. Robert Gordon University, Aberdeen, Scotland.

Kelly, H. (2004) 'Enhancing interpersonal interaction in online courses', *Educational Technology*, 44(1), 53–6.

Khan, A. W. and McWilliam, P. (1998) 'Application of interactive technologies in open and distance learning: an overview', *Indian Journal of Open Learning*, 7(1), 7–21.

Laurillard, D. (1993) 'Balancing the media', *Journal of Educational Television*, 19(2), 81–93.

Liaw, Shu-Sheng and Haung, Hsin-mei (2000) 'Enhancing interactivity in Web-based interaction: a review of the literature', *Educational Technology,* 40(3), 41–5.

McCrosky, J. C. and Anderson, J. F. (1976) 'The relationship between communication apprehension and academic achievement among college students', *Human Communication Research*, 3, 73–81.

McLaughlin, C. and Oliver, R. (1997) 'Maximising the language and learning link in computer learning environments', *British Journal of Educational Technology*, 24(4), 1–12.

Mishra, S. (2001) 'Designing online learning', *Knowledge Series of the Commonwealth of Learning*. Online. Available at: http://www.col.org/knowledge/.

Mishra, S. and Jain, S. (2002) 'Designing an online learning environment for participatory management of displacement, resettlement and rehabilitation', Paper presented at the Pan-Commonwealth Forum on Open Learning held at Durban, 29 July–3 August 2002.

Moore, M. G. (1983) 'The individual adult learner', in M. Tight (ed.), *Adult Learning and Education*, London: Croom Helm.

Moore, M. G. (1989) 'Editorial: three types of interaction', *American Journal of Distance Education*, 3(2), 1–6.

Parer, M. S. (1994) 'Towards a theory of open and distance learning', in M. S. Parer (ed.), *Unlocking Open Learning*, Churchill: CDE, Monash University.

Paulsen, M. F. (1997) 'Teaching method and techniques for computer mediated communication', Paper presented at the 18th ICDE World Conference: The New Learning Environment, A Global Perspective, ICDE, Pennsylvania State University, 29–31 May.

Piskurich, G. M. (2001) 'Facilitating synchronous WBT', *Infoline 0112*, December, 1–16.

Pulist, S. K. (2001) 'Staff Development for online learning', *Staff and Educational Development International*, 5(1), 59–70.

Ragan, L. C. (1998) 'Good teaching is good teaching: an emerging set of guiding principles and practices for the design and development of distance education', *DEOSNEWS*, 8(12). Online. Available at: http://www.ed.psu.edu/acsde/deos/deosnews/deosnews8_12.asp (Accessed on 3 November 2004).

Salmon, G. (2000) *E-moderating: The Key to Teaching and Learning Online*, London: Kogan Page.

Tiffin, J. and Rajasingham, L. (1995) *In Search of the Virtual Class: Education in an Information Society*, London: Routledge.

Vygotsky, L. (1978) *Mind in Society: Development of Higher Psychological Process*, Cambridge, MA: Harvard Business Press.

Wagner, E. D. (1989) 'Interaction: an attribute of good instruction or characteristics of instructional technology', Paper Presented at the Annual Meeting of the National University Continuing Education Association, Salt Lake City, UT, April.

Wagner, E. D. (1994) 'In support of a functional definition of interaction', *American Journal of Distance Education*, 8(2), 6–29.

Wallace, R. M. (2003) 'Online learning in higher education: a review of research on interactions among teachers and students', *Education, Communication and Information*, 3(2), 241–80.

Chapter 10

Interactions in online peer learning

Charles Juwah

Peer learning is a dynamic form of learning in which learners are actively engaged in a diverse range of interactions intellectually, emotionally and socially to construct knowledge, make new meanings and develop skills and abilities. The involvement of information and communications technology in online peer learning has the potential to transform student learning through increased engagement and interactivity. This chapter presents the underpinning theory and range of interactions and complexities (challenges and risks) involved in peer learning in an online learning environment. It also presents insights into innovative technologies that can be used to promote effective peer interactions online. The chapter concludes with hints and an agenda for further research into online peer interactions.

Introduction

Context

Competitiveness and survival in today's knowledge economy requires the acquisition, development and regular updating of knowledge, skills, competences and the ability to work in cross-cultural contexts or situations. Higher education aims to promote scholarship, the development of higher order skills and employability as well as promote social inclusion. However, the massification of contemporary higher education in recent years as a result of increased large class sizes, diverse student population due to widening participation, reduced resource allocation (or reduced unit cost) and the rapid evolution of technology has created the need for different strategies of teaching and learning such as peer learning to meet the intended learning outcomes.

Lave and Wenger (1991) and Wenger (1998) provide useful insights into the apprentice-to-apprentice interactions which underpin peer learning in contrast to the more prominent master-to-apprentice interactions.

Peer learning can be defined as learning in which participants of approximate equality (regardless of status) collaborate to learn with and from each other in authentic situations to leverage their educational experience and socio-cultural gains. It involves learning in a non-threatening environment or learning community; the removal of power domination by the teacher over the student and the involvement of the student(s) in the assessment process (Topping, 1998). Examples of the types of educational experience and socio-cultural gains that may be derived from peer learning include: the development of knowledge – principles, concepts and theories; development of skills (interpersonal, project management, peer support, reflection, self-directed skill), abilities and a diverse range of competencies; and the provision of immediate response and feedback to participants (Anderson and Boud, 1996).

Smith (1983) posits that the key to peer learning lies in the mutually supportive climate which the learners themselves construct and in which they feel free to express opinions, test ideas and request and offer help as needed (p. 91). This form of active, collaborative and cooperative learning is underpinned by constructivism (Piaget, 1963; Bruner, 1966; Vygotsky, 1978) – a phenomenon in which the learners are actively engaged in situational learning and through social discourse, dialogue, talk and negotiation construct knowledge and make new meaning. Doolittle and Camp (1999) posit that constructivism is underpinned by a set of theoretical principles, which are:

- Learning should take place in authentic and real-world environments;
- Learning should involve social negotiation and mediation;
- Content and skills should be made relevant to the learner;
- Content and skills should be understood within the framework of the learner's prior knowledge;
- Students should be assessed formatively, serving to inform future learning experiences;
- Students should be encouraged to become self-regulatory, self-mediated, and self-aware;
- Teachers serve primarily as guides and facilitators of learning, not instructors;
- Teachers should provide for and encourage multiple perspectives and representations of content (paragraph 29).

The different models of peer learning have been well documented by Anderson and Boud (1996) and Griffiths *et al.* (1995) (see Table 10.1).

Managing peer learning

There is much information in the literature about group learning (Jaques, 2001). However, for peer learning to be successful, it needs to be managed. The following factors are important in designing peer learning into a course:

Table 10.1 Models of peer learning

• Student-led workshops • Learning exchanges • Seminar presentations • Work-in-progress reports • Debriefing sessions • Peer feedback • Study groups • Learning partnerships Anderson, G. and Boud, D. (1996).	• Proctor model of peer tutoring – in which senior students tutor junior students • Partnerships between same year students • Discussion seminars • Private study groups • Peer counselling • Peer assessment schemes • Collaborative project or laboratory work • Projects in different size groups • Workplace mentoring • Community work Griffiths *et al.* (1995).

Identify what the learning is about

In any learning activity, it is critical to identify what needs to be learned, whether it is knowledge, skills, abilities, competences, etc. The nature of the learning may be formal (structured and assessed) or informal.

Learning skills

For learners to participate and gain positive experience from online peer learning, they must be skilled in 'learning how to learn' and in the effective use of information technology. The US National Research Council (1999) identified three key principles for effective learning:

- *Principle 1*: Students bring to the classroom (or new learning) preconceptions of how the world works (or prior knowledge). Engaging this prior knowledge is critical if the learner is to grasp and comprehend new concepts.
- *Principle 2:* For students to develop competence in an area of inquiry they must have: a deep foundation of factual knowledge of the subject matter; a thorough grasp and comprehension of facts and ideas in the context of a conceptual framework; and the ability to organise knowledge in ways that facilitate retrieval and application.
- *Principle 3:* An approach to instruction that will enable learners to take ownership of their own learning via defining learning goals (outcomes), and monitoring progress and evaluate the achievement of their learning. In essence, learning should be active, self-regulated and underpinned by reflection (see Figure 10.1 from Jackson, 2004). It is important that the instructional approach must be constructively aligned to the intended learning outcomes to enable the learners to understand and consolidate,

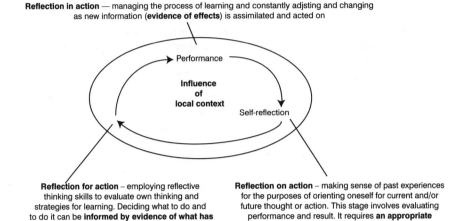

Figure 10.1 Model of self-regulated learning (Zimmerman, 2000 p. 226) coupled to notions of reflection (Ertmer and Newby, 1996) (Source: Jackson, 2004)

connect, interpret, validate, reflect on and apply knowledge in different contexts (Biggs, 1999; Boud *et al.*, 1985; Kolb, 1983; Schon, 1987). Also, learners must have evidence to draw on to ensure that their learning is meaningful, effective and that they have achieved the intended learning outcomes.

Use of information technology

Equally important as 'learning how to learn', is the ability to use information technology effectively. Thus, it is important that learners have the required skills to enable them to access, navigate and utilise the diverse range of educational technologies and the facilities they offer in meaningful learning. In addition, the learners must be information literate – that is being able to source, retrieve, evaluate and apply information appropriately.

Group formation and socialisation

In peer learning, groups are formed through self-selection or people are allocated to a group by a structured or randomised approach. For groups to cohere and perform effectively, it is important that they are appropriately formed and socialised. Tuckman (1965) has identified four stages of group dynamics: forming, norming, storming and performing. Socialisation of the group is critical in helping to ensure good group dynamics as participants get acquainted with individual, social and cultural differences, expectations, ground rules, etc. The group's performance can be limited by the number of participants. Too few participants within the group may result in very limited interactions, whilst a very large group may result in too many interactions, ultimately bordering on chaos. Equally too, some participants may find they are unable to actively participate and learn effectively within such groups. An important aspect of group socialisation is that it provides the platform early on in the learning process of modelling the 'good behaviours and attributes' you would like learners to acquire.

Contextualisation

The context in which the learning is to take place should be well understood by the learners and should provide the essential resources in terms of content, infrastructure and facilities (for example technology) and scaffolding required to make learning meaningful. Where appropriate, learners should be encouraged to bring their own intended outcomes to the group learning. By so doing they learn to share knowledge and resources thus enhancing collaborative learning. It is important to maintain a consistency of approach in the mode of delivery be it asynchronous or synchronous. If the mode of delivery is asynchronous, do ensure that synchronous (real time) activities are adequately planned and that learners are well informed of such sessions.

Interactions in peer learning

In contemporary distance and online education, computer mediated conferencing (CMC) is the dominant technology used in the delivery of instruction. The mode of delivery can be either asynchronous or synchronous or both. However, the asynchronous mode of delivery is limited by the lack of non-verbal information and the lack of this information may in some instances result in terse interchanges or 'flame' wars (Sproull and Keisler, 1986). CMC they argued, is sufficient for effective communication when the messages are simple and unequivocal but are inappropriate for ambiguous, empathic or emotional messages. Peer learning is underpinned by a range of complex interactions, which include: intellectual (reading, reviewing, conceptualising, critiquing), emotional, social, manipulating objects, questioning, responding, etc. Thus, for peer learning to be effective in a technology-enhanced environment, it is important that the interactions consist of three core components: cognitive presence, teaching presence, and social presence (Garrison et al., 2000 cited in Rourke et al., 2001).

Cognitive presence

Cognitive presence is defined as the extent to which participants in a community of learning engage in sustained dialogue and discourse (conversation), and through this engagement are able to negotiate and construct meaning.

From the above, it is evident that conversation is a key interaction in peer learning. Also, conversation is central to information sharing. Klemm (1999) states that conversation consists of: monologue; dialogue; dialectic; and construction. He defines these processes as follows:

- Monologue – involves only oneself in the exchange of opinion and supposition. The positions taken may sometimes be rigid.
- Dialogue – involves a group or community in exchanging ideas and building shared views to reach a consensus.
- Dialectic – involves distilling the conversation or discourse into 'facts', 'truth' or 'correctness' from logical argument. The focus of the dialectic is on analytical thought and factual information.
- Construction ('Design') – involves the use of conversation to construct new knowledge and new meaning making.

He further states that conversations between learner and learner and learner and tutor/facilitator 'contribute to learning in many ways: rehearsal of facts to expedite memorization, exposure to a broad range of information and perspective, deeper understanding, a stimulus for insight and creative thought, and a basis for assessment of learning' (Klemm, 1999).

As part of conversation, dialogue in peer learning in an online setting is also very important. Mercer (2000) identifies three forms of dialogue: disputational, cumulative and exploratory.

Disputational dialogue is very much less productive than exploratory dialogue, as individuals engage more in non-productive argument. Whereas in exploratory dialogue, learners engage in a more critical, constructive and reflective learning. The different forms of dialogue provide learners with alternative views/perspectives and feedback. It enables the learner to recognise and resolve inconsistencies, and revise and/or reject initial beliefs, views or hypotheses based on reasoned judgement. Hence, it is the nature and quality of the dialogue/interactions and feedback inherent in the discourse that enhances learning rather than the amount (or quantity).

Whilst self-reflection or reflective discussion is critical in learning, Hartley and Ravenscroft (1993) state that self-reflection or reflective discussion between students may not be effective in changing beliefs and their organisation into conception. This requires dialogue with a teacher. This statement predicates that certain types of learning can only take place when there is dialogue between teacher and learner as the teacher will bring to the learning situation his expertise and experience. The dialogues between teacher and learner not only establish the foundation for learning but also extend the possibilities for knowledge creation and knowledge acquisition (Purnell *et al.*, 2004). Bakhtin (1981) and Mercer (2000) attribute the effectiveness of dialogue in promoting learning to the concept of control, i.e. ability to exert and retain control in context rather than the issue of 'power and authority' by the teacher over the learner. Therefore, to ensure effective and meaningful learning, it is appropriate to design in access to the tutor or tutor support in peer learning.

Dialogue which can be written and mediated by technology enables the learner to:

- verbalise and articulate their learning needs and understanding;
- question, analyse and synthesise information to make new meaning;
- reflect (Cook, 2002; Vygotsky, 1978).

Thus, for dialogue to engender effective knowledge construction and skills development in peer interactions, it is important to provide the necessary scaffolding. The epistemological approach in providing appropriate scaffolding to support deep learning includes questioning, analysing and representing, i.e. presenting and structuring activities within appropriate contexts and authentic situations (see Chapter 5). These scaffolds are the cognitive tools or anchors which learners use as points of reference to structure, analyse, sequence, contextualise, develop, adapt (for example, object oriented activity), mediate and reflect on their learning. Scaffoldings can be categorised as:

- Conceptual – these guide the learner in what to consider, particularly when the problem/task is defined. They provide explicit hints and examples.
- Metacognitive – these guide the learner in how to think in considering the problem/strategies, for example, framing the problem. They provide suggestions for planning ahead, modelling cognitive strategies, providing a regulatory process and evaluation.
- Procedural – these guide the learner in how to utilise information, i.e. provide on-going help and advice, and may include tutoring (see next section on teaching presence).
- Strategic – these guide the learner in analysing and approaching the problem with a strategy. They provide a basis to seeking solutions as well as enabling focused responses to the problem (Juwah, 2002).

However, the threaded discussion boards used in most proprietary online learning environments to support dialogue in online learning do not lend themselves to linking of thoughts and responses as well as focusing learners' attention. I shall return to this issue in the section dealing with technology for peer learning.

Teaching presence

Teaching presence is defined as the ability to design, structure and facilitate learning processes through social interactions with a view to achieving intended and meaningful learning outcomes.

The strategy of facilitating effective peer learning is underpinned by collaboration and engagement. Vygotsky (1978) in his theory of 'zone of proximal development – ZPD' posits that children learned skills more effectively when collaborating with adults (*or a more experienced or competent peer*). The effectiveness of their learning was predicated on the process of engagement enabling the children to refine their thinking and performance. Similarly, situated cognition theory (situated learning), a variant of constructivism, highlights that the structure of the learning is implicit in the experience of learning rather than the way the subject matter is structured (Stein, 1998). This model posits that knowledge is obtained via '*way in*' and '*practice*'. In '*way in*', the learner watches the master and through '*practice*' makes use of acquired knowledge and refining and perfecting of the same to solve the problem. This master–novice/apprentice model engages both the master and learner in dialogue, questioning and practice that promotes learning through explanation of and reflection on process. The type of dialogue and sequence of discussion and questioning have important effects on learning. Thus, the learner is able to draw on the implications for learning from previous experiences. As Mazur (1997) observes Socratic–dialogic approach enables learners to learn best when they:

- are engaged in real life (authentic) challenges or activities; and
- exchange feedback with others in similar situations through questioning.

This process of questioning (and giving and receiving feedback) encourages the students to think through the argument being developed as well as enables them to assess their understanding of principles and concepts.

These interactions are similar to the processes inherent in apprentice-to-apprentice learning (peer learning) within a community of learning (Lave and Wenger, 1991; Wenger, 1998).

The key elements of this situational paradigm of learning are: *content*, *context*, *community of practice* and *participation*.

The *content* focuses on subject/discipline facts, principles and concepts and the *context* deals with situations, cultural issues, values, beliefs and environmental cues within which learners master the subject/discipline content. In peer learning, learners are expected to engage with a variety of activities, for example: brainstorming exercises, case studies, debates, decision making, writing reports, projects, portfolios, problem-based scenarios, etc. It is imperative that both the content and context of the learning activities are authentic and relevant (see Chapter 5). The *community of practice* provides the forum in which the learners interact, and to some extent the context and content to enable them to create and negotiate meaning. Within the community of practice, interaction and engagement are underpinned by *participation*, the process in which learners working together with peers and experts in a social organisation learn to solve problems.

Social presence

Social presence is defined as a phenomenon in which participants project their individuality, socio-emotional content and personal identities online. This is underscored by affective responses, social cohesion, and interactive responses.

Social interaction is a critical component of peer learning in an online setting. However, engagement in computer mediated asynchronous discourse will not suffice for quality learning. Thus, to create the context in which online peer interactions foster quality discourse, the creation of knowledge, development of skills and abilities, sharing of values and practices, promoting diversity and inclusion and high quality learning (Lowell and Persichitte, 2000), it is important to:

- provide an induction to familiarise learners with the concept and benefits of peer learning underscored by cooperative and collaborative learning;
- define the technical requirements and prerequisite skills;
- provide an orientation to familiarise learners with using the technology and the new learning environment;
- coach learners on how to facilitate learning activities and discourses, assess, give and receive peer feedback, evaluate and reflect on own learning.

(Krauth and Carbajal, 1999)

Sustaining the process

Dialogic strategies which focus on questioning, informing, discussions (which promotes negotiation and challenges the learner to think and to enhance performace), giving and receiving feedback, providing encouragement and motivation, and reflection are paramount in sustaining interest and participation in peer learning. Also, assessment, be it informal or formal, contributes in motivating and sustaining learning.

Assessment

Online peer learning operates in a social, cultural and technological setting, thus, assessment of learning within the sociocultural context should assess both process and product (Gipps, 1999). Such assessment should be interactive, involve group collaborative activity and be integral to learning. It should focus on the development of: the learner's mental function, their knowledge of the subject matter, skills and abilities, identity formation and the use of auxiliary tools in the form of peer and tutor support in setting and clarifying the rule to elicit elaborate performance.

In such assessment, as in instruction using group approaches, the student can observe how others reason and can receive feedback on his or her own efforts. In this context, not only performance, but also the facility with which a student adapts to help and guidance, can be assessed.

(Glaser and Silver, 1994, pp. 412–13)

However, assessment for many technology-enhanced and online courses is based on tests, quizzes, multiple-choice questions, essays and problem type examinations. These assessments are very limited in effectively testing and developing higher order skills, for example, critical thinking, analysis, evaluation, creativity and reflection (Elton and Johnston, 2002, p. 7). In addition, these assessment methods tend to demotivate students as they lack relevance to real-life situations. Therefore, to use peer assessment to promote effective individual and/or group learning, it is imperative that the curriculum/course is constructively aligned to meet the intended learning outcomes of developing the learners' knowledge, skills and desired capabilities. However, as learners are central in this assessment process, concerns are often raised regarding both their expertise in the knowledge content of the subject matter and their assessment skills to ensure reliability, validity and fairness. Juwah (2003) outlines a seven-stage peer assessment process in an online context which focuses on developing high order skills and capabilities. The process involves learners in assessing, critiquing and making value judgements on the quality and standard of work of other learners, as well as providing feedback to peers to enable them to enhance performance.

Technology for peer learning

In my view, a key weakness in the teaching method used in higher education lies in the huge reliance on lectures. Whilst this method of delivery may have been adopted because of 'economic reasons', to deliver a body of information to a large number of students within a very short space of time, there is little or no interaction between the teacher and the learner. The lack of interaction will be even more compounded if the same transmissive, content-focused delivery method is used for e-learning courses and curricula.

Until recently, the use of technology in education and training has focused in the main on mass education. However, with increased understanding and integration of appropriate pedagogy into new technologies, new learning environments are being developed, and these new technologies have revolutionised the way education and training is delivered. In addition, the new technologies can support a diverse range of teaching and learning methods, in particular peer and collaborative learning, as well as 'offer facilitating strategies and tactics that support learners as multi-dimensional participants in sociocultural processes and social-dialogical activities' (Harper and Hedberg, 1997). Also, the new technologies enable structuring of the learning environment to provide: (a) open ended contexts and (b) sophisticated multiple media and tools that enable the dextrous use of ideas, textual, visual and dynamic representations, audio, simulations, graphic and knowledge construction in real or differed time (Harper and Hedberg, 1997; Laurillard, 2001). The contexts and facilities provide a rich, stimulating and interactive learning environment that offers close to real life situations which make learning more authentic and engaging.

Table 10.2 lists a range of technologies which support and enhance online peer learning.

The next section reports on a case study on peer learning at The Robert Gordon University.

Table 10.2 Technology for peer learning

Tool	Description	Source of further information
Email	Facility for sending and receiving electronic mail through the Internet.	http://www.aol. com; www.mail. com; www.hotmail. com
Discussion Tools (Discussion Lists/ Listserv)	These are used to engender and encourage debate, the exchange and negotiation of meanings.	http://www.phpbb. com http://webtc. gatech/edu/help/ faculty/discussion. shtml http://www. blackboard.com/ extend/b2
Threaded Discussion Software	These are available on most proprietary VLEs (FirstClass, Blackboard, WebCT etc.) and can be used in the making of meaning. They are often asynchronous (the sender and the receiver do not communicate at the same time) but may be used synchronously (in real time). They are mainly text-based and some cannot cross-reference messages. In addition, they are limited in handling data and cannot handle images.	
Shared-Document Computer Conferencing (SDCC)	SDCC systems provide shared workspaces for groups of individuals co-located at a site or at a distance. They allow sharing, annotations and editing of documents. They permit: organisation of information; responses to previous points/messages to be made in context e.g. in the form of pop up notes and embedded as appropriate; cross-referencing of messages; and maintenance of working memory of content in a self contained document thus enabling the construction of new knowledge, intellectual products. They can handle text, data, spreadsheets, graphics, and sound or video clips. They can make links to Web pages and perhaps to other documents in the system. These systems overcome the limitation of discussion boards.	Examples of SDCC include: Forum Matrix – http:// www.foruminc. com. Knowledge Forum – www. knowledgeforum. com
White Boards Software	These provide a visual, sharable forum for synchronous, collaborative project work. They can handle graphics, images and synchronous text discussion but are limited in that they cannot cross-reference messages. This facility can be used to promote critical and creative thinking, analysis, manipulation of objects and reflection.	http://www. groupboard.com/ whiteboard.html

continued...

Table 10.2 continued

Tool	Description	Source of further information
Knowledge Forum Software	This advanced software is database-driven and allows for the creation of knowledge through meaning making, collaboration and connecting ideas to previous ideas. It provides for the labelling and annotation of entries. It can also handle images and graphics. This tool provides facilities for collaboration, building idea networks in the form of nodes (or nexuses) and super discussions (in which information can be referenced; issues or arguments are supported or refuted; ideas are connected; and the ideas of other individuals can be built-on to advance knowledge), storing notes, retrieving, identifying knowledge gaps or advances and viewing knowledge from multiple perspectives.	www. knowledgeforum. com
Dropload	This is a facility which enables individuals with an email address to drop off and upload (usually very large files) any type of file, mp3, movies, docs, pdfs, up to 100MB each.	http://www. dropload.com/
Blog	Tool for gathering field data for research (for example – keeping a daily critical reflection diary of field observations). Instructional or curricula designers use this or similar tools with their students as an active learning tool for developing reflection.	http://www. blogger.com/start
Podcasting	This is a process for the automatic distribution of audio programs over the Internet using a collection of technologies and a publisher/subscriber model.	http://en.wikipedia. org/wiki/Podcasting
Wiki	This is a server software which enables individuals to freely create and edit Web pages. This facility can be used for collaborative working.	http://wiki.org/wiki. cgi?WhatIsWiki
Concept (Mind) Mapping Software	Similarly, this provides a visual forum for the mapping of concepts, understanding and agreement. The software also provides facilities for synchronous text discussion, project management tools, and can handle data, graphics and hyperlink functions.	http://www. inspiration.com/
Peer to Peer Radio	This tool enables the distribution of and offers the capacity to listen to audio streams. It provides the facility to broadcast educational materials as well as the facility for users to engage in a dialogue or discussion on the broadcast material. This facility can be used to promote reflection and support metacognitive processes for measuring understanding through super discussion.	Once installed, and provided a player such as *Winamp* is available, users can listen to several radio stations. An example of P2P radio software is Streamer. This is a freeware product and can be downloaded from http://streamerp2p. com/

continued...

Table 10.2 continued

Tool	Description	Source of further information
Video-conferencing	This offers collaborative technologies for audio, video, images, graphic and data transmission. It offers a diverse range of uses in teaching, learning and research.	http://www.videnet.gatech.edu/cookbook.en/
Peer to Peer Telephony	This tool allows users to conduct voice/text chat. This facility can be used to promote reflection and support metacognitive processes for measuring understanding through super discussion.	An example of this software is Skype. It is freeware and can be accessed at: http://skype.com
Peer to Peer Messenger	This is an Instant Messenger tool which enables users to send/receive instant messages and files from an individual to another whilst the program is running. It also has the potential to broadcast video images swiftly to other users.	This software can be accessed at: http://p2pmessenger.com/
Classroom Communication Systems (CCSs) and Personal Response System (PRS)	These are communication tools which enable and process in real time, the students' responses to questions posed by the instructor. The tool can be used to support collaborative learning in a range of pedagogic areas: • Assessment: both formative and summative • Formative feedback on learning • Formative feedback on teaching • Peer assessment • Community building • Experiments using human responses • Initiation of discussion	http://www.tomlinsonproject.mcgill.ca/classroom_communication_systems.htm
Computer Mediated Communications	The computer mediated communications tool provides flexibility of time and space, allowing collaboration both synchronously (in real time) or asynchronously (in deferred time) regardless of distance and geography. It provides facilities which allow students to brainstorm, collaborate in a group project, share files, text and images, to engage in group discussions and to keep track of the progress of their work.	An example of a peer to peer computer mediated communication tool is Groove – http://www.groove.com/
Assessment Tools	These tools are necessary for assessing learning and in providing immediate feedback to enable learners to monitor their progress. Technology-enhanced assessment is effective in allowing for continuous formative and summative assessment with appropriate, individualised guidance and immediate feedback. In addition, it could also be used by a group of learners to attempt and complete real-life or simulated activities collaboratively.	Computer Assisted Assessment Centre, University of Luton at http://www.caacentre.ac.uk/ and Question Mark Corporation at http://www.questionmark.com/uk/home.htm

continued...

Table 10.2 continued

Tool	Description	Source of further information
Agent Technology Software (or Avatars)	These are tools that serve as prompts and guides and are used for creating simulations in a learning environment to ensure that learning is focused. The agent technology may be used to introduce complexity to the problem within the learning environment. These technologies help create interest, variety and motivation in learning as both audio (speech) and visual images are incorporated into the environment. Regardless of the role and function of the agent technology or avatars, they do not erode the critical role of the human expert and guide.	http://www. avatarity.com
ePortfolios (including Webfolios)	These are electronic information management tools that enable learners to create and maintain a digital repository of resources to support and to evidence their learning, competence, personal and professional (career) development.	http://www. deskootenays.ca/ wilton/eportfolios/ whatitis.php http://www. elearnspace. org/Articles/ eportfolios.htm

Case study

In keeping with its mission – *To transform individuals, business and communities* – the RGU strives to produce graduates that can use knowledge in new domains, synthesise information, problem solve and work effectively in teams in both real and virtual settings with a focus on online peer learning. Equally important too, is the university's new focus in expanding the range of its provision both for on-campus and distance learning via distributed, networked technologies. This case study reports on the development of faculty to better support peer learning online. Drawing on research on professional development, a collaborative pedagogic approach, underscored by peer and action learning, was identified as the most appropriate method for supporting faculty development in the acquisition of the desired skills and repertoire.

The participants were a mix of both experienced and new, inexperienced individuals from a diverse range of disciplines and different geographic locations. Their level of knowledge and experience about peer learning in face-to-face settings was very varied and ranged along a continuum from novice to expert.

The course was delivered via a networked virtual learning environment, which provided the learner management system. The course consisted of both asynchronous and synchronous activities underpinned by a diverse range of interactions.

Group formation and socialisation

Socialisation of the group is critical in helping to ensure group dynamics (Tuckman, 1965), interactions and performance. The socialisation process was very important in raising participants' awareness of issues of individual and cultural diversity (e.g. language, gender, disability, etc.). Also, the process provided the opportunity of promoting desired behaviours. For example, modelling good practices of providing support and feedback through giving reassurance, encouragement, praise, insights or alternative perspectives to issues provides sources of learning. If learners feel confident and well supported, they feel motivated and perform better. Thus, it is good early on in the process to model the type of behaviour you would like learners to demonstrate through your responses.

Contextualisation

The context in which the learning is to take place should be well understood by the learners and should provide the essential resources in terms of: content, resources (for example, technology) and scaffolding required to make learning meaningful, as well as contribute to the development of learners' meta-communicative and meta-cognitive skills.

Pedagogy

For effective online peer learning, the platform for delivery must be based on sound and appropriate collaborative pedagogy. Like most proprietary VLEs, ours has a 'set' pedagogy and was inappropriate for a peer learning context. The VLE did not provide alternative approaches that are central to the intended learning/training event. However, such limitations can be overcome through appropriate adaptation and re-orientating of tasks/activities to enable participants to collaborate effectively.

Learning and assessment on the course were *formalised* and *learner-centred*. This was to ensure that the learning was structured to meet both the individual's needs and the intended course learning outcomes. Immersion and action learning (i.e. learning by doing) was critical in enabling the participants to engage with and to experience online peer learning. Learning was underpinned and enhanced by the following interactions: dialogic iterations, critique of others' work, questioning, analysis, synthesis, the effective use of technology in teaching and learning, construction of new knowledge and making of meaning, sharing of resources, assessing own and peer learning, and reflection.

The dialogic iterations and reiterations were important in enabling the participants to engage in deep learning and reflection, and to acquire the desired repertoire for effectively supporting online peer learning. Thus, both context and reflection were very important aspects of the course (Sorensen, 2003).

Through sharing of information and resources and social interactions, the participants learned to motivate and support each other. Also, the pooling of different roles engendered genuine interdependence within the group thereby promoting the individual's zone of proximal development (Marton and Saljo, 1984).

Both the context and activities provided sources of social learning from and with peers, coupled with regular and timely feedback. Learning from and with others was also based in most part on role modelling and coaching. The provision of appropriate scaffolding in the form of context and interventions was critical in promoting and supporting the development of learners' meta-communicative and meta-cognitive skills. Wilson (1997) has shown that students need training in understanding concepts, and that they accomplish this more effectively through interactive engagement in intellectual discourse with their tutor, peers and guided learning materials/objects than merely listening and taking notes in lectures.

We observed how participants grew in confidence in their learning to engage in the development of content through sharing resources and expertise. This obviously was an emergent and not an intended outcome. An entry in the learning journal of one course participant read:

> This course has clarified some of the potential pitfalls and made me think about what might work in an online environment and how it might be designed to maximise the opportunities the new technologies create. The design of any online materials has to be carefully considered to match the pedagogical needs of the students to allow them to fulfil their potential. Personalities and the needs of the individual must be taken into consideration as much as they would in a traditional teaching environment.

Also, sustaining the group learning is a critical success factor of online peer learning. Sustaining the group learning was ensured through creating interest and motivation and providing relevant learner support to meet both individual and group needs. However, it is important that the tutor does not intervene so frequently as to infringe on the group's learning. Here, effective resource management regarding tutor's/facilitator's time is paramount. Good planning is required to ensure that the tutor/facilitator provides prompt responses and interaction times to learners and this is even more important when participants come from across multiple time zones.

Assessment in both formative and summative modes was pivotal in providing effective feedback to the learners to enable them to improve and enhance their performance. The participants were coached in giving feedback underscored by the seven principles of good feedback as identified by Nicol and MacFarlane-Dick (2004).

The seven principles of good feedback are:

1 Facilitates the development of self-assessment (reflection) in learning.
2 Encourages teacher and peer dialogue around learning.
3 Helps clarify what good performance is (goals, criteria, expected standards).
4 Provides opportunities to close the gap between current and desired performance.

5 Delivers high quality information to students about their learning.
6 Encourages positive motivational beliefs and self-esteem.
7 Provides information to teachers that can be used to help shape the teaching.

Technology

For online peer learning, it is important that the platform for delivery is fit-for-purpose and designed with the correct pedagogical underpinning to support group, collaborative learning. The availability of new peer-to-peer technologies (see Table 10.2) permit sharing of documents and collaborative learning. Such technologies now permit learners to create 'content' through sharing of knowledge and resources (including re-using learning objects).

Conflict resolution

We observed aspects of conflict amongst participants during the various stages in the learning process. However, these were easily managed and resolved within the group. It was apparent that the process of socialisation at the start of the course provided the participants with the ground rules and tools to manage conflicts within the group.

Conclusion

This case study illustrates that interactions are a critical successful factor in online peer learning. There is evidence from faculty evaluation of:

- improvement in skills and abilities to use technology as both a teaching and learning tool;
- changes in perception about e-learning and organisational culture in using peer learning to meet the needs of our diverse audiences in both on-campus and distance learning courses;
- use of e-learning to add value and to diversify context in teaching and learning.

The case study has highlighted the potential of the apprentice–apprentice mode of learning in enhancing the knowledge and skills base of learners if applied in the right context, with the correct pedagogy, technology and support. However, it raises key fundamental questions and areas of further research relating to:

- how students learn within a group;
- what environment can best support peer collaboration online?;
- what kind of additional support is required to foster effective and efficient online peer learning?

References

Anderson, G. and Boud, D. (1996) 'Extending the role of peer learning in university courses', *Different Approaches: Theory and Practice in Higher Education*. Proceedings HERDSA Conference 1996. Perth, Western Australia, 8–12 July. Online. Available at: http://www.herdsa.org.au/confs/1996/anderson.html (Accessed 20th July 2004).

Bakhtin, M. (1981) *The Dialogic Imagination: Four Essays by M. Bakhtin*, Trans. Emerson, C. and Holquist, M. Ed. by Holquist, M. Austin, TX: University of Texas Press.

Biggs, J. (1999) *Teaching for Quality Learning at University*, Buckingham: Society for Research into Higher Education, RHE and Open University Press.

Boud, D., Keogh, R. and Walker, D. (1985) *Reflection: Turning Experience into Learning*, London: Croom Helm.

Bruner, J. S. (1966) *Toward a Theory of Instruction*, Cambridge, MA: Belknapp Press.

Cook, J. (2002) 'The role of dialogue in computer-based learning and observing learning: an evolutionary approach to theory', *Journal of Interactive Media in Education*, 5, 1–15.

Doolittle, P. E. and Camp, W. G. (1999) 'Constructivism: the career and technical education perspective', *Journal of Vocational and Technical Education*, 16(1), 23–46. Online. Available at: http://scholar.lib.vt.edu/ejournals/JVTE/v16n1/doolittle.html (Accessed 10 July 2004).

Elton, L. and Johnston, B. (2002) *Assessment in Universities: A Critical Review Assessment Research*, York: LTSN Generic Centre. Online. Available at: http://www.ltsn.ac.uk/application.asp?app=resources.aspandprocess=full_recordandsection=genericandid=13 (Accessed 10 July 2004).

Ertmer, P. A. and Newby, T. J. (1996) 'The expert learner: strategic self-regulated, and reflective', *Instructional Science*, 24: 1–24.

Gipps, C. (1999) 'Sociocultural perspectives on assessment', *Chatbook*, Chapter 6. Online. Available at: http://people.ucsc.edu/~gwells/CHATbook/Ch6.Gipps.html (Accessed 17 October 2004).

Glaser, R. and Silver, E. (1994) 'Assessment, testing and instruction: retrospect and prospect', *Review of Research in Education*, 20, 393–421.

Griffiths, S., Houston, K. and Lazenbatt, A. (1995) *Enhancing Student Learning Through Peer Tutoring in Higher Education*, Coleraine: Educational Development Unit, University of Ulster.

Harper, B. and Hedberg, J. (1997) 'Creating motivating interactive learning environments: a constructivist view', Paper presented at Ascilite 97 Conference. Online. Available at: http://www.curtin.edu.au/conference/ascilite97/papers/Harper/Harper.html (Accessed 25 July 2004).

Hartley, R. and Ravenscroft, A. (1993) 'Computer aided reflection: an overview of SCILAB'. Paper presented at the SMILE Workshop, 29 September–1 October, Computer Based Learning Unit, University of Leeds, UK.

Jackson, N. (2004) Keynote Speech presented at the Higher Education Academy Conference on enhancing student learning through effective formative feedback, London, 7 June.

Jaques, D. (2001) *Learning in Groups*, 3rd edn, London: Kogan Page.

Juwah, C. (2002) 'Using information and communication technology to support problem based learning', a commissioned article by the Institute for Learning and Teaching in Higher Education (ILTHE – now the Higher Education Academy). Online. Available at: http://www.heacademy.ac.uk/embedded_object.asp?id=21658andfilename=Juwah (Accessed 10 October 2005).

Juwah, C. (2003) 'Using peer assessment to develop skills and capabilities', *Journal of the United States Distance Learning Association*, January, 39–50. Online. Available at: http://www.usdla.org/html/journal/JAN03_Issue/article04.html (Accessed 20 October 2005).

Klemm, W. R. (1999) 'Building global community over the Internet: what is right about shared-document conferencing'. Online. Available at: http://www.friendspartners. org/GLOSAS/Global_University/Global%20University%20System/UNESCO_ Chair_Book/Manuscripts/Part_III_Global_E-Learning/Klemm,%20W.%20R./ Building%20Community/Klemm_B-C_web/Klemm.B-C.D7.html.

Kolb, D. (1983) *Experiential Learning: Experience as the Source of Learning*, New York: Prentice Hall.

Krauth, B. and Carbajal, J. (1999) *Guide to Developing Online Student Services*, The Western Cooperative for Educational Telecommunications. Online. Available at: http:// www.wcet.info/resources/publications/guide/guide.htm (Accessed 10 March 2004).

Laurillard, D. (2001) 'The E-university: what have we learned', *The International Journal of Management Education*, 1(2), Spring, 3–7.

Lave, J. and Wenger, E. (1991) *Situated Learning: Legitimate Peripheral Participation*, Cambridge: University of Cambridge Press.

Lowell, N. O. and Persichitte, K. A. (2000) 'A virtual ropes course: creating online community', *ALN Magazine*, 4(1). Online. Available at: http://www.sloan-c.org/ publications/magazine/v4n1/lowell.asp (Accessed 12 March 2004).

Marton, F. and Saljo, R. (1984) 'Approaches to learning', in F. Marton, D. Hounsell and N. Entwistle (eds), *The Experience of Learning*, Edinburgh: Scottish Academic Press.

Mazur, E. (1997) *Peer Instruction: A User's Manual*, New York: Prentice Hall. Online. Available at: http://galileo.harvard.edu/ (Accessed 15 June 2004).

Mercer, N. (2000) *Words and Minds: How We use Language to Think Together*, London: Routledge.

Moon, J. (1999) *Reflection in Learning and Professional Development*, London: Kogan Page.

Nicol, D. and MacFarlane-Dick, D. (2004) 'Principles of good feedback', in C. Juwah, D. Macfarlane-Dick, B. Matthew, D. Nicol, D. Ross and B. Smith (eds), *Enhancing Student Learning Through Effective Formative Feedback*. Online. Available at: www.ltsn.ac.uk/ embedded_object.asp?id=20876andfilename=ASS096 (Accessed 27 October 2004).

Piaget, J. (1963) *The Psychology of Intelligence*, New York: Routledge.

Purnell, K., Callan, J. and Whymark, G. (2004) 'Managing learner interactivity: a precursor to knowledge exchange', *Studies in Learning, Evaluation Innovation and Development*, 1(2), 32–44. Online. Available at: http://sleid.cqu.edu.au (Accessed 20 October 2004)

Rourke, L., Anderson, T., Garrison, D. and Archer, W. (2001) 'Assessing social presence in asynchronous text-based computer conferencing', *Journal of Distance Education*. Online. Available at: http://cade.athabascau.ca/vol14.2/rourke_et_al.html (Accessed 20 October 2005).

Schon, D. (1987) 'Educating the reflective practitioner', Paper presented to the American Educational Research Association, Washington, DC. Online. Available at: http://educ. queensu.ca/~russellt/howteach/schon87.htm (Accessed 10 October 2005).

Smith, R. M. (1983) *Learning How to Learn*, Buckingham: Open University Press.

Sorensen, A. (2003) 'Intellectual amplification through reflection and didactic change in distributed collaborative learning', *International Journal of E-learning*, July–September, 37–43.

Sproull, L. and Keisler, S. (1986) 'Reducing social context cues: electronic mail in organizational communication', *Management Science*, 32, 1492–513.

Stein, D. (1998) 'Situated learning in adult education', *ERIC Digest*, No. 195. Online. Available at: http://www.ericfacility.net/databases/ERIC_Digests/ed418250.html (Accessed 24 October 2004).

Topping, K. (1998) 'Peer assessment between students in colleges and universities', *Review of Educational Research*, 68, 249–76.

Tuckman, B. W. (1965) 'Developmental sequences in small groups', *Psychological Bulletin*, 63, 384–99.

US National Research Council (1999) 'How people learn: brain, mind, experience and school', Expanded edition. Committee on Developments in Science of Learning and Committee on Learning Research and Educational Practice. J. D. Bransford, A. Brown and R. R. Cocking (eds). Commission on Behavioural and Social Sciences and Education. Washington, DC: The National Academy Press.

Vygotsky, L. S. (1978) *Mind in Society*, Cambridge, MA: Harvard University Press.

Wenger, E. (1998) *Communities of Practice: Learning, Meaning, and Identity*, Cambridge: Cambridge University Press.

Wilson, J. (ed.) (1997) *Conference on the Introductory Physics Course: On the Occasion of the Retirement of Robert Resnick*, New York: Wiley.

Zimmermann, B. J. (2000) 'Self-regulatory cycles of learning', in G. A. Straka (ed.), *Conceptions of Self-directed Learning, Theoretical and Conceptual Considerations*, New York: Waxman.

Chapter 11

Interactions in teaching by videoconferencing

Wolfgang Greller

Introduction

Videoconferencing (VC) has been around in UK Higher Education for many years. High hopes and promises of ubiquitous usage and access have been following the technology ever since. However, due to the traditional single-campus focus of most universities and colleges it hardly made it into the institutional mainstream anywhere. The reasons for this have been related to cost, the complexity of the technology, a lack of demand, and a resulting slowness in understanding the pedagogic setting exacerbated by a lack of training and support for the lecturer. Even where there were multi-site institutions, the demand for remote visual connectivity was low, because courses were either duplicated locally or local by discipline. With the advent of the Internet, widening access initiatives in the sector focused on Web-based delivery, rather than videoconferencing, due to the high bandwidth requirements that were unavailable at the time and the restricted flexibility of the medium. It left videoconferencing a fancy but sporadic and expensive tool at the periphery of educational delivery. Only with the rise of networked universities and increased networked operations of traditional universities has videoconferencing become an option to supplement face-to-face and Web-based provision.

Despite an abundance of videoconferencing how-to guides and manuals, both online and in print, surprisingly few pedagogic studies have been carried out into the effects of this delivery mode on distance learning and learning outcomes. This study explores the pedagogy and psychology of interactive teaching by videoconferencing in the remote delivery of Higher Education courses and aims to illustrate its practical application by example of UHI Millennium Institute, a regional Higher Education network covering the Highlands and Islands of Scotland. The chapter focuses on the pedagogic environment of the technology rather than the technology itself.

Terminology

Videoconferencing has been described most appropriately as a 'function' which can be hosted on a variety of technologies, but not a technology in itself (Coventry,

1996, p. 7). I fully subscribe to this definition, but for the purpose of this chapter, I shall refer to videoconferencing as a network-based communication technology using either the H323 or H320 protocol over IP or ISDN.

The use of the term has become more widespread and blurred as new carriers of image-supported communication become available such as mobile phones. Taking the perspective of its most common manifestation in current learning and teaching rather than its audience or its technology, I will distinguish only between desktop systems and studio systems.

Streaming video is another multimedia technology that is currently being explored for its potential role in learning and teaching (see Thornhill *et al.*, 2002). The term is somewhat misleading since videoconferencing too is streamed video and uses the same carriers. I believe it to be more accurate to distinguish between non-interactive video on demand (VoD) and videoconferencing (VC). While the latter allows synchronous two-way communication, the former is solely a mono-directional stream which can be both synchronous and asynchronous. Interactivity for learning and teaching in the case of VoD comes from the combination with other communication tools. The term 'interactive videoconferencing', mainly used in the US, is a tautology because its characteristics as a synchronous conversation tool inevitably make videoconferencing interactive.

When talking about 'videoconferencing' in teaching, what is usually meant is a whole range of different technologies playing together to produce the learner experience. This may include presentation tools such as a VCR or collaborative tools such as whiteboards and document cameras. It can even go as far as including a computer in the setup in order to support either presentation (e.g. PowerPoint™) or collaboration.

Although this blended videoconferencing experience of the learner or group of learners could be dissected into technological components that determine the interactivity of the session, this study will stick with the holistic notion to keep the focus on the learner. It has to be noted, however, that the pedagogic strategies may vary according to the tools available, which may not be a direct reflection on the adequacy or inadequacy of videoconferencing. This applies to both desktop and studio systems.

Pedagogy and interactivity by videoconference

A number of studies suggest that videoconferencing requires a different pedagogy to traditional face-to-face teaching in a classroom (e.g. Amirian, 2003, p. 7). Without rejecting this out of hand, I feel that there is frequently confusion between pedagogy and presentation (e.g. Rees, 2003, p. 1) as well as between the delivery itself and the management of that delivery.

If one compares the parameters of the learning environment and the learning processes involved in face-to-face delivery and teaching by videoconference, it soon becomes apparent that it is primarily the presentation and articulation of the delivery that actually changes. The educational objectives remain the same, as do the learning goals and assessment criteria. Equally, the raw content does not require addition or deduction. According to research findings by Reiserer *et al.* (2001) there is no significant difference in collaboration or the processes of knowledge construction. It would then seem that the use of videoconferencing favours the same learning styles as face-to-face teaching and does not significantly impact on achievement and learning outcomes. This makes it the closest emulation of live instruction (Rees, 2003, p. 1).

The literature repeatedly points to interaction as the critical distinguishing factor between videoconferencing and classroom teaching. However, various influential learning theories such as Constructivism, Vygotsky's Social Development Theory (1978), or Conversation Theory (Pask, 1975) suggest that the pedagogic strategy of interactivity in instruction is just as beneficial to the learner in a classroom as to one in a remote session, and indeed one can expect a good classroom teacher to also perform well in a videoconferencing setting (Amirian, 2003, p. 7).

The understanding that learners benefit most from being actively engaged in the learning process has, at least in Higher Education in the Anglophone world, led to a cultural shift and the revision of pedagogic practice, both within and outside the classroom, and even led to concrete pressures to this end from quality assurance authorities. This change in teaching culture towards interactivity and active learning would, I believe, lead to a departure from the results of various surveys from the early 1990s, summarised in Coventry (1996, p. 26 ff), which suggested that videoconferencing, as perceived by lecturers and students then, was less effective for group discussions and seminars and best for delivering lectures. But now the tables have turned in favour of discourse based learning and collaborative knowledge construction (see Burnett, 2001, p. 3).

So what does really change in a videoconferencing learning environment? The following spheres of impact can be identified:

- *The psychology of the space*
  Desktop videoconferencing does not normally support continuous presence, but even when available in studio systems it may not be possible or practical depending on the number of participating sites. The lack of appearing on screen all the time can lead to the feeling of isolation with some participants. It also puts an extra mental effort on the tutor for making sure everyone takes part in the group (see Schiller and Mitchell, 1993, p. 46). The perception of the medium and environment will be discussed in more detail below.
- *Planning and administration*
  There is clearly a greater necessity of pre-delivery planning which includes activities such as scripting a videoconferencing session, preparing the material and sending it out in good time before the class. Organising peripheral equipment, technical support, and perhaps local moderators needs to be planned.

- *Adaptation of content presentation*
  For videoconferencing the format and strategy of content presentation might require adaptation, e.g. larger fonts in PowerPoint™ presentations or testing demonstration objects under the document/3D camera. Some materials may have to undergo change in format, e.g. conversion of 35mm slides to digital images. Lengthy pieces of video suitable in a classroom should be sectioned into smaller chunks interrupted with time for questions so the contact between members of the group does not get lost for too long.
- *Guidance and support requirements*
  Using videoconferencing requires additional training in the technology and the appropriate communication protocols for interaction with the group.

The areas highlighted here demonstrate that course delivery by videoconferencing requires a special approach to the presentation of the pedagogic strategy rather than to the pedagogy itself. Improvements or failures in students' attitudes and learning cannot simply be attributed to the technology (Coventry, 1996, p. 28). The learning outcomes should not be compromised if these are appropriately addressed.

Among the planning challenges to the tutor is mixing and matching the most appropriate and right quantity of supportive technology. It has to be said, though, that showing a video clip or PowerPoint™ presentation over videoconferencing is not more interactive than in a classroom and it has to be embedded in an interactive environment to accommodate active learning. Unless provided on an additional video channel, e.g. via a networked PC or extra monitor, supportive technology may cut the tutor off from vital visual information on the students' reception and hides the tutor from the students. Therefore, it is recommended to deliver such presentations in shorter than usual chunks or in a way where the communication between tutor and students is not lost at any time.

To determine the right mix of tools remains a challenge and can be daunting to less technically inclined tutors.

ARCS model of motivation

Following on from the issues raised in the section above, we can hold videoconferencing against Keller's ARCS motivation model and compare how the medium impacts on the motivation for learning (see Dabbagh, 1999). In brief, Keller's model references four sequential conditions which occur in a cyclic order: Attention – Relevance – Confidence – Satisfaction (ARCS).

Videoconferencing as transmission medium impacts mainly on the attention and confidence conditions, where presentation and interaction come into play over and above relevant content. The practical application of Keller's model suggests varying the presentation methods to gain and retain the learner's attention. In videoconferencing this has to be done within the constraints of the technology and protocol. Encouraging students' participation through personally addressing them takes a rather greater effort as the tutor might not be in the position to see all students on screen all the time, so cannot react to physical signs of mental fatigue or distraction.

In a constructivist setting another useful way of retaining attention is to vary the presenter, for example through individual site feedback and rotating moderation of discussions. It is worth noting that small group tasks are generally site specific due to the limitations of the technology. This means that instead of being able to match individual students on pedagogic considerations when dividing them up into small groups, the tutor has to go with individuals that are present at each site – even if there is only one student at a particular site.

The confidence condition of learning may not be directly affected by the technology in question but indirectly, videoconferencing can be a barrier to confidence building which needs to be addressed through training (see Coventry, 1996, p. 35). Confidence in the technology is achieved when the students forget that they are on camera.

Learning design

When planning the delivery modes to achieve particular learning outcomes, the lecturer has to carefully define the role of complementary tools (a) within the videoconferencing environment, e.g. document camera, whiteboard, VCR, etc.; and (b) in the wider blended learning context, e.g. e-mail, Web-based, printed materials, etc. If a tool is not used according to its strength or over-used this may be harmful to the learning experience of the students. Gagné's nine instructional events (see Bostock, 1996) can help in a SWOT analysis for a particular learning context and the level of interactivity required. Planning which tools to use is of great benefit to the learners and should take into account the proposed learning outcomes, the particular target group, and the learning context (Bostock, ibid.).

Videoconferencing not only enables remote access to tutor-led learning sessions and to external experts (see the Motivate Project, Gage et al., 2002), but can also be used successfully to support cooperative learning and facilitate collaborative knowledge construction. Using reciprocal teaching as a pedagogic technique between different groups of students in order to measure the achieved learning outcomes, Reiserer et al. (2001, p. 4) conclude that there is no significant difference in collaboration between videoconferencing and face-to-face settings. Supporting interaction through pre-structured content or cooperation scripts, they also found that scripting cooperation supports learners in interacting with each other more efficiently.

The medium and its perception

The physical environment of videoconferencing and its perception has an unspecified impact on the learning situation and the interactivity happening in class. A lot of the success depends on managing initial user expectations – much like in a traditional classroom environment, but of a different kind.

Different types of videoconferencing are perceived differently by the users in terms of expectation of quality and engagement with the medium. When making a choice between studio based videoconferencing and desktop for learning situations, some psychological considerations have to be taken into account.

Studio based videoconferencing

The main reference points for users of this type of delivery come from television. Studio based VCs have a strong notion of formality and protocol attached. This should not be seen as a disadvantage, though, as it distinguishes the teaching situation from informal learning. The perception of formality of the situation comes from a variety of sources:

- *Space*
  Studio space is accessed through time-tabling procedures that are usually carried out through an institutional booking system. In addition, the tutor and students are moved physically into a purpose-built room with a different layout to ordinary classrooms. Personal space, light settings and audio capture may differ from what students are used to and therefore have an influence on how they settle into the learning environment (Childs, 2003).
- *Protocol*
  Studio based VC requires observation of specific protocols even going as far as suggesting a dress code (see UKERNA VC manual, 2003, p. 1) or restricted movements (ibid., p. 3). Common good practice of muting the microphone when you are not talking is generally accepted by the users, but can be an obstacle to less forthcoming communicators and requires the moderator to be more proactively inviting.
- *Monitor*
  Especially in group situations the appearance on the remote monitor matters to the flow of discussion. Often the camera is set to capturing the whole presence in a room, which leads to tiny undistinguishable figures appearing remotely with a lot of wasted monitor space taken up by ceiling, floor and table. This makes it harder for listeners to identify who is speaking. Another distraction one may find is the 'voice with no face', i.e. a participant is off camera. Quick changes of the camera view can solve both of these and give a positive impression of fluid interaction. However, the absence of a dedicated cameraman can lead to a struggle between focusing on the transmission as opposed to focusing on the content.
  A mistake that can easily be avoided is the 'squint eye syndrome' where due to the camera position, there appears to be no eye contact between speaker and audience. This can be corrected by positioning the camera directly above the window or monitor showing the remote site.
  Additionally, it is a well-known fact that looking at a monitor for a long time is tiring and affects students' concentration and attention span. Despite

this knowledge, videoconferencing sessions still largely aim to imitate normal classroom times.

* *Quality*

In our modern hi-fi environment, where live television coverage from the remotest and most undeveloped places on the planet comes across to the consumer in crystal clear quality, with perfect lip sync and direct interaction, the expectations of a similar experience are put forward at least by first time users. However, even with high level ISDN transmission it is impossible to get a similar quality. This may lead to disappointment and in certain cases where lip sync and transmission without delay is an essential component – such as language learning or music – may lead to the failure of the delivery.

Audio quality is even more important, and it is usually a sign of insufficient technical setup if the lack of clarity in transmission has to be compensated by human efforts such as speaking up, speaking slowly and in a more pronounced way, the above mentioned un/muting of the microphone, or the need for introductory protocols for voice switching (ranging from 'This is Bob from Thurso here. Can I come in? ...' to 'cough cough'!).

* *Technology*

A historic prejudice about the lack of robustness of the technology can still be found with some lecturers. However, the technology today is much more stable than before. There are fewer outages and breaks in connection, and connecting up sites does not normally take as long as it used to.

In my own institution, UHI, the institutional videoconferencing service provides users with a 'walk-in walk-out' solution, so when lecturers and students arrive, the sites are already connected.

Desktop videoconferencing

Desktop videoconferencing is not suitable for large groups of students. The video normally runs in a small window on a desktop computer or laptop and due to bandwidth implications does not provide the same quality as dedicated ISDN lines in studios. The image can be pixelated and choppy even on high bandwidth connections and there is a greater time lag. However, it provides a suitable medium for collaborative work which is complemented by a set of tools to engage students with.

Compared to the aspects discussed above, some contrasts to studio based videoconferencing can be identified, notably the following:

* *Space*

Sitting at a computer desk is a common activity for students and therefore feels quite familiar, even if they do not sit at their 'own' desk. Since desktop videoconferences work best on a point-to-point connection, i.e. with only two parties involved, no special booking procedures are usually required.

Some tools such as online address books can show who else is online and contactable, which may lead to spontaneous interaction happening.

- *Protocol*
  The informality of the tool, which is portrayed by its visual environment, does not specifically ask for a protocol to be observed, unless special requirements come into play. In some instances there may be no full duplex audio available because of lack of bandwidth, in which case only one party can take the word at a time.

- *Monitor*
  In desktop videoconferencing the video component plays a lesser role and mainly acts as a visual stimulant. The interaction primarily happens via the collaborative tools such as whiteboard, chat, or document sharing (Coventry, 1996, p. 8). In this scenario the picture quality is less relevant in fact often redundant.

  In many classes I could observe students grabbing the camera and swerving it around the room, which confirms the hands-on environment of desktop VCs.

- *Quality*
  Because of the *ad hoc* and informal environment, no high expectations are raised regarding the quality. Even when audio fails, communication can swiftly move onto the chat tool. When desktop cameras are in short supply, tutors can still use applications such as Netmeeting® for delivery (see Greller and MacKay, 2002).

All of these factors are examples of the psychological influences the environment exercises over the delivery mode. The combination of these is reflected in student behaviour and participation. With regards to studio based videoconferencing a passive consumption is often the result whereas desktop videoconferencing stimulates interaction. To overcome this deficit of room-based systems an extra effort is required by the lecturer to foster student participation, motivation, and learning (Morgan, 2000, p. 2 ff).

Case study: videoconferencing in UHI

UHI is a networked Higher Education Institution (HEI) based upon the partnership of fourteen local colleges and research institutions together with a network of some 80 local learning centres. Its institutional mission is to overcome remoteness and geographical isolation in the Highlands and Islands of Scotland, which has traditionally been an area of educational emigration. The UHI network covers the North and West of Scotland, an area approximately the size of one-fifth of the UK.

Some compare UHI to virtual universities, but UHI sees itself as a networked partnership to top up local Further Education provision with trans-regional Higher Education and research. The majority of UHI's networked modules are delivered using blended learning modes with only very few courses solely online (see Greller, 2003, p. 67). The typical blend would include elements of face-to-face and online, including videoconferencing.

UHI operates a regional Metropolitan Area Network (MAN) on a WAN infrastructure that connects all the academic partners and the Inverness-based Executive Office. The videoconferencing delivery between the main sites uses the H323 protocol over the IP network which produces the equivalent of ISDN12 transmission quality or six double telephone lines. However, in some of the remoter learning centres H320 using an ISDN2 dial-up connection is still in use and will be for some time to come. These conferences are translated into the main network via a Gateway.

The type that is most often used in course delivery is studio based videoconferencing in specially designed class- and conference rooms. In addition, there are a number of individual desktop cameras around, but these are mainly used for meetings and less for teaching. The driving policy behind the distribution of desktop equipment is the freeing up of VC studio space.

The use of videoconferencing has increased rapidly over the past few years and is expected to grow further. It has led to UHI being one of the biggest users of this technology in UK Higher Education, which demonstrates a firm commitment to this delivery mode.

Of the 2,330 annual videoconferences that are routed through the multipoint control unit (MCU) or bridge, around 60 per cent are teaching related, while another 30 per cent are connected to course administration and institutional management (see Figure 11.1). These statistics only capture traffic at the videoconferencing bridge, usually multi-point conferences with more than two sites involved. In addition, there are a substantial number of point-to-point conferences that are not routed through the MCU but established directly, internally or externally, and which are not captured in statistics.

When it comes to the right choice of technology, which in videoconferencing terms can mean choosing between studio based, mobile, or desktop, we often find ourselves limited by what is institutionally available, rather than what would be

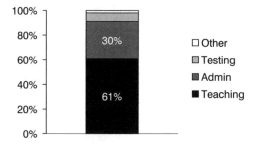

Figure 11.1 Use of videoconferencing in UHI

the best tool for the purpose. In an ideal world, this choice would depend on the participants and their specific educational requirements, taking into account the factors outlined in the previous chapters.

Opponents to the technology in UHI have often argued that it is restrictive in its use and therefore could not replace face-to-face contact. While this is difficult to deny, it is equally recognised that videoconferencing may be the *only* way of providing high quality contact hours to remote students. It also offers educational *additionality*, e.g. the possibility of bringing in outside experts or the collaboration with peer groups in other countries.

Educational complexity

There are a number of typical scenarios representing teaching and learning situations by videoconference in UHI. As our understanding of the technology grows, these are used more deliberately to support specific strategies. As has been mentioned above, they are mostly embedded in a blended learning environment. To achieve successful learning outcomes, offline communication and preparation of sessions are just as critical as determining the best blend of technology.

A number of settings can be identified for remote delivery by videoconference, each with a different aspect of complexity posing different challenges, but also with potential for added educational value. The challenges mainly originate from the type of interaction wanted and the coordination of offline and online preparations and planning activities that are needed to successfully achieve learning goals.

The model most commonly found in UHI is tutor to students. The formats for this model can fall within the following range of scenarios (cf. Coventry, 1996, p. 25):

- lecturer delivers to a remote class; example: bringing in an outside expert speaker
- lecturer delivers locally and remotely; example: widening access to other locations
- lecturer delivers to dispersed students; example: networked courses.

Another model, up until now less often used – and rarely without any tutor involvement – is students to students. Its main goal being student collaboration, this model can also be used as a support mechanism for remote students, for example to facilitate remote student involvement in representative bodies and committees, or for personal guidance. Scenarios include:

- peer presentation; students presenting their work to others (tutor is normally present)
- student meeting; example: UHISA, the UHI Student Association, representing the distributed student body; another example would be peer support

- tutor-led student group collaboration; example: students from different institutions collaborating on a single project.

The last scenario is arguably the most complex in terms of planning and preparation as it requires the tutors at all ends to come to an agreement on common learning outcomes and the provision of equitable support to all students involved. UHI has not engaged in this type of delivery a great deal, but collaborative classes have been conducted this way under the MA in Professional Development with institutions in Iceland and Scandinavia (O'Miadhachain *et al.*, 2004, p. 99 ff). This was supported offline through additional technologies such as e-mail, the web, and locally where possible.

The remaining set up of tutor-to-tutor is primarily used for curriculum support mechanisms, such as course tutor meetings, curriculum planning, course validation or staff training. In situations where a remote facilitator is employed this forms an important part in course delivery preparations.

Networked courses

The networked character and complexity of a course come to light when looking at the delivery structure from different viewpoints. From the lecturer's point of view the students are dispersed around different sites varying in numbers at any location. At the same time, for students on a networked course, the delivery of individual modules comes from different lecturers based at different locations elsewhere.

Good examples of such course structures can be found in UHI and the University of the Arctic, a university network delivering a Bachelor degree in Circumpolar Studies to students in all Arctic countries. While UHI operates within one time zone and relies heavily on videoconferencing in its provision of Higher Education, in the case of UArctic asynchronous delivery is preferred due to the time differences involved.

The networked structure of courses has its own challenges for all the stakeholders. In brief they can be summarised as:

- for the lecturer: to communicate with dispersed students in a balanced fashion and to provide an equitable learning experience
- for the student: to get access to the lecturer and communicate with peers
- for the institution: to assure appropriate quality of delivery at all end points.

Unlike most other institutions with an outreach environment, UHI courses are networked in such a way that course teams do not normally find themselves in one location, but spread out through different academic partners. This requires an additional effort to maintain quality and communication between colleagues.

UHI staff are using different methods of asynchronous and synchronous communication with their dispersed students. The wide ranging and ever growing choice of tools available offers the opportunity of suitable delivery, but can also lead to a lack of in-depth understanding of any of these. Videoconferencing has had a fairly stable presence within the provision and has therefore allowed pedagogy and expertise to develop.

Conclusion

Videoconferencing neatly combines traditional methods of delivery with modern technology. It is the link between the classroom and the fully online environment: situated between face-to-face and independent self-paced learning; between class timetables and round-the-clock provision; between classroom walls and global access. It combines the private atmosphere within a classroom with the technological reach of networked learning.

Videoconferencing supports all interactive strategies of the face-to-face delivery: its great advantage is that it removes the geographic boundaries of the classroom. Research has found no significant difference to classroom delivery in terms of pedagogic application and enabling successful learning. It also supports the same learning styles as face-to-face teaching. These findings are confirmed by the UHI experience.

The challenges for effective use of the technology by the tutor come from managing the psychological impact of the environment on the learners, from adjusting the presentation of their pedagogic strategy, and from planning and administering the sessions. There is a significant amount of training needed to achieve this. From the points raised in this study, here are some points of advice:

- Make your sessions interactive.
- Use collaborative knowledge construction techniques: provide students with a collaboration script and structured content (e.g. graphs) they can discuss.
- Make sure everyone can participate equally. If you are teaching a local class at the same time, do not forget the remote attendants.
- Break up long parts of monologue or presentation into small digestible chunks interrupted by interactive parts such as questions. Try not to lose contact with your learners for too long and use extra equipment for presentations if available.
- Make sure demonstration materials are seen clearly at the remote site. Test this with someone before the class. Adjust font size etc. appropriately. Send out learning materials well in time.
- Do not overdo technology. Let the audience get acquainted with one tool before moving to the next.
- Vary the presenter. Remove yourself at times and let students collaborate on their own across the sites.

- In studios: ease the formality imposed by the environment, use ice breaker techniques at the beginning of a session. Be relaxed when students forget to keep to the communication protocol. Allow and encourage spontaneous interaction.
- In the desktop environment: encourage the use of collaboration tools rather than the video component. The low video quality does not support long viewing.

Videoconferencing has undoubtedly great potential in widening access to education in remote areas or for non-traditional students. Because of its synchronicity it does not in itself extend business continuity of institutions to 24/7 like Web-based delivery, but it provides a personal and supportive 'almost-face-to-face' learning route which can easily be complemented by remote asynchronous and independent learning provision. While videoconferencing and online learning are at present mostly kept apart, integration with online learning platforms (virtual learning environments or VLEs) is desirable and efforts to this end are currently being undertaken.

References

Amirian, S. (2003) Pedagogy and Video Conferencing: A Review of Recent Literature. Online. Available at: www.iclassnotes.com/amirian_handout.pdf (Accessed 1 August 2004).

Bostock, B. (1996) Instructional Design – Robert Gagné, The Conditions Of Learning. Online. Available at http://www.keele.ac.uk/depts/cs/Stephen_Bostock/docs/atid.htm (Accessed 14 May 2004).

Burnett, K. (2001) Interaction and Student Retention, Success and Satisfaction in Web-based Learning. Paper presented at the 67th IFLA Council and General Conference, Boston, 16–25 August.

Childs, M. (2003) Teaching Using Videoconferencing. Introduction to Videoconferencing. PALATINE workshop: University of Warwick, May 2003. Online. Available at: http://www.lancs.ac.uk/palatine/reports/video.htm (Accessed 9 March 2004).

Coventry, L. (1996) Videoconferencing in Higher Education; Institute for Computer Based Learning, Heriot Watt University, Edinburgh. Online. Available at: http://www.agocg.ac.uk/reports/mmedia/video3/contents.htm (Accessed 1 August 2004).

Dabbagh, N. (1999) Attribution Theory and Keller's ARCS Model of Motivation. In EDIT 704: Instructional Technology Foundations and Theories of Learning. Online. Available at: http://chd.gse.gmu.edu/immersion/knowledgebase/strategies/cognitivism/keller_ARCS.htm (Accessed 14th May 2004).

Gage, J., Nickson, M. and Beardon, T. (2002) Can Videoconferencing Contribute to Teaching and Learning? The Experience of the Motivate Project. Paper presented at the Annual Conference of the British Educational Research Association, Exeter, September 2002. Online. Available at: http://www.leeds.ac.uk/educol/documents/00002264.htm (Accessed 25 July 2004).

Greller, W. (2003) Institutional Challenges of Distributed Higher Education Institutions by Example of UHI Millennium Institute. In *Bridging the Digital Divide – Proceedings of the SCOPE – UArctic Workshop* 9–12 May 2003, Mpumalanga, South Africa, pp. 67–73.

Greller, W. and Mackay, M. (2002) Using Netmeeting for Learning and Teaching at the UHI Millennium Institute. In ScotFEICT Autumn 2002. Online. Available at: http://www.scotfeict.ac.uk/journal/autumn2002/NetMeeting/index.htm (Accessed 30 March 2004).

Moore, M. and Kearsley. G. (1996) *Distance Education – A System View.* Belmont, CA: Wadsworth Publ.

Morgan, T. (2000) Increasing Student Interaction in the Interactive Video Classroom Setting. Dakota State University.

O'Miadhachain, S., deFresnes, J and Hughes. A. (2004) Lessons from the Edge: Building Networks between Remote Learning Centres and their Members Located in the Circumpolar North. In L. Pekkala, W. Greller, A. Krylov, L. Kullerud, S. Mýrdal, O. Snellman, and J. Spence (eds) *Overcoming the Challenges of ICT and Distance Education in the Arctic.* Rovaniemi, Finland: University of the Arctic Press and the University of Lapland Faculty of Education, pp. 99–109.

Pask, G. (1975) *Conversation, Cognition and Learning: A Cybernetic Theory and Methodology.* Amsterdam and New York: Elsevier.

Rees. F. J. (2003) Hitting the Right Note with Video Conferencing. In *Syllabus*, June. Online. Available at: http://www.syllabus.com/article.asp?id=7767 (Accessed 27 July 2004).

Reiserer, M., Ertl, B. and Mandl, H. (2001) Fostering Collaborative Knowledge Construction in Desktop Videoconferencing. In Research report no. 143, LMU Munich. Online. Available at: http://epub.ub.uni-muenchen.de/archive/00000251/01/FB_143.pdf (Accessed 25 July 2004).

Schiller, J. and Mitchell, J. (1993) Interacting at a Distance: Staff and Student Perceptions of Teaching and Learning via Video Conferencing. In *Australian Journal of Educational Technology*, 9(1), 41–58. Online. Available at: http://www.ascilite.org.au/ajet/ajet9/schiller.html (Accessed 14 August 2004)

Thornhill, S., Asensio, M. and Young, C. (2002) *Video Streaming – A Guide for Educational Development; JISC Click and Go Video Project.* Manchester: UMIST.

UKERNA (2003) How to get the best out of a video conference meeting. Online. Available at: http://www.video.ja.net/usrg/U_page4.html (Accessed 28 March 2004).

Vygotsky, L. S. (1978) Mind in Society: The Development of Higher Psychological Processes. M. Cole, V. John-Steiner, S. Scribner and E. Souberman (eds). Cambridge, MA: Harvard University Press.

Part IV

Professional development

The fourth section examines the professional development models from the works of Schon and Moon, and from a constructivist professional development framework. Based on this backdrop, the authors offer a framework for effective professional development for enhancing interaction, engagement, reflection and transformative learning in an online setting both within a community of learning and community of practice. In addition, the section examines the diverse range of skills and competencies (for example videoconferencing, computer mediated conferencing, interactive radio, etc.) used in facilitating learner engagement in online education. It concludes by suggesting strategies for developing faculty to acquire required competencies to facilitate distance and online education.

Chapter 12

Professional development of online facilitators in enhancing interactions and engagement

A framework

Santosh Panda and Charles Juwah

Introduction

The increased use of the web for teaching, learning, training and development has necessitated a re-look at some of the foundational issues concerning online learning and mentoring, and the continuing professional development of online facilitators. This chapter reflects on some of the fundamental issues defining online learning, and provides a framework for the professional development of online facilitators, relating online mentoring/facilitation to situated learning, transformation in professional practice and a pan-global community of learning/ community of practice (both on- and offline). It also highlights reflection as a critical element in enhanced professional learning and practice.

Online learning/professional development

Learning today is taking place in a variety of flexible ways: fully online (web-based), classroom-based, distance learning, blended learning, work-based learning, etc. In all these settings, learning involves interactions. In the literature on online learning environments, interaction is described as involving the content, the facilitators and participants, and the context (Berge, 1996). Although in the design of curricula and content the teacher is involved in developing the pre-produced content (or content generation), the teacher as online facilitator is also involved in interpersonal interactions with the participants. In the context of online professional development, interactions often involve the community of practice (CoP). And some of the interactions may be offline. Thus, in both online learning and professional development it will be too naive to construe that learning and development takes place entirely online. In reality, much of this process encompasses the offline contexts and the individual learner as a professional. Therefore, besides the interactions between the facilitator and the participants, interactions also take place with oneself. The framework of professional development of online facilitators outlined in this chapter involves the rectangle of: the curriculum and content design, the design of the online learning community, the offline communities of practice including their cultures, and the 'self' engaged in constant 'reflection' in relation to the rectangle. The framework provides the basis of engagement and online interactions for both the facilitators and learners engaged in online learning.

Conceptual frameworks explaining the process of online learning and the formation of online learning communities are limited, and vary from each other based on the assumptions as to:

- how learning takes place;
- the process of formation of an online learning community and collaboration; and
- the end product of the online interactions.

Although theoretical foundations of distance education have been significantly developed over the last three decades, similar works on online learning are limited and still unfolding.

So, theoretical discourses on online learning concentrate more on the formation and interactions within the online learning community, the course design considerations and online mentoring, amongst other things. We focus on three works which have made significant contributions to the theory of online professional learning, Barab *et al.* (2003), Salmon (2000, see also 2004) and Anderson (2003), and describe a derivative framework of online constructivist professional development of online facilitators, and its implication for professional practice.

In a recent work on improving inquiry-based pedagogical practices for mathematics and science teachers, Barab *et al.* (2003) developed and tried out an Inquiry Learning Forum (e-ILF), a web-based professional development system to support a CoP of teachers. The CoP was characterised by sharing of knowledge, values and beliefs; overlapping histories among members and mutual interdependence; mechanisms for reproduction; and common practice/mutual enterprise with opportunities for participation, meaningful relationships and respect for diverse perspectives. The e-ILF had four principles of design: fostering ownership and participation, focusing on inquiry, visiting the classroom through video streaming and web-based technologies to situate the participants in their social context, and supporting the communities around some collective experience/ practice. Barab and colleagues used the term 'web-supported communities', instead of 'online communities', since the success was more when e-ILF was used as an extension of face-to-face (f2f) workshops or when those in online interactions were extended to develop relationships outside the e-ILF. The discussion by the authors on six dualities, designed/emergent, participation/reflection, local/global, identification/negotiability, online/face-to-face, and diversity/coherence, and the tensions involved within the situations will greatly help in facilitating the design of the system dynamics for the online learning community. Such a discourse has considerable implications for the converging online professional community and offline community of practitioners.

Salmon (2004), in an exciting work on the training of tutors/facilitators (or as she calls them 'e-moderators'), developed a five-stage e-moderating model: access and motivation, online socialisation, information exchange, knowledge construction, and development. She suggests that while motivating the online participants, their technology difficulties may be identified; personal problems on socialising in the cafe may be attended to; problems in information exchange can be dealt with by structuring exchanges and interactions; knowledge construction may be facilitated and strengthened by playing a very sensitive but critical role; and learning and development can be facilitated by critical response, encouragement, sharing of own experiences, and indicating to the participants that they are growing in their understanding. She also underlines that at stage five, the participants are encouraged to look for achieving personal goals, integrate e-learning with other forms of learning, and also reflect on the learning process. The e-moderators need different skills at each of these five stages, and the last stage of development is essentially an individual activity. This is a comprehensive work on online participation in which both technological and e-moderating supports by the e-moderators are well defined and articulated.

In so far as interaction is concerned, Anderson (2003) outlined a comprehensive model encompassing in essence two models: the community model (through community of enquiry) and the independent learning model (through structured learning resources). Six forms of interactions are described: student–content, student–teacher, student–student, teacher–content, teacher–teacher, and content–content. Anderson uses Tim Berners-Lee's original coinage of the term 'semantic web' to locate online learners. In the semantic web, the format and structure of the content are so formatted that they can be searched and acted upon by autonomous agents. The learners, the teachers and the content interact in a community of enquiry; and though learning is largely an individual activity, professional and other support in family, office and across the Net is available to the learner. The theory of online learning interaction 'suggests that the various forms of student interactions can be substituted for each other, depending on costs, content, learning objectives, convenience, technology, and available time' (Anderson, 2003, p. 53).

Online mentoring and the role of facilitators

Teaching in an online learning context involves a variety of skills and activities often non-existent in face-to-face classroom teaching. The detailed discussion (Berge, 1996) on the role of online instructors in a computer conferencing environment shall be very useful to the online facilitators. There are pedagogical (task-based, intellectual), social (human relationship in the learning community), managerial (administrative, organisational, procedural), and technical (ease in use of hardware and software) roles to be played by each online instructor. In addition, confidence and communicative competences are prerequisites to successful online interactions (Berge, 1996). A clear distinction in the dual roles played by e-moderators – technical support and e-moderating – has been highlighted by Salmon (2000). At each of the five stages the dual roles (technical support, and e-moderating, respectively) prescribed by her include the following:

- Access and motivation: setting up system and accessing/welcoming and encouraging.
- Online socialisation: sending and receiving messages/familiarising and providing bridges between cultural, social and learning environments.
- Information giving and receiving: searching, personalising software/facilitating tasks and supporting use of learning materials.
- Knowledge construction: conferencing/facilitating process.
- Development: providing links outside closed conferences/supporting, responding.

Further, students' perceptions of teachers' interactivity affects their learning; and therefore strong teacher presence (and professional development therein) is needed for developing and sustaining online learning communities (Wilson and Stacey, 2004). The facilitators need to be aware of online teaching strategies: 'You can probably only develop online "antennae" with experience, but it is useful to be aware of possible online teaching strategies so you can draw on these to change tack, or to prevent unhelpful trends becoming established' (Gustafson and Gibbs, 2000, p. 208). They further suggest that there may be mentor-observers to stimulate and facilitate collaboration online and offline, thereby contributing to the transformation of the professional practice of the facilitators. The mentor-observer needs to combine the skills of a 'techie' (Rogers, 2003), as early adopters of innovation in online learning, and an expert in social construction of knowledge in the CoP (Vygotsky, 1978; Wenger, 1998). As suggested by Herrington and Oliver (1995), there are in fact two kinds of observers: mentor-observer and apprentice-observer and both have their respective roles at the various stages of online and offline interactions, knowledge construction and formation of identity in the community. In some situations or contexts, an individual may fulfil both roles of mentor-observer and apprentice-observer. Also, it is important that the formation of professional development communities online and the convergence of CoP offline need to be done by the online facilitators themselves (Barab et al., 2003). The peers have important roles to play – for both in online interactions and collaborations within the CoP the learners' contributions, practice and performance need to be continuously peer-critiqued to enable acquisition of professional knowledge and enhancement of performance (Gustafson and Gibbs, 2000). Equally, reflection plays a critical role in this process.

Role of reflection in learning and professional development

Contrary to popular belief, professional development involves much more than mere acquisition of skills. It encompasses change in attitude and practice, beliefs, and values. As Guskey argues, 'it also involves learning how to redesign educational structures and cultures' (1999, p. 160). Reflection is central to professional development, and as a reflective practice, it is intentional, continuous, and systemic. Reflection in contexts of professional practice involves engagement in exploring one's experiences. And as Boud *et al.* (1985) note, it consists of three interrelated stages: returning to the experience, attending to feelings, and re-evaluating the experience. For Dewey (1933), reflection is a process of the manipulation of knowledge and is goal-directed. One thinks at times of uncertainty and reflection as secondary experience that is used to make sense of the world by using the environment as the object of reflection. For Habermas (1971), human beings adopt reflection as one of the processes in the generation of particular forms of knowledge and evaluative processes of enquiry are equated with reflection. In educational practice this is used to find correspondence between the actual phenomenon, the practice and one's own understanding of the phenomenon, and reflection also facilitates location of ideological distortions. Rather than the individual processes, Habermasian reflection has much to do with social processes. While 'interpretive enquiry reflection' provides for finding the best solution, 'critical reflection' facilitates evaluation of the status of knowledge and theory building.

Reflection in contemporary professional development practices relies largely on the work of Schon (1987) which categorises reflection into: 'reflection-in-action' and 'reflection-on-action'. It is argued that the espoused theories taught to novices to graduate as professionals are rarely applied in professional practices that are based on context-specific practical ways of performing the profession. Rather, individual professional practitioners acquire understanding and competence through situated learning – the epistemology of professional knowledge and practice is guided more by theories-in-use rather than the undeveloped espoused theories. 'Reflection-in-action' occurs at the time of action with unexpected consequences, and guides the process of professional action through 'knowledge-in-use' (derived from theories-in-use and therefore has very little to do with espoused theories), while 'reflection-on-action' occurs when the action has already taken place, and is therefore retrospective. Reflective practitioners are developed through the process of contextualising the reflective knowing-in-action into the structured context of that profession, and this is shared by the community of practitioners.

A critical work on a model of learning/professional development and the role of reflection in it is that of Moon (1999) who argues about the inconsistency in the use of terminologies in Schon's works, and points out that the mental framework of individual professionals has not been analysed in interpreting how reflection occurs. She has further drawn on works of others to provide both a theoretical stance and a practical stance for reflective practice in the professions, and therefore for professional development. In fact, reflection has been used more for professional development rather than facilitating student learning. Based largely on the work of Moon (1999), and drawing from the critical works of Mezirow (1990, 1991) on transformative learning and that of Richardson (2000) on learning styles of both campus-based and distance learners, a framework of reflective and transformative professional development is presented in Figure 12.1.

The framework is grounded in the constructivist view of learning in that the focus shifts from the structured teaching of the teacher to learners' construction of their own knowledge organised in a network called cognitive structure. The cognitive structure given in Figure 12.1 (comprising guidance, assimilation, and accommodation) is spiral in nature and goes on at every stage of learning (see Moon, 1999, p. 110 for its original version). The cognitive structure stores the newly learnt material, accommodates and readjusts itself in response to new ideas, and actively guides the individual in the learning of new material. Cognitive structure is central to individual construction of knowledge/meaning and group negotiation of meaning considered from the constructivist view of learning. Meaning perspective is used by Mezirow (1990) to explain the role of cognitive structure and individuals who get trapped in their meaning perspective (and do not open up to new ideas and meanings) should be supported to be emancipated – and

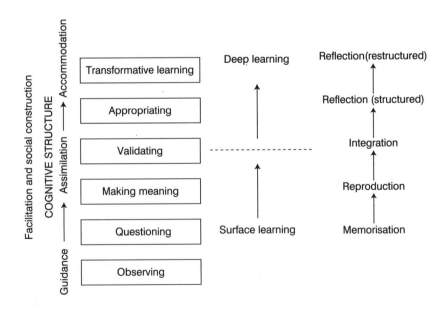

Figure 12.1 Cognitive structure, reflection and transformative learning/professional development (Sources: Mezirow, 1990, 1991; Moon, 1999; Richardson, 2000; Juwah and Panda, 2005)

that is what transformative learning does, and this is where social construction/ negotiation of meaning assumes significance (Panda, 2004).

The six stages of mental processes depicted in the framework (see Figure 12.1) are described as follows:

- at the stage of 'observing', the cognitive structure facilitates the individual to observe and recognise what is to be learnt; attitude, motivation and emotion play important roles in this process;
- at the stage of 'questioning', the learner uses questions to clarify areas of doubt, uncertainty, to seek affirmation and reassurance of their understanding or actions;
- 'making meaning' involves the learner building on prior knowledge, identifying possible links, establishing connections with present materials and assimilating new materials into the cognitive structure, and relating the new meaning to the established discipline;
- at the next stage of 'validation' the materials learnt are applied and validated in real life situations, processes and practices; this process also involves the private process of construction of meaning;
- 'appropriation' involves using learnt material and the knowledge gained in new contexts and situations;
- the final stage of 'transformative learning' involves the extensive use of the cognitive structure; the learner becomes capable of evaluating their own frame of reference, and others' knowledge and process of knowing.

The framework also shows the role of deep and surface approaches to learning (Marton *et al.*, 1984; Marton and Saljo, 1997; Entwistle, 1997; Ramsden, 1992; Biggs, 1993; Richardson, 2000) and these may affect individual thinking, reflection and professional development. The approach to learning adopted by the learner determines the best possible representation (BPR) of learning (from 'memorization' to 'restructured reflection') *vis-à-vis* the stages of learning. For instance, even if one has reached the third stage of 'making meaning' (in the stages of learning), because of adoption of a surface approach, one will be simply reproducing unrelated ideas in the BPR because new learning cannot be related to the existing learning. A deep approach to learning will have greater use of cognitive structure in regard to new materials of learning. At the stage of memorisation, what one is doing is observation and peripheral participation (Lave and Wenger, 1991). Progression towards restructured reflective practice enables one to become a reflective professional. It is contended that reflection is involved at stages of making meaning, working with meaning, and transformative learning. There is a possibility that reflection facilitates the cognitive structure to upgrade to a higher stage of learning. For example, when reflection takes place during making meaning, learning progresses to a higher stage in which the cognitive structure further accommodates what is reflected on and therefore re-interpreted/ re-learnt. This in turn enhances practice or performance. Jonassen (1994), in the schematic web of constructivism, underlines the role of articulation and reflection in both internal negotiation and social negotiation of meaning, and distinguishes between experiential knowledge and reflective knowledge.

Cowan (2002) posits that we can facilitate the improvement of an individual's learning and the development of their capabilities through structured varieties of reflection. He identifies the types of reflection as:

- Reflective process analysis – here the question focuses on 'How do I (do something)?' This enables learners to derive a refined generalisation in their minds of how they can apply their generalisation methodically to future tasks/examples.
- Reflective self evaluation – this type of reflection answers the question 'How well I do' or 'How well could I do (something)?' This enables the learner to understand outcomes and standards. With time the learner notices deviations from desired outcomes and will modify their behaviour and activity, and through self-directing monitor and manage their own learning.
- Critical incident analysis – this type of reflection involves learners in situations which puzzle or perturb and enables them to consider 'What should I take from considering this incident?' This type of reflection enables the learners to progress from intense consideration of issues at the time of the event to a more generalised and transferable appreciation of issues and possibilities (Moon, 1999, pp. 209–10).
- Open-ended reflection – this enables the learner to engage with and tackle questions/situations whose answers they cannot predict and/or anticipate. This form of reflection can facilitate dramatic changes in ability, attitude and values.
- Serendipitous reflection – the outcome of this type of reflection is based on chance and therefore cannot be purposefully planned for.

Cowan (1998) also proposed the term 'reflection-for-action'. This involves using knowledge and understanding gained (or constructed meaning) to improve practice and performance.

Online professional development: a framework

As outlined above, professional practitioners strive towards transformative learning through change in their cognitive structure and reflection. Mentor facilitation plays an important role in upgrading learning, representation of learning (or evidence of achievement of professional knowledge) and enhancement in the quality of professional practice. Although knowledge construction/construction of meaning is an individual affair, this process takes place within a social setting or context, and, therefore, there is always an interaction between the professional and the context.

Context

The context for our framework for the professional development of online facilitators (Figure 12.2) involves: the online learning community (OLC), the community of practice (CoP), and one's social community/culture. Therefore, all three aspects need to be taken into consideration while designing for online professional development. We have also argued that 'reflection' plays a prime role in bringing coherence to the meanings derived from all the three aspects. Hence, in the context of online professional development and the framework of cognitive structure, constructivist and reflective professional development need to be extended to include situated learning, community of practice, culture, and social construction of knowledge.

In 'situated cognition' (and situated learning), context plays an important role in learning since it forms an integral part of the knowledge base which guides that learning (Brown *et al.*, 1989). Thus, in providing the context for a 'cognitive apprenticeship' approach to learning, Collins *et al.* (1987) argue that instead of using pre-determined instructional sequences, learning should take place through solving real world problems. Jonassen (1994), in discussing the design of learning environments and the web of constructivism, presents three common elements: context, collaboration, and construction. Herein, construction involves both internal and social negotiations, with social negotiation being mediated by articulation and reflection. In Jonassen's elements for designing learning environments, situated learning defines the context. In our framework we have

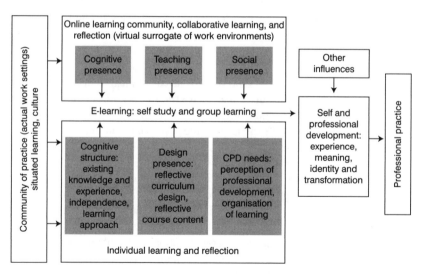

Figure 12.2 Constructivist online continuing professional development of online facilitators: a framework (Sources: Dewey, 1933: Garrison and Anderson, 2003; Habermas, 1971; Jonassen *et al.*, 1995; Gunawardena *et al.*, 2003; Lave and Wenger, 1991; Mezirow, 1990, 1991; Moon, 1999: Richardson, 2000; Salmon, 2000; Schon, 1987; Wenger, 1998)

identified three types of contexts: culture, community of practice, and online learning community (Figure 12.2). This is consistent with Brown *et al.*'s (1989) idea that knowledge is contextually situated, and influenced by activity, context and culture. In instructional design for situated learning in a multimedia environment, Herrington and Oliver (1995) have argued that learning and development will be more meaningful if they are embedded in the social and physical contexts in which they are to be used. Thus, professional development for online facilitators needs to be embedded in the social and physical contexts of OLC and CoP – though there might be virtual surrogates of online and offline work environments (Figure 12.2). Since online professional development does not exclusively involve activity but encompasses online socio-cultural interactions and the social and physical contexts of the CoP, professional development programmes for online facilitators will be more effective and meaningful if they incorporate both contexts of online and offline CoPs. Hence, the observer-facilitators need to have strong design and teaching presence as well as the capability of creating and embedding the appropriate contexts in the learning process.

Lave and Wenger (1991) talked of situated learning as situated activity through legitimate peripheral participation (LPP) – the latter provides for relationships between newcomers and old timers, and leads the newcomers to become part of the community of practice. In this regard, learning is an integral part of social practice, and in situated ways is transformative. Thus, situated learning provides a bridge between cognitive processes (and learning) and social practice, and LPP is the process of situated learning in social practice. In the wider context of the development of online facilitators, the apprentice-observers move from peripheral participation to become reflective professionals in both the OLC and the CoP.

Community

While Garrison and Anderson (2003) have used 'critical thinking' to define individual responsibility, and 'discourse' as a group activity in the community of inquiry, we have used 'reflection' for both individual and group interactions in the framework of online professional development. Garrison and Anderson take the discussion on discourse and meaning making in online learning communities further through their framework of cognitive presence, teaching presence and social presence. In a text-based collaborative online learning environment or critical community of inquiry, cognitive presence of the participants refers to the extent to which they can continuously use reflection and discourse to be able to analyse, construct and confirm meaning and understanding. Teaching presence involves three elements: i) instruction design and organisation, ii) facilitating discourse, and iii) direct instruction. Since the online learning community is to engage in discourse and reflection, which needs to be sustained and which has precedence in and is followed up by the community of practice, their collaboration is therefore essential; and their social presence (affective presence, open communication, and cohesive presence) sustains such a collaborative community. In their online community of inquiry, cognitive independence and social interdependence occur simultaneously. In cognitive presence particularly, there is provision of time for self-reflection, and provision for modelling and reflecting upon the process of critical thinking; but there has not been any indicator or provision for facilitating reflection. Though the authors mention challenging ideas and precipitating reflection in the attempt to ensure cognitive presence, it is not clear how this precipitation is possible. Further, the community of inquiry model is a model of learning or professional development online, while most of the learning as such − whether in online or traditional distance education, or face-to-face education contexts − takes place offline (i.e. when one goes through the content and other sources, interacts with the community of practice and culture, and reflects upon the experiences individually and in group contexts). Garrison and Anderson's model suggests to us that within the individual cognitive structure, one can maintain independence and employ reflection even while undertaking online and offline collaboration.

In our framework of online constructivist continuing professional development, reflection is assumed to play the major role in underpinning the change in cognitive structure through independent study, online collaboration and negotiation, collaborative group/project work, knowledge construction and negotiation in the community of practice.

Professional identity

Change of professional identity is visualised as the goal of professional development for online facilitators. 'Identity' as a social process (Wenger, 1998) includes: membership of the community, a learning trajectory, negotiation of experience with others, and many forms of membership in relation to local and global contexts. An individual may actively engage in the community, have an imaginative engagement with its ideas, or align with the aims of the community. In professional practice, any of the above three is possible, and more so at a distance through online interaction. Negotiation of meaning is possible through participation and reification. Participation has to be necessarily in (cyber) 'communities' rather than networks and reification is the consolidation and transmission of meaning through the production or outcome of something. Therefore, professional development involves participation in the CoP, transformation of knowledge in the form of experiencing one's identity and change in both individual and community identities. So, there must be a context in which the change takes place: the context being the transformative practice of the professional community. In the case of professional development of the professional community, changes in individual cognitive structure (and so, professional practice) and in transformative practice of the professional community are possible through transformation of individual cognitive structures due to individual reflection and social negotiation of meanings. And, if the community of practice is scattered over places (maybe, all over the globe), the cultures of the communities play an important role in affecting individual cognitive structure, social construction and negotiation of meaning in both online and offline interactions and collaborations.

In online professional development contexts, the members of the online community also belong to other institutional communities. Hence it is important to take a holistic view of the learning community. For instance, misrepresentation and pseudo-representation by the members of the community in the virtual world is possible. The community of inquiry suggested by Garrison and Anderson (2003) sufficiently guards against this, but does not translate the transfer of 'identities' to the community of practice. It is therefore suggested that 'reflection' can play even a broader role beyond the online learning community − it can connect the learning community and online mentoring with the reflective activities/projects of the community of practice. This also authenticates the validity of knowledge created in the online learning community.

With regard to community, Brown and Duguid (2000) have further argued that the Internet provides an excellent context for communication in local communities where reciprocal relationships and activities exist, but it fails to do so in the global community. The creation of information networks seems to be more appropriate for a global community. They further suggest that any educational provision must have access to an authentic learning community, authentic resources for the creation of knowledge and accreditation of the process and product. In the case of online professional development, therefore, the Internet can support the existing professional community of practice as an online learning community. The existence of the local community of practice and its working on collaborative reflective projects will ensure credibility, authentication and accreditation.

Culture

Culture is defined as a code of ethical values underpinned by respect, truth, sincerity, fairness, equality of participation, tolerance and accountability. In a community or culture, these norms are regulated through the protection of practice and mutual understanding of norms from other cultures (Habermas, 1990, pp. 65, 85, 86–94, 158–9).

In our framework of online constructivist professional development (see Figure 12.2), culture is an important component of 'context' (the other two components being 'community of practice' and 'online learning community'). Though it was pointed out earlier that the development of the individual cognitive structure is an outcome of one's interaction and growing up with one's own culture, the role of culture within the above framework has been examined from the point of view of its direct effect on presence in and interactions within the online learning community. In the case of adult learning, Brookfield (1995) notes that the variables of culture, ethnicity, personality, and political ethos are more important than chronological age in explaining how learning occurs and is experienced. Further, one is influenced by different cultures at the same time and from that point of view, the community of practice may have its own culture (Rogers and Steinfatt, 1999). Based on the authors' experience, a sustained online community of online facilitators develops and is influenced by its own culture and modus operandi. The influence of culture is/may be evidenced in the cultural 'form' of behaviour, meaning attributed to a given form of behaviour and the patterned distribution (or frequency) of the behaviour in both online and offline interactions (Lado, 1986).

In designing and administering programmes for the development of online facilitators, particularly programmes which cut across national and cultural boundaries, it is extremely important that both the design presence (Figure 12.2) (comprising the curriculum and course design), and the design of content and activities (specific to each of the different cultures) take into consideration the values, beliefs and past social experiences of the participants, as in the case of diffusion of innovations (Rogers, 2003). Therefore, for a meaningful professional development of online facilitators, the programmes should be grounded in the relevant aspects of culture, community of practice, situated learning, online learning community, and individual cognitive structure.

Labour *et al.* (2000) have covered in more depth aspects of culture and ethics in online learning as well as useful hints and tips for facilitating online learning.

Collaboration and dialogue

In web-based professional development, collaboration requires an environment of shared goals, peer learning (see Chapter 10), use of personal experiences and problems, and dialogue. The online environment also promotes and facilitates dialogue and discourse among participants, in which they openly contribute to the meaning created by each other, and in the process reconstruct their mental models or frames of reference. Skilled online discussion maintains a balance between participants' advocacy and the inferences that they draw. Mentor-observers can facilitate this by encouraging diversity of views and advocacy, expansive questioning, making provision for constructive feedback on each other's views and performance as well as engendering reflection. Participants can also be assigned the responsibility of leading and facilitating parts of the skilled discussion/dialogue, commenting on the content and group dynamics, providing constructive feedback, moderating the process, and summarising at the end (see Chapter 10). 'Dialogue for critical thinking requires two processes – the making of meaning that accompanies the use of language and the public recognition of that meaning' (Burge and Haughey, 1993, p. 103).

Transformative practice

It has been appropriately noted by van Halen-Faber (1997) that, 'Critical reflection and transformative learning are the tenets of reflective practice' (p. 52). Mezirow underlines the statement by positing that, 'to facilitate transformative learning, educators must help learners become aware and critical of their own and others' assumptions' (1997, p. 10). Learners must be helped to transform their frames of reference so that they can best appreciate and understand their own experience. To do this, both observer-mentors and facilitators need to do more critical reflection themselves. Burge and Haughey emphasised 'We believe that if we are to encourage transformative learning and critical self-reflection in our learners, then we had better do the same for ourselves' (1993, p. 93). Pallof and Pratt (1999) consider transformative learning as the final form of learning and 'real' learning that takes place online, and which 'represents a self-reflective process that occurs at several levels' (p. 129). Therefore, transformation of online facilitators is the goal visualised in the framework discussed above. The framework has further been operationalised in a schema (Figure 12.3) showing the linkages of various variables operating in the professional development of the facilitators.

The schema

The framework for the online constructivist continuing professional development given in Figure 12.3 explains that the individual cognitive structure of the professional (i.e. online facilitator) which has in the past been shaped by culture, previous (situated) learning/education and the community of practice undergoes transformation in the online leaning environment. The variables that affect the professional cognitive structure and identity include:

- the continuing professional development needs, perception of the value of professional development and its organisation;
- the design presence of the curriculum and the course content;
- cognitive presence (i.e. the intellectual environment in which the professionals individually and collectively construct knowledge and negotiate meaning – the nature of collaboration, interaction and engagement – and which leads towards meaning making and transformative learning);
- teaching presence through the direct instruction, and mentoring and facilitation of discourse/reflection by the instructor/mentor; and social presence of the participants and the mentor.

Also, the framework depicts the causal relationship amongst the various variables involved in online professional development. The individual cognitive structure and professional identity of the facilitators undergo change and transformation through collaboration and the various forms of interactions: participation, negotiation and ratification of meaning, and reflection. Lastly, both the individual and collaborative reflection contribute in:

- enhancing the quality of the learning experience;
- empowering and emancipating the individual and transforming their professional practice of online facilitation.

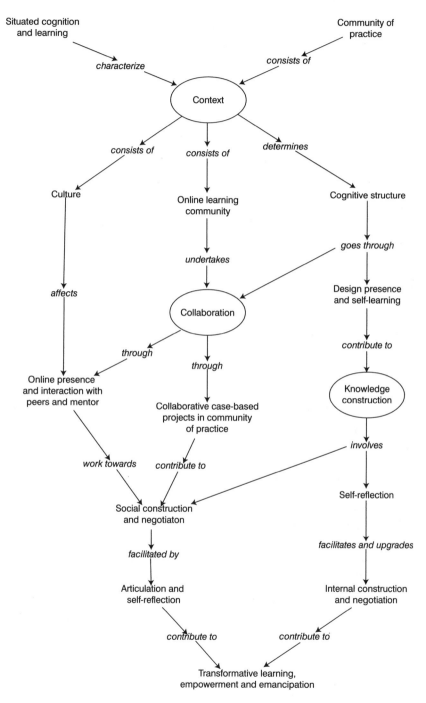

Figure 12.3 Online constructivist professional development schema (© Panda, 2003)

From the framework, it is evident that a deeper approach to learning and transformative professional development as well as the transformation of the professional identity can be made possible through enhanced facilitation of various learning activities and encouraging reflection by the mentor-observer (see case study below).

Case study

Developing online facilitators at Robert Gordon University

The Robert Gordon University (RGU), Aberdeen is located in a sparsely populated region of the North East of Scotland, in the United Kingdom. RGU is a global provider of education and training in specialist and niche areas of energy-based courses (oil, gas and tidal wave engineering), business administration, nursing and midwifery, and information and publishing studies. Increasing our market share of students particularly through the postgraduate and continuing professional development provision resonates in the university's 2010 mission and vision statement. Due to our geographic location and to ensure flexibility of delivery, ease of access to and equality of participation on our courses, the strategy was adopted to deliver most of our courses online via the University's Virtual Campus. The adoption of an e-based strategy of delivery therefore required that our staff are skilled and competent in the use of new technologies in facilitating teaching and learning online.

To ensure that staff are proficient in facilitating learning online, a five-week course in developing online tutoring skills was introduced in 2002. The course was designed to develop staff's skills in:

- using virtual/online learning environments (VLEs/OLEs – Internet, virtual universities or intranets) in teaching, learning and assessment;
- appraising the pedagogy underpinning online teaching and learning;
- designing fit-for-purpose online course(s) and activities;
- embedding information and communication technologies in the curriculum and using innovative technology in teaching and supporting learning;
- developing effective facilitator roles of moderating, reviewing and summarising;
- assessing and giving feedback on individual and group performance; and
- reflecting on own personal and professional practice and development.

The five-week course is delivered entirely online through the FirstClass software or through blended learning (a mixture of face-to-face meeting and online attendance).

Learning was underpinned by the following interactions:

- reading appropriate set text to provide the theoretical basis;
- using technology to engage with and to facilitate learning;
- critiquing and responding to posts on a one-to-one basis within the group;
- summarising the group's deliberations;
- sharing the group's summary with other groups and providing an overall summary for the large group;
- self reflection;
- using feedback from other learners to enhance own learning and reflection.

Participants were supported through a variety of mechanisms including tutor and mentor support, the learning community and community of practice.

Community of learning and community of practice

Both the communities of learning and practice provided forums for formal and informal socialisation and interactions, frames of reference, peer learning, peer support and encouragement. The community provided the setting for situated learning in which participants learnt by doing in a safe and 'realistic, learning environment'. Participants learnt by being immersed in the roles of facilitators, moderators and summarisers. Feedback from peers was critical in providing the much needed motivation and encouragement, and in contributing to the transformative development of the participants.

> There was much that was positive about the course, the supportive learning community, the introduction to a completely new environment and the opportunity to take on different roles were all very much appreciated in enhancing the learning experience. The negative aspects that I experienced had more to do with my own fears and the volume of work with which I had to cope at the time. I have much to consider regarding my own time management skills and I will need to give much more consideration with regard to my own motivation and commitment before agreeing to take on further courses of study. I feel there were aspects that I could have handled better by being more focused and meeting deadlines. Missing them just added to the stress levels!

Tutor and mentor support

The tutor role focused on facilitating, monitoring and assessing participants' learning and being a co-learner. For this course, the mentor-observer and apprentice-observer roles were fulfilled by individuals. Both the tutor–learner and mentor–learner interactions provided opportunities for: a) initiating dialogue and discourse, b) questioning, c) probing and challenging assumptions, and d) prompting analytical and in-depth reflection thus enabling the learner to develop beyond the ZPD (Vygotsky, 1978) (see Chapter 1). Online tutorials and comments from mentors provided constructive feedback that enabled the participant to assess his/her performance or progress against the standard as well as use the information gained to work towards closing the gap between current and desired learning outcomes.

> My learning log is very revealing! Now, looking back at the experience, with the benefit of hindsight and feeling far more relaxed, I am actually rather taken aback at the levels of stress that I was experiencing. This was very much as a result of the pressures of family life around the Christmas period combined with my anxieties about my lack of expertise in I.T. in general. I considered giving up the course. This is the first time that I have felt like this about any course of study. It has given me an insight into the way a number of my 'return to practice' students feel about combining distance learning with full time employment. I can now truly empathise with the students who struggle with their studies and feel that I can offer them constructive advice directly from my own experiences. I can now also appreciate the significance and motivating effect of regular tutor/moderator contact and have reviewed my own tutorial support for students as a result. The support of my co-student was also very important. His input, enthusiasm and constructive feedback really did have a positive, motivating effect upon me. The importance of peer support has been reinforced and I will be encouraging my distance learning students to set up peer support groups as a result and facilitating them to do so, if requested.

> I found that once confidence started to build the final sections of the course were progressed through very rapidly indeed, but getting started was the biggest hurdle.

The course focused on reflection as a key competence of professional online facilitators. This was to ensure that facilitators engage with analytical and evaluative reflection to enhance practice and performance. The major issues and findings from our study included a) overcoming staff's resistance to engage with the training partly due to their limited experience in using technology and wanting not to be exposed to their colleagues as being technologically non-competent, b) the challenge of getting the participants to engage in meaningful reflection, and c) dealing with large numbers of participants. Researching the development of online facilitators from diverse backgrounds, it is apparent that engaging novice facilitators in meaningful reflection should be underpinned and progressed through positive regard, empathy and congruence (Rogers, 1980). Effective methods identified in promoting reflection included: the use of questioning (trigger questions) (Cowan, 2002); coaching novices to write reflective accounts through providing scaffolding (e.g. providing exemplars of good practice); and tutors acting as role models for novice apprentices. Our study revealed that group numbers impacted on the quality of interaction and learning. Group interactions beyond ten participants were often bordering on being chaotic when all participants were really participative. In some instances some participants tended to act as freeloaders. Too few participants, less than five, provided a much narrower range of discourses. We found a group size of seven to be the optimum number for good peer interactions and learning, for providing effective feedback and good peer support. Group sizes of more than ten individuals become fairly unmanageable for effective interactive online discussions and assessment of performance.

Conclusion

As part of grounding the course in best practice, it was fundamental that staff were trained online, in the same medium through which they will deliver their own teaching. This makes learning more authentic and provides staff with prior experience in understanding and being better able to facilitate quality learning, as well as helping them empathise with and support learners in an online learning environment. Tutor, mentor and peer support provided invaluable interactions and opportunities that enabled learners to achieve transformative learning. This study has given insight that transformative learning can be charted through the processes of observing, questioning, making meaning, validation and appropriation.

References

Anderson, T. (2003) Towards a theory of online learning. In T. Anderson and F. Elloumi (eds), *Theory and Practice of Online Learning*. Athabasca: Athabasca University.

Barab, S. S., MaKinster, J. G. and Scheckler, R. (2003) Designing system dualities: characterising a web-supported professional development community. *The Information Society*, 19(3), 237–56.

Berge, Z. L. (1996) The role of the online instructor/facilitator. Online. Available at: http://www.emoderators.com/moderators/teach_online.html (Accessed 15 July 2002).

Biggs, J. (1993) From theory to practice: a cognitive systems approach. *Higher Education Research and Development*, 12, 73–85.

Boud, D., Keogh, R. and Walker, D. (1985) Promoting reflection in learning: a model. In D. Boud and D. Walker (eds), *Reflection: Turning Experience into Learning*. London: Kogan Page.

Brookfield, S. (1995) Adult learning: an overview. In A. Tuijnman (ed.), *International Encyclopedia of Education*. Oxford: Pergamon.

Brown, J. S. and Duguid, P. (2000) *The Social Life of Information*. Boston, MA: Harvard Business School Press.

Brown, J. S., Collins, A. and Duguid, P. (1989) Situated cognition and the culture of learning. *Educational Researcher*, 18, 32–42.

Burge, L. and Haughey, M. (1993) Transformative learning in reflective practice. In T. Evans and D. Nation (eds), *Reforming Open and Distance Education*. New York: St Martin's Press.

Collins, A., Brown, J. S. and Newman, S. E. (1987) Cognitive apprenticeship: teaching the craft of reading, writing, and mathematics. In L. Resnick (ed.), *Learning, Knowing, and Instruction*. Hillsdale, NJ: Lawrence Erlbaum.

Cowan, J. (1998) *On Becoming an Innovative University Teacher*. Buckingham: Open University Press.

Cowan, J. (2002) Facilitating development through varieties of reflection. Higher Education Academy Resources on Reflection. Online. Available at: http://www.heacademy. ac.uk/resources.asp?process=full_recordandsection=genericandid=481 (Accessed 24 October 2005).

Dewey, J. (1933) *How we Think*. Boston, MA: D.C. Heath and Co.

Entwistle, N. (1997). Contrasting perspectives on learning. In F. Marton, D. Hounsell and N. Entwistle (eds), *The Experience of Learning*, 2nd edn. Edinburgh: Scottish Academic Press.

Garrison, D. R. and Anderson, T. (2003) *E-learning in the 21st Century*. New York: RoutledgeFalmer.

Gunawardena, C. N., Wilson, P. L., and Nolla, A. C. (2003) Culture and online education. In M. Moore and B. Anderson (eds), *Handbook of Distance Learning*. Mahwah, NJ: Lawrence Erlbaum.

Guskey, T. R. (1999) *Evaluating Professional Development*. Thousand Oaks, CA: Corwin Press.

Gustafson, P. and Gibbs, D. (2000) Guiding or hiding? The role of the facilitator in online teaching and learning. *Teaching Education*, 11(2), 195–210.

Habermas, J. (1971) *Knowledge and Human Interests*. London: Heinemann.

Habermas, J. (1990) *Moral Consciousness and Communicative Action*. Amherst: MIT Press.

Herrington, J. and Oliver, R. (1995) Critical characteristics of situated learning: implications for the instructional design of multimedia. *Proceedings ASCILITE '95*. University of Melbourne.

Jonassen, D. (1994) Thinking technology: towards a constructivist design model. *Educational Technology*, 34(4), 34–7.

Jonassen, D., Davidson, M., Collins, M., Campbell, J. and Haag, B. (1995) Constructivism and computer-mediated communication in distance education. *American Journal of Distance Education*, 9(2), 7–26.

Juwah, C. and Panda, S. (2005) Cognitive structure, reflection and transformational learning. In C. Juwah (ed.) *Reflection and Professional Development* (work in progress).

Labour, M., Juwah, C., White, N. and Tolley, S. (2000) Culture and ethics: facilitating online learning. In *Online Tutoring e-Book*, Chapter 6. Online. Available at: http://otis. scotcit.ac.uk/onlinebook/otist6cs.htm (accessed 3 September 2005).

Lado, R. (1986) How to compare two cultures. In J. M. Valdes (ed.), *Culture Bound. Bridging the Cultural Gap in Language Teaching*. Cambridge: Cambridge University Press.

Lave, J. and Wenger, E. (1991) *Situated Learning: Legitimate Peripheral Participation*. Cambridge: Cambridge University Press.

Marton, F., Hounsell, D. and Entwistle, N. (1984) *The Experience of Learning*. Edinburgh: Scottish Academic Press.

Marton, F. and Saljo, R. (1997) Approaches to learning. In F. Marton, D. Hounsell and N. Entwistle (eds), *The Experience of Learning*. 2nd edn. Edinburgh: Scottish Academic Press.

Mezirow, J. (1990) How critical reflection triggers transformative learning. In Jack Mezirow and Associates (eds), *Fostering Critical Reflection in Adulthood*. San Francisco, CA: Jossey-Bass.

Mezirow, J. (1991) *Transformative Dimensions of Adult Learning*. San Francisco, CA: Jossey-Bass.

Mezirow, J. (1997) Transformative learning: theory to practice. In P. Cranton (ed.), *Transformative Learning in Action: Insights from Practice*. San Francisco, CA: Jossey-Bass.

Moon, J. (1999) *Reflection in Learning and Professional Development: Theory and Practice*. London: Kogan Page and Sterling: Stylus.

Palloff, R. M. and Pratt, K. (1999) *Building Learning Communities in the Cyberspace*. San Francisco, CA: Jossey-Bass.

Panda, S. (2003) Training needs analysis and development and tryout of a constructivist online model of continuing professional development of special educators. *Fulbright Post-Doctoral Research Report*. University of New Mexico, Albuquerque.

Panda, S. (2004) Reflection and continuing professional development: implications for online distance learning. *Indian Journal of Open Learning*, 13(1), 63–77.

Ramsden, P. (1992) *Learning to Teach in Higher Education*. London: Routledge.

Richardson, J. T. E. (2000) *Researching Student Learning: Approaches to Studying in Campus-based and Distance Education*. Buckingham: SRHE and Open University Press.

Rogers, C. R. (1980) *A Way of Being*. Boston, MA: Houghton Mifflin.

Rogers, E. M. (2003). *Diffusion of Innovations*. 5th edn. New York: Free Press.

Rogers, E. M. and Steinfatt, T.M. (1999) *Intercultural Communication*. Prospect Heights, IL: Waveland.

Salmon, G. (2000) *E-Moderating: The Key to Teaching and Learning Online*. London: Kogan Page.

Salmon, G. (2004) *E-Moderating: The Key to Teaching and Learning Online*. 2nd edn. London: RoutledgeFalmer.

Schon, D. (1987) *Educating the Reflective Practitioner*. San Francisco, CA: Jossey-Bass.

van Halen-Faber, C. (1997) Encouraging critical reflection in preservice teacher education: a narrative of a personal learning journey. *New Directions for Adult and Continuing Education*, 74, 51–60.

Vygotsky, L. S. (1978) *Mind in Society*. Cambridge, MA: The MIT Press.

Wenger, E. (1998) *Communities of Practice: Learning, Meaning, and Identity*. Cambridge: Cambridge University Press.

Wilson, G. and Stacey, E. (2004) Online interaction impacts on learning: teaching the teachers to teach online. *Australian Journal of Educational Technology*, 20(1), 33–48.

Chapter 13

Developing competencies for online and distance education teaching

Ramesh C. Sharma and Charles Juwah

The changing role of the distance educator from a teacher to a facilitator of learning (manager of knowledge) in the context of ICT and enabling technologies calls for the acquisition of certain competencies to effectively support the learner. In this chapter, we discuss how enabling technologies promote the development of appropriate competencies for distance education teaching. Competencies can be developed in the case of those technologies that can penetrate the target groups as against those that fail to do so. This chapter examines the range of skills and competencies (for example videoconferencing, computer mediated conferencing, interactive radio, etc.) used in distance and online education.

Introduction

The student support services in all sectors of education, especially in open and distance education, have been greatly influenced by the emerging information and communication technologies (ICTs). Graziadei (1996) reported a significant effect of communication technologies on the manner in which learning occurs. The introduction of radio counselling, teleconferencing, Internet, web-based computer conferencing etc. has converted the colleges and universities into a 'global village' promoting collaborative learning and teaching. In open and distance education system, a counsellor or tutor is the main contact point for obtaining instructions (Sewart, 1978). Tait (2000, p. 289) identified three fundamental functions of student support: cognitive (sustaining learning through course materials and learning resources), affective (creating commitments, and enhancing self-esteem), and systemic (putting in place effective, transparent and student-friendly administrative procedures and information management systems). This student support is provided in the form of a human support, which is identified differently in different open universities across the globe: tutor counsellor, course tutors, subject matter specialist, student counsellor, tutor counsellors, mentor, demonstrator, and assessor or evaluator.

Distance educator in changing times

The methodology of instruction in distance education is very different from that of conventional education. Stevenson *et al.* (1996) highlighted the general acceptance that the distance tutoring role is, to a large extent, self-taught. The distance education system is more learner-oriented and a student is an active participant in the learning process. The teaching process is aimed at imparting education from a distance and at reducing structure and increasing dialogue. Distance education uses various media for instruction that includes print material, audio-video material, counselling sessions, interactive radio sessions, interactive television sessions etc. With the introduction of information and communication technologies and methodological changes there has been a paradigm shift and the traditional learner has metamorphosed into a 'new learner'. This new learner does not accept whatever is provided to him in a predetermined fashion. As the gainer of knowledge, he knows exactly what he wants and will only accept what he needs. He also does not adhere to any limits to learning. For him/her, learning cannot be limited to formal settings alone. The whole world is a university that is at hand to offer limitless opportunities for learning.

The role of academic counsellor

The role of academic counsellor is based on the fact that the students need a high level of support at various stages in their pursuit of higher education. The support takes into account the various experiences the student has come to bear in his education process. These include the kind of schooling the student has had, the family background from which he comes etc. Thus the role of an academic counsellor is seminal to the existence of the university.

The role of an academic counsellor is more crucial at the preparatory stage of a learner when he or she is academically immature. The student may not possess the requisite study skills, they may be joining studies after a long gap and they may be confronted with a wide range of problems which could be academic, social, professional, psychological etc. Once the preparatory stage is over, the student would have developed certain study skills. Moreover they would be academically better equipped and therefore the task of an academic counsellor becomes easier. The academic counsellor undertakes counselling, and uses media as support mechanisms for instruction and evaluation of assignments (IGNOU, 2001; RGU, 2005).

Activities of academic counsellors

The major activities of an academic counsellor are informing, advising and discussion.

- *Informing*

  At this stage the counsellor provides information to the students about the programmes of the university, qualifications prescribed by the university for admission and about different regulations of the university. To cater for this need the counsellor should have complete and accurate knowledge about the rules and regulations of the university.

- *Advising*

  Advising is the aspect of helping the students in adopting the right approach, for example the selection of the right courses within a programme. The counsellor has to advise based on the requirements and abilities of the students.

- *Discussing*

  Discussions initiated by the counsellor should consider all relevant factors that are required to reach a decision. Through the discussions, the students should be in a position to adopt the right direction for a variety of issues.

- *Facilitating*

  As students in their course of study encounter some difficulties with their academic work, the counsellor, by using a diverse range of skills, strategies and interventions facilitates the resolution of academic problems. The strategies and interventions employed are targeted towards empowering the student to enable them to resolve the issues themselves.

- *Referral*

  As students' needs and demands may require specialist help and trained skills, the academic counsellor, in ensuring that the student receives effective and efficient support, refers the student to the necessary services and resources within or outwith the university.

- *Advocating*

  This involves advocating on behalf of the student on academic matters requiring specialist knowledge and skills that the student lacks. For example, counsellors may advocate on behalf of or represent the student in academic matters requiring full interpretation of the university's academic regulations at Board of Studies and/or Assessment Boards.

Changing face of distance teacher/teaching: emergence of new technologies

Distance teaching has undergone a great metamorphosis from simple correspondence teaching to virtual/online teaching over the last two decades. The distance teaching institutions have empowered themselves with modern communication technologies, opening new avenues for education and training for learners. Taylor (1995) traced out the evolution of distance education operations through four generations: starting with the Correspondence Model (print technology based); moving on to the Multi-media Model in the second phase (print, audio and video technologies based); then in the third phase came the Tele-learning

Model (introduction of telecommunication technologies enabling synchronous communication); and arriving at the fourth phase of the Flexible Learning Model (based on online delivery via the Internet). Professor Taylor (2001), working again on his model, reported the emergence of the fifth generation, taking advantage of Internet and Web technologies. He found that although many institutions still belonged to the fourth generation, work was already in progress for fusion of interactive multimedia and distance teaching (see Figure 13.1).

He predicted that 'Effective implementation of fifth generation distance education technology is likely not only to transform distance education, but also to transform the

---

FIRST GENERATION – [The Correspondence Model]
- Print

SECOND GENERATION – [The Multi-media Model]
- Print
- Audiotape
- Videotape
- Computer-based learning (e.g. CML/CAL/IMM)
- Interactive video (disk and tape)

THIRD GENERATION – [The Telelearning Model]
- Audio-teleconferencing
- Videoconferencing
- Audiographic communication
- Broadcast TV/Radio and Audioteleconferencing

FOURTH GENERATION – [The Flexible Learning Model]
- Interactive multimedia (IMM) online
- Internet-based access to WWW resources
- Computer mediated communication

FIFTH GENERATION – [The Intelligent Flexible Learning Model]
- Interactive multimedia (IMM) online
- Internet-based access to WWW resources
- Computer mediated communication, using automated response systems
- Campus portal access to institutional processes and resources

---

Figure 13.1 Models of distance education and associated delivery technologies (Source: Taylor, 2001)

experience of on campus students' (Taylor, 2001, p. 4). Under these circumstances, the teacher educator's role is a key element of success as they are at the forefront to explain to the students how ICT constitutes one of the important tools they could use to meet their pedagogical goals and responsibilities. Jung (2000) proclaimed that Internet-based education is an effective means of distance education as it provides a better platform for learning dialogue and learning communities. Since open universities are increasingly acquiring communication technologies for instruction, there has been a growing apprehension about drawing the maximum benefits of such practices until the teachers are adequately charged with the necessary skills to use them. Taylor Northrup and Little (1996) undertook a study to find the success indicators as regards the ICT integration into the programmes related to the training of teachers, and reported attempts being made by universities towards that end.

Competencies for the information age distance teaching

To empower teachers to take on the digital era technologies easily and effectively, they must be provided with the necessary skills and roles to lead the students to the fifth generation distance education. This seems to be inevitable, because the way the new technologies are being developed and advanced, if the teachers are not adequately prepared to use them, they and the students are making sure of staying back in the dark ages.

Cyrs (1997) stressed that distance education teachers need to have the proper skill level in the areas of course planning and organization, verbal and non-verbal presentation, collaborative teamwork, and questioning strategies. A great amount of work exists about course planning and its distance delivery (e.g. Willis, 1994; Paulsen, 1995; de Verneil and Berge, 2000). Cyrs's meta-analysis (1997) advocated a strong case for making provision for developing skills in handling different technologies by the teachers, which was otherwise found to be lacking. Thach (1994) expressed that an instructor's ignorance and lack of familiarity about different mechanisms of synchronous and asynchronous communication may not yield full results during teaching. Technology is always a tool to the teachers to enhance the learning and provide new vistas of education to the learners. Each of such technology, be it print-based, audio, video, multimedia or web-based, demands certain instructional skill on the part of teacher to take maximum gain out of it. Technologies dealing with audio mode require skills in verbal cues whereas those that are web-based need understanding of online communities. While dealing with teaching a distance education course through audiographics conferencing and computer mediated communication (CMC), Gunawardena (1992) stated that 'one of the most important skills I had to develop as a distance teacher was the ability to use the technology to effectively mediate the communication process' (p. 59).

Bates (1995), Paulsen (1995) and Simonson et al. (2000) also expressed the necessity of having adequate knowledge of technical and communications problems that the students may encounter. The teachers also need to be ready with back-up plans in case of exigency or failure of some process or product. Thus the teacher needs to develop certain competencies to deal with teaching through telecommunications, certainly a different situation from teaching in a traditional setting.

Defining competency

Competency has been defined by various persons in the form of abilities, skills or related to doing some activity with some element of quality in it. According to the International Board of Standards for Training, Performance and Instruction (IBSTPI), a competency involves a related set of knowledge, skills and attitudes that enables a person to effectively perform the activities of a given occupation or function in such a way that meets or exceeds the standards expected in a particular profession or work setting (Richey *et al.*, 2001). Buford and Lindner (2002) define competencies as a group of related knowledge, skills, and abilities that affect a major part of an activity such as going to school. A simple search on Google (google.com) provided the following definitions for competency:

- A knowledge, skill, ability, personal quality, experience, or other characteristic that is applicable to the profession of teaching (www.wmich. edu/evalctr/ess/glossary/glos-a-d.htm).
- A characteristic of an employee that contributes to successful job performance and the achievement of organizational results. These include knowledge, skills, and abilities plus other characteristics such as values, motivation, initiative, and self-control. Competencies may be defined organizationally or on an individual basis (www.goer.state.ny.us/workforce/glossary.html).
- (1) Areas of personal capability that enable people to perform successfully in their jobs by completing a task effectively. A competency can be knowledge, attitudes, skills, values, or personal values. Competency can be acquired through talent, experience, or training. (2) Competency comprises the specification of knowledge and skill and the application of that knowledge and skill to the standard of performance required in employment (www. neiu.edu/~dbehrlic/hrd408/glossary.htm).
- Describes the work related skills and behaviour needed to effectively perform in a role. Core competencies are required for all role profiles. Specific competencies are required for some role profiles (www.mcgill.ca/ hr/mcompensation/terms/).
- Specific skill or knowledge related to the performance of a task, usually related to a job-related task (CLDT) (freire.cascadia.ctc.edu/ePortfolioWeb/ glossary.htm).
- The ability to perform a particular skill or to demonstrate a specified level of knowledge (highered.mcgraw-hill.com/sites/0072484918/student_view0/ glossary.html).

- Specialist knowledge or skills required to perform a job function (erin.gov. au/industry/finance/glossary.html).

The above definitions indicate that specialized knowledge and skills in a job setting form the core competencies.

Competencies of a distance teacher

Determining competencies required for a given job is an important activity. Different universities and researchers have been engaged in documenting roles, skills and competencies for years. Sewart (1993) emphasized that there is a requirement to provide a role definition for those engaged in the student support services. These can be used as a tool to improve curricula, teaching materials, evaluation processes and instructional delivery methods. On the basis of studies on competencies to teach at a distance (Cyrs and Smith, 1988, 1990; Thach, 1994; Chute et al., 1988), Cyrs (1997) identified the following broad areas as important elements for developing competencies in distance teachers: course planning and organization; verbal and non-verbal presentation skills; collaborative team-work; questioning strategies; subject matter expertise; and involving students and coordinating their activities at field sites. O'Rourke (1993, p. 10), for a project for the Commonwealth of Learning, identified some roles and competencies in distance education for distance teachers, providing tutoring and student support. Expertise in the teaching subject area; knowledge about how distance education works, and about the kinds and timeframes needed for distance education course delivery; openness to new ideas, new perspectives on one's discipline; willingness to learn new approaches to teaching and learning; and the ability to communicate the needs of learners to institutions and institutions' perspectives to learners, were reported to be essential roles and skills. On the basis of a survey of students' expectations, Stevenson and Sander (1998) suggested some qualities of a good tutor. These are:

- must be sensitive to students' problems;
- is a good communicator;
- provides detailed feedback;
- gives constructive criticisms;
- has a good sense of humour; and
- is available and helpful.

Ally (2000) also reported on some significant tutoring skills as required in distance education. Dooley and Lindner (2000) suggested six core competencies of distance educators: adult learning theory, technological knowledge, instructional design, communication skills, graphic design and administrative issues. Williams (2000, 2003) recognized 30 competencies as a set of foundational skills needed in higher education institutions to implement and manage distance education programmes. He grouped them into communication and interpersonal skills, administration and management, technology and instruction.

Competencies for online instructors

For teachers dealing with distance education courses to become effective online instructors, Schoenfeld-Tacher and Persichitte (2000) suggested the following set of skills and competencies:

- familiarity with basic research on the characteristics of distance learners, their needs, and how these differ from those in face-to-face settings;
- application of basic principles of instructional design (e.g. congruence of content, activities, media, assessment, selection of appropriate media for the content);
- thorough knowledge of subject matter and common misconceptions;
- deep understanding of the necessity of a learner-centred environment in online settings;
- ability to design a constructivist learning environment;
- practical applications of adult learning theories, self-paced instructions and computer mediated communication;
- appropriate selection of online strategies and tools that promote reflection and deep processing of content (e.g. synchronous discussion, asynchronous discussion, alternative assessment);
- adaptability and flexibility with the capabilities and limitations of the delivery media;
- sufficient familiarity with the delivery medium to provide basic trouble-shooting;
- ability to multi-task;
- time management (e.g. respond to students in a timely manner, extensive advance preparation and planning).

Shank (2004) classified different actions involved in online instructions into five competency areas: administrative, design, facilitation, evaluation, and technical. The individual actions are general and apply mainly to asynchronous instruction.

- *Administrative* (needed for smooth course operations and to help reduce instructor and learner overload)
  - Providing an unambiguous roadmap through the instruction.
  - Providing clear objectives, expectations, and policies.
  - Posting course materials (syllabus, assignments, discussion topics, etc.) in advance so learners can plan.
  - Ensuring that all learners are 'on board' at the beginning of a course.
  - Returning learner calls/emails quickly to allow learners to progress.

- Referring problems to appropriate sources and following up to assure resolution.
- *Design* (targeted towards bringing adequate learning outcomes and satisfaction)
  - Plans activities that allow learners to attach personal meaning to content.
  - Provides opportunities for hands-on practice and application.
  - Balances design to help learners manage load.
  - Helps learners assess their learning and attain personal learning goals.
  - Incorporates social aspects to improve satisfaction, provide a realistic environment, present multiple viewpoints and overcome anonimity.
  - Assures materials are easy to use.
- *Facilitation* (presenting social benefits to students and enhancing learning in them)
  - Sets or facilitates setting of communication rules and group decision-making norms.
  - Provides compelling opportunities for online discussion, negotiation, debate.
  - Moderates discussion, contributes advanced content knowledge and insights, and models desired methods of communication.
  - Fosters sharing of knowledge, questions, and expertise.
  - Contributes outside resources (online, print-based, others) and encourages learners to do so as well.
  - Responds to discussion postings adequately without 'taking over'.
  - Provides acknowledgment of learner contributions.
  - Moderates disagreements and group problems.
- *Evaluation* (pertains to defining evaluation strategies and achieving course objectives)
  - Provides learners with clear grading criteria. Uses rubrics, grading criteria, or examples to help learners recognize expectations.
  - Assists learners who are having problems completing the assignments.
  - Allows learners to track assignment completion and impact on final grade.
  - Quickly acknowledges receipt of assignments.
  - Provides feedback and help with remediation, as needed.
  - Contacts learners who have not completed assignments and helps them plan to complete assignments.
- *Technical* (aimed at removing the hurdles arising out of technical components)
  - Becomes proficient with all technical systems used in the course.
  - Helps learners troubleshoot technical systems.
  - Refers problems to appropriate sources and follows up to assure resolution.

Competencies for e-moderators

Another outstanding work in identifying competencies for e-moderators was carried out by Salmon (2000).

She developed a broad-sheet of competencies for e-moderators which can be adopted by online trainers for designing professional development plans for faculty members, distance teachers for developing teaching material, and administrators for enabling online recruitment of personnel. These competencies are as follows:

- *Understanding of online processes* – understand how to promote group work, pace online discussions, experiment with new ideas.
- *Technical skills* – use software to facilitate student interaction by monitoring student messages, and create conferencing opportunities.
- *Online communication skills* – able to effectively interact with students by using concise and clear messages that encourage academic dialogue and personalize the online experience.
- *Content expertise* – credible subject matter knowledge and experience to share comments/questions that stimulate lively debate.
- *Personal characteristics* – able to adapt to different teaching situations and demonstrates a genuine excitement about online learning.

Competencies for web-based instructional designer

Parhar and Mishra (2000, p. 420) also identified the following competencies that instructional designers may have in order to design web-based instruction:

- state the objectives in behavioural terms;
- sequence objectives in logical order;
- design instructional materials to the level of learners;
- develop the performance measures;
- judge the validity and reliability of the measures used;
- use software application packages;
- explain the process of video production;
- develop formative and summative evaluation plan;
- communicate effectively by visual, oral and written form;
- establish rapport with individuals and groups;
- develop test items and write interactive feedback;
- demonstrate organizational skills and time management skills;
- demonstrate problem solving abilities;
- design textual messages;
- apply principles of page layout design;
- apply current research and theory to the practice of instructional design;

- apply fundamental research skills to instructional design projects;
- design curriculum or programme;
- identify the target learners and conduct needs analysis;
- analyse the characteristics of existing and emerging technologies;
- evaluate instruction;
- use Internet and develop educational web sites;
- use web-based course management tool.

Competencies for online discussions and chat sessions

The distance teacher assumes a very significant role in online learning because in that capacity the teacher has to remove the barriers occurring due to technology, time, space and the interaction patterns amongst learners and with the teacher. Collison *et al.* (2000), Kearsley (2000) and Rosenberg (2001) suggested that for teaching in online environments, the teacher must develop competencies which are distinctive of online environments. Here the teacher can moderate online discussion and chat sessions either synchronously or asynchronously. These researchers reported that in online asynchronous discussions, the moderator's competencies involve:

- allowing learners time for reflection;
- keeping discussions alive and on a productive path; and
- archiving and organizing discussions to be used in subsequent lessons.

In the case of online synchronous discussions (e.g. chat), the moderator must:

- establish ground rules for discussion;
- facilitate interactions with minimal instructor intervention;
- sense how online text messages may appear to distant learners; and
- be aware of cultural differences.

Competencies for web-based computer conferencing (WBCC)

Sharma (2002) reported the following performance indicators needed for WBCC in terms of WBCC requirements, efficacy of communication channel and interaction analysis. He indicated that a successful WBCC needs a well planned web site and depends on internal (user-controlled) and external (driven by visitors and Internet itself) issues. These performance indicators reflect the competencies as these affect the output of the system, provide directions toward the right methodology leading to successful completion of a task and can act as quantitative measures to improve the efficiency of a system.

- *WBCC requirements*
  - clear statement of learning objectives;
  - clear statement of characteristics and prerequisites of learners;
  - clear statement of entry and terminal behaviour of learners;
  - relevance of WBCC to professional activities after a study stage;
  - statement of characteristics and feasibility of WBCC (programme based, technology based etc.);
  - statement of strategies involved (methodologies, time, costs, venue, experts etc.) in implementing the model;
  - concept map of the programme;
  - sequencing of content;
  - identification of activities;
  - design of placement activities;
  - array of graphic support capabilities;
  - geographical spread of learners;
  - composition (homogeneous/heterogeneous);
  - cultural barriers (language/traditions);
  - use of Internet mail during/after WBCC;
  - familiarity with WBCC equipment;
  - building of rapport;
  - fear of being spotlighted;
  - offer trans-national programmes;
  - statement of existing and perceived constraints and alternative strategies to implement the plan;
  - reference to and use of learners' experience;
  - compatible with students' discipline;
  - compatible with existing course material;
  - basic didactic options.
- *Efficacy of communication channel*
  - permission to read/write/download data;
  - appropriate design of learners' feedback mechanism;
  - method of logging and user identification;
  - invoking FTP session to allow file download;
  - encouraging group learning activities;
  - enables user to engage in individual activities;
  - enables user to engage in collaborative group activities;
  - enables user to engage through various media formats.
- *Interaction analysis*
  - mode of response e.g. taking printout, thinking and then replying;
  - replying on-line as the question comes in;
  - peer counselling;
  - facilitate tutor's functions;
  - facilitating team approach.

Competencies for interactive radio

'Interactive Radio Counselling (Live)' is the latest effort in the direction of minimizing the distance in open and distance learning. It provides occasions for learners for live, real-time interaction with experts and with peers at different locations, even as they stay comfortably where they are. In a sense, it provides a platform for the learners and teachers to 'meet', for the learners to know about the other learners and for the administrator to get feedback from learners and teachers. Radio lessons are not self-contained whole units, in the sense that self-instructional materials are. They are not intended for use at initial levels of exposure to a learning content; rather, they are used to further understanding, application or consolidation after the initial exposure. Hence successful interactive radio counselling depends on the competencies of the anchorperson, subject expert/resource person and the organizer, e.g. distance education functionaries working at a distance education centre.

- *Competencies for anchorperson:*
  - possess adequate background on radio operations;
  - can interpret the questions emanating from the receiving ends;
  - coordinate effectively between the resource persons.
- *Competencies for radio officials and distance education functionaries:*
  - finalisation of subjects/topics for a counselling programme;
  - pinalisation of participating experts for each counselling programme;
  - preparation of question bank based on queries received from students or clarifications sought by them;
  - training of counsellors in undertaking 'live' broadcast;
  - release of advertisement in the local press in order to create awareness among the student community;
  - identifying the producer, the anchorperson, the engineer and the production assistant;
  - devising a plan for publicizing the programme including the methodology/procedure to be followed by the students while phoning, including dos and don'ts;
  - working out a hassle free procedure for handling incoming telephone calls.

Competencies for teaching in a videoconferencing classroom

Cyrs (1997) identified competencies for teaching in a videoconferencing setting and grouped them in five areas pertaining to: course planning and organization; verbal and non-verbal presentation skills; questioning strategies; involving students and coordinating their activities; and design of study guides. Cyrs asserted that the same competencies may be applied to the tele-teaching settings. These are:

- *Course planning and organization*
  - an understanding of how tele-teaching differs from traditional teaching;
  - awareness of the advantages and disadvantages of the delivery system and how it affects the course plan;
  - logistical knowledge – has knowledge of copyright issues; use of site coordinators or facilitators (or lack of); technical details such as getting instructional materials (handouts, homework, exams) between sites;
  - basic course design strategies – this includes how to build interactive teaching/learning strategies into the course; how to use technology effectively;
  - general knowledge of instructional development and system theory, and learning theories.
- *Verbal and non-verbal presentation skills*
  - it is important for all teachers to be able to construct organized presentations, to project enthusiasm for the topic and be able to pace lectures appropriately;
  - coordinate presentation with a study guide or handout;
  - operate with a reduction in feedback cues from learners;
  - be aware of how, as an instructor, you look, sound and move on TV monitor;
  - how to manage discussion among sites as well as with originating site.
- *Questioning strategies*
  - tele-teachers need to know how to construct questions at a variety of intellectual levels for a variety of instructional purposes and how to move among these levels and purposes during a question period;
  - establish ground rules for asking and answering questions and how to signal individuals and sites to respond to questions;
  - encourage students to ask questions and elicit positive feedback from students.
- *Involving students and coordinating their activities*
  - this is one of the key differences between tele-teaching and classroom instruction;
  - managing student involvement could take up to 30–50 per cent of class time;
  - need to understand how to select, design, or adapt exercises to match the domain, intellectual skill level, and cognitive level of course objectives while still engaging remote students.
- *Design of study guides*
  Study guides should be readily accessible to the students and easy to understand. Study guides should provide students with:
  - relevant information on how to study, how to take notes and how to manage their time effectively;

- information on how to engage with tasks and assignments, and hints on examination techniques;
- information on sources of academic support, guidance and technical help;
- information on personal development and career planning.

Cultural competencies

As both the Internet and the WWW have increased access to education on a global scale, individuals who engage in distance and online education come from a diverse range of cultures, backgrounds and beliefs. To this end, it is important that facilitators of online education are culturally competent to enable them to value differences, be responsive to diversity and to ensure an inclusive learning environment.

The cultural competencies that the online facilitators should have to enable them to deliver quality focused services include:

- Being ethically aware of cultural, ethnic, racial, linguistic and disability matters and how these could impact on the quality of students' learning.
- Valuing and incorporating multi-perspective views in the curriculum and course materials as appropriate.
- Providing support and interventions that meet the needs of cultural, ethnic, racial, linguistic and disability diversity within your student/learner group.
- Developing and using communication and information technology that effectively and appropriately delivers information to individuals and communities of diverse racial/ethnic/cultural/linguistic backgrounds (see Labour *et al.*, 2000 – http://otis.scotcit.ac.uk/onlinebook/otisT606.htm).

Drawing on our experiences of professional development at The Robert Gordon University, UK, the strategies for developing faculty to acquire required competencies to facilitate distance and online education must include:

- A needs analysis to determine the knowledge, skills and competencies required by faculty in facilitating online and distance education;
- Aligning training and development to meet both organizational/institutional and individual needs;
- Identifying appropriate training and development to match identified training needs;
- Using available and standardized competence frameworks to inform staff and faculty development for online teaching programmes. This enables staff and faculty to gain accreditation for their learning;
- Senior management's commitment. This should include commitment of resources and where possible a 'Development Champion';
- A systematic staff and faculty development that is operationalized along a continuum from the novice at one extreme to the expert at the other. A staged and incremental approach in providing online development reduces the risk of aversion and failure. Also, use a diverse

range of delivery methods to meet the learner's needs, for example – face-to-face, online and blended delivery (a combination of face-to-face and online interactions). A one-size-fits-all approach is a recipe for disaster. However, it is important to stress that staff learn online, as this enables them to experience online education as a learner;

- A range of strategies or approaches for overcoming resistance and fear of change. For example, using the *4I* change management strategy of *Inform* (through awareness raising); *Involve* (all relevant stakeholders through meaningful dialogue); *Implement* (change processes via innovative curricular development, training and development, and quality systems) and *Incentivize* (via rewards and recognition: these need not be financial);
- Implementing training and development within a community of learning and community of practice (where the knowledge and practice already exist). This is important in providing appropriate context for authentic learning and the opportunities for individuals to: share experiences and ideas; see and hear alternative perspectives; and share their reflections on practice and performance. Where appropriate, focus on the discipline-based or local practice(s) and customs;
- Providing a diverse range of learning support, e.g. peer support, mentorship, post course support, etc., to further help develop confidence and professional knowledge in the novice/new practitioner as well as enhance good and reflective practice (see Chapter 12);
- Supporting faculty in the effective management of time online. This is to ensure that students are encouraged and supported to develop as autonomous learners but also to help prevent 'burn out' for faculty;
- Providing regular, just-in-time, top-up sessions for up-skilling and acquisition of new competencies to ensure that faculty are up-to-date in their knowledge (pedagogy), practice and use of emerging new technologies/methods in handling new challenges and situations. The trick is to focus on innovative teaching methods rather than on technologies. If the reasons for innovation are properly analysed, evaluated and communicated, this provides a good rationale for staff to adopt new teaching methods and practices;
- Evaluating the effectiveness and efficiency of the training and development programmes.

Endnote

The incorporation of ICT into distance education has gradually metamorphosed the instructional and learning strategies leading to the development of cognitive, affective and psychomotor skills in the learners. To seek fullest development of such skills in the learners, the distance teachers need to be equipped with proper competencies as related to the technology. The competencies form the base from which to ascertain how to communicate effectively, manage the instructions and learning within norms of 'learner autonomy' and exploit the resources fully. Thus, various authorities and bodies involved in distance teaching like instructional managers, educational technologists, web designers and developers, learners etc. must have a proper evaluation and determination of all concerns, including technological and non-technological factors, e.g. quality facilitation; learner experience; learning environment, etc.

References

Ally, M. (2000) Tutoring skills for distance education, *Open Praxis*, 1, 31–4.

Bates, A. W. (1995) *Technology, Open Learning and Distance Education.* New York: Routledge.

Buford, J. A. Jr., and Lindner, J. R. (2002) *Human Resource Management in Local Government: Concepts and Applications for Students and Practitioners.* Cincinnati, OH: Southwestern.

Chute, A., Balthazan, L. B. and Poster, C. O. (1988) Learning from tele-training, *American Journal of Distance Education*, 2(3), 55–63.

Collison, G., Elbaum, B., Haavind, S. and Tinker, R. (2000) *Facilitating Online Learning: Effective Strategies for Moderators.* Madison, WI: Atwood Publishing.

Cyrs, T. (1997) Competence in teaching at a distance. In T. E. Crys (ed.), *Teaching and Learning at a Distance: What it Takes to Effectively Design, Deliver and Evaluate Programs. New Directions for Teaching and Learning.* Number 71, Fall. San Francisco, CA: Jossey-Bass Publishers.

Cyrs, T. and Smith, F. A. (1988) Faculty training for television teaching: State of the art, Paper presented at the Annual Conference of the Association for Educational Communication and technology, New Orleans, January.

Cyrs, T. and Smith, F. A. (1990) *Teleclass Teaching: A Resource Guide*, 2nd edn. Las Cruces, NM: New Mexico State University.

de Verneil, M. and Berge, Z. L. (2000) Going online: guidelines for faculty in higher education. *Educational Technology Review*, 13, Spring/Summer, 13–18.

Definitions of Competency on the Web (2004) Online. Available at: http://www.google.co.in/search?hl=enandlr=andie=UTF-8andoi=defmoreandq=define:Competency (Accessed 27 September 2004).

Dooley, K. E. and Lindner, J. R. (2000) Competencies for the distance education professionals: A self-assessment to document professional growth. *Journal of Agricultural Education*, 43(1), 24–35.

Graziadei, W. D. (1996) VICE in REST part IV. In J. M. Harison and D. Stephen (eds), *Computer Networking and Scholarship in the 21st Century University.* New York: SUNY Press.

Gunawardena, C. N. (1992) Changing faculty roles for audiographics and online teaching. *The American Journal of Distance Education*, 6(3), 58–71.

IGNOU (2001) *Academic Counselling in Open and Distance Learning* (STRIDE Handbook #3), New Delhi: IGNOU.

International Board of Standards for Training, Performance and Instruction (1999) The IBSTPI 1998, instructional design competencies. Online. Available at: http://www.ibstpi.org/98comp.html (Accessed 20 August 2004).

Jung, I. (2000) Online distance education: annotated bibliography (1997–1999). Online. Available at: http//www.ed.psu.edu/ascade/annbib/parta/doc (Accessed 20 August 2004).

Kearsley, G. (2000) *Online Education: Learning and Teaching in Cyberspace.* Belmont, CA: Wadsworth.

Labour, M., Juwah, C., White, N. and Tolley, S. (2000) Culture and ethics: facilitating online learning. In C. Higginson (Ed.), *Online Tutoring e-Book.* Online. Available at: http://otis.scotcit.ac.uk/onlinebook/otisT606.htm.

O'Rourke, J. (1993) *Roles and Competencies in Distance Education*. Vancouver: The Commonwealth of Learning. Online. Available at: http://www.col.org/10th/about/images/Roles_Competencies.pdf (Accessed 20 August 2004).

Parhar, M. and Mishra, S. (2000) Comepetencies for web-based Instructional designers. *Indian Journal of Open Learning*, 9(3), 415–22.

Paulsen, M. F. (1995) *The Online Report on Pedagogical Techniques for Computer-mediated Communication*. Online. Available at: http://www.nettskolen.com/alle/forskning/19/cmcped.html (Accessed 15 May, 2000).

Richey, R. C., Fields, D. C. and Foxon, M. (2001) *Instructional Design Competencies: The Standards*, 3rd edn. ERIC Clearinghouse on Information and Technology, Available online at http://eric.ed.gov/ERICWebPortal/contentdelivery/servlet/ERICServlet?accno=ED453803 (Accessed 11 June 2006).

Rosenberg, M. J. (2001) *E-learning: Strategies for Delivering Knowledge in the Digital Age*. New York: McGraw Hill.

RGU (2005) *Handbook for Personal Tutors*. Centre for the Enhancement of Learning and Teaching (CELT). Aberdeen: Robert Gordon University.

Salmon, G. (2000) *E-moderating: The Key to Teaching and Learning Online*. London: Kogan Page.

Schoenfeld-Tacher, R. and Persichitte, K.A. (2000) Differential skills and competencies required of faculty teaching distance education course. *International Journal of Educational Technology*, 2(1). Online. Available at: http://www.ao.uiuc.edu/ijet/v2n1/schoenfeld-tacher/ (Accessed on 4 October 2004).

Sewart, D. (1978) Continuity of concern for students in a system of learning at a distance. *ZIFF Paper No. 22*, Hagen: ZIFF. Online. Available at: http://www.fernuni-hagen.de/ZIFF/ZP_022.pdf.

Sewart, D. (1993) Student support systems in distance education. *Open Learning*, 8(3), 3–12.

Shank, P. (2004) *Competencies for Online Instructors*. Online. Available at: www.learningpeaks.com (Accessed 20 August 2004).

Sharma, R. C. (2002) Professional performance determinants in web based learning. *Journal of Distance Education*, 9(1), 51–63.

Simonson, M., Smaldino, S., Albright, M. and Zvacek, S. (2000) *Teaching and Learning at a Distance: Foundations of Distance Education*. Upper Saddle River, NJ: Merrill.

Stevenson, K. and Sander, P. (1998) How do Open University students expect to be taught at tutorials? *Open Learning*, 13(2), 42–6.

Stevenson, K., Sander, P. and Naylor, P. (1996) Student perceptions of the tutor's role in distance learning, *Open Learning*, 11(1), 22–30.

Tait, A. (2000) Planning student support for open and distance learning. *Open Learning*, 15(3), 287–99

Taylor, J. C. (1995) Distance education technologies: the fourth generation. *Australian Journal of Educational Technology*, 11(2), 1–7. Online. Available at: http://www.ascilite.org.au/ajet/ajet11/taylor.html (Accessed 11 june 2006).

Taylor, J. C. (2001) Fifth Generation Distance Education. Keynote Address presented at the 20th ICDE World Conference, Düsseldorf, Germany, 1–5 April.

Taylor Northrup, P. and Little, W. (1996) Establishing instructional technology benchmarks for teacher preparation programs. *Educational Leadership*, 47(3), 213–22.

Thach, E. C. (1994) Perceptions of distance education experts regarding the roles, outputs and competencies needed in the field of distance education. Doctoral Dissertation, Texas AandM University, 1994/1995. Dissertation Abstracts International, 55/10, 3166.

Williams, P. (2000). Making informed decisions about staffing and training: roles and competencies for distance education programs in higher education. *Online Journal of Distance Learning Administration*, 3(2). Online. Available at: http://www.westga. edu/~distance/williams32.html (Accessed 4th December 2004).

Williams, P. E. (2003) Roles and competencies for distance education programs in higher education institutions. *American Journal of Distance Education*, 17(1), 45–57.

Willis, B. (ed.) (1994) *Distance Education: Strategies and Tools*. Englewood Cliffs, NJ: Educational Technology Publications.

Conclusion

Charles Juwah

In previous chapters the authors described a diverse range of issues that underscore and impact positively or negatively on interactions in online education and the learner's experience. The discourses which draw on evidence-based practice, research and experiential learning highlight the importance of the phenomenon of interactions in online education from the theoretical, pedagogical, design, educational and socio-cultural perspectives.

The aim of this concluding chapter is to reflect the key issues which impact on online interactions, to identify the challenges which these represent, and to provide an account of why we think they arise and how to resolve some of them. The chapter will also attempt to identify key areas of research in providing a way forward for effective and quality interactions in online education.

What have we learnt

Key issues

It is evident from the examples and case studies highlighted in the book, the importance of pedagogy in informing the nature, sequence and effectiveness of interactions in online education. Interactions are critical in providing the link between pre-existing knowledge, the form of the new information, how the information is analysed and incorporated into a schema for constructing new meaning and knowledge as well as in the development of relevant skills and capabilities. These therefore require that learning activities/tasks should be authentic, engaging and contextualised to ensure meaningful learning.

Learning is always situated in a social context (see Chapter 1). In such settings and more importantly within a group/community context, dialogue is critical for negotiating and making new meaning, for providing feedback and alternative perspectives and for promoting and engendering reflection. Thus, to produce learners who can regulate their own learning, it becomes increasingly important that we should focus on the design of student-centred methods and pedagogies (problem-based and enquiry-based learning, simulations, role plays, peer learning and peer assessment, etc.), the learning environments and placing emphasis on feedback and reflection (see Chapters 1, 5, 6, 7 and 10). With online education being largely underpinned by constructivism, the learning activities should be interactive, motivating and engage the students in deep, reflective and transformative learning. This can be regulated through coaching and provision of relevant scaffolding as the learner moves from novice towards gaining mastery of the subject matter.

We have observed that the success criteria for 'interactive-centric' learning are dependent on the method of instruction, the learning environment, the context, the activities, the learner, other participants (including designers) and the role that the above factors play in the learning interactions. According to Dewey (1938), the learning context is most effective when an interaction between the social, physical and the learner's internal world is established. Thus enabling the learner to interpret the experience of the educational function.

Quality interactions lead to quality learning experience. As Dewey further stated, the quality of the learning experience is dependent on the initial and immediate appeal to the learner, particularly 'if an experience arouses curiosity, strengthens initiative, and sets up desires and purposes that are sufficiently intense to carry a person over dead places in the future, continuity works in a very different way. Every experience is a moving force. Its value can be judged only on the ground of what it moves toward' (p. 38). Thus, positive learning experiences stimulate and enhance the quality of future experiences.

As eloquently articulated in Chapters 4 and 5, motivation and engagement are important factors in the learning process. However, research reports the lack of engagement by college and university students in online courses (e-learning) as a result of de-contextualisation and lack of focus on authentic tasks (see Chapter 5). Motivation and engagement in learning can be influenced by 'value', 'meaning', 'relevance', 'cultural expectations' and practices associated with the 'learned skill in the real world' (see Chapter 5). Thus, educators need to be mindful of and to address relevant socio-cultural values in the learning process. As is evident from the book, games and simulations in online education are important in providing and supporting a diverse range of interactions. Examples of the types of interactions include exploration, visualisation, dialoguing with self and others, manipulating objects or artefacts, control, and reflection as well as providing opportunities for learners to practise and perfect their skills in a safe learning environment.

Also, evidence available both in the literature and from practice suggests that learning objects are important both for creating content and in underpinning some types of interactions within an online learning context, as well as enhancing the quality of learning (see Chapter 8). Advances in technology and knowledge management are providing opportunities for sharing, re-using and for effectively managing learning content (see Chapter 9). However, the form, granularity and purpose of learning objects are critical for determining levels of re-usability and interactions. Thus, to ensure that learning objects meet their intended objectives in learning situations, further research is needed to define different classes of learning objects that best suit different communities of users.

Design of the learning environment

Fundamental to promoting effective learning and enhancing online learners' experience is a fit-for-purpose learning environment. Such an environment should not focus exclusively on technology to the detriment of learning. Rather, it should be based on sound pedagogical principles and incorporate a mix of materials, content, multiple media, facilities and resources to suit different learning contexts and situations. As highlighted in Chapter 2, a major challenge arises in that most proprietary virtual learning environments, current practices, and frameworks used to support the design and implementation of online teaching and learning systems may not be the most appropriate for understanding the dynamics of virtual and predominantly asynchronous online learning. Thus, there is the need to design fit-for-purpose, robust and seamless learning environments based on encounters and interactions between all stakeholders, as well as the needs and expectations of all participants in the learning situation. As a general principle therefore, the learning environment should be designed to support strategic encounters and choice and directions for subsequent learning experiences. In so doing, educators should ensure that learning is situated, contextualised and characterised by:

- authentic activities;
- learner-focused interactions;
- guidance provided by expert facilitators;
- appropriate use of scaffolding and the shift in the locus of control to the learner as s/he acquires competency (Vygotsky, 1978).

Learner–environment interactions (e.g. visiting labs, clinics, etc.) provide a rich source of materials in the learning process, as well as contribute towards developing certain skills and capabilities. However, a majority of online course and training programmes, either because of logistics due to geographic spread of the learners or cost, fail to address this form of interaction in their provision (see Chapter 3). It is critical that designers of learning ensure a balance in providing *Learner–self interactions; Learner–Interface interactions and Learner–Instruction interactions* in their course design (see Figure 3.1), as lack of such interactions in the learning design may impact on learners' engagement and the quality of learning. Further research in this area is necessary to help inform on the impact of learner–environment interactions on the quality of learning.

In designing learning environments, designers must ensure equality of access and opportunity for all to participate in education and training (including individuals with disabilities). In the UK, as in most advanced Western countries, it is now a legal requirement that individuals are not denied access to learning as a result of their disabilities (Disabilities Discrimination Act 1995, 2005). All the above leads one to pose the following questions:

- How interactive is our learning environment?
- Do our learning environments provide appropriate space to support authentic, collaborative learning and a networked community of learning/practice suitable for all users, including individuals with disabilities?
- How do we provide a robust, seamless environment that can support a diverse range of interactions (including learner–environment interactions) to ensure effective learner-centred learning?

Peer learning

Peer learning is key in supporting collaborative learning and development of desirable high order skills. However, the effectiveness of peer learning is dependent on a variety of factors: the nature of the learning, context, the group and group dynamics, culture, emotions, technology, etc. In formalised online peer learning, structured learning plays a vital role in helping learners to meet the intended learning outcomes.

> Thus the discovery was made that learning is best facilitated in an environment where there is dialectic tension and conflict between immediate, concrete experience and analytical detachment. By bringing together the immediate experiences of the trainees and the conceptual models of the staff in an open atmosphere where inputs from each perspective could change and stimulate the other, a learning environment occurred with remarkable vitality and creativity.
>
> (Kolb, 1984, p. 10)

Also, the facilitator/more experienced learner's role in sustaining and enhancing reflection is critical in some context of peer learning (Hartley and Ravenscroft, 1999). Although a significant proportion of college and university students are 'digital natives' as it relates to the use of information and communication technology (ICT), most still lack information literacy and the essential skills of group/collaborative work. The case study reported in Chapter 10 illustrates how structured coaching in peer learning and peer assessment can be used to support and enhance the development of the students' knowledge, skills and professional repertoire (Juwah, 2003). The evolution of technology, in particular, peer-to-peer technologies (see Table 10.2) continues to broaden the boundaries, possibilities and opportunities of collaborative and cooperative learning. However, educators must ensure that automated, adaptive or intelligent tutoring systems do not diminish social interactions and discourses that are critical in social learning.

Professional development

Professional development for the acquisition of relevant knowledge and competencies for effective facilitation of online learning is a *sine qua non*.

The rapid expansion of online education and the use of educational technologies in on-campus, face-to-face courses has had a significant impact on staff. Such impact ranges from designing new curricula for online delivery, adopting new methods of teaching, learning to use new technologies, assessing learning online, managing time online, to monitoring and managing learning, and record keeping. All of which involve change.

Faculty need robust support to help them engage with and assimilate new ways of working, but more importantly to continue to ensure the quality of provision as well as enhance the students' experience. In our observations and experience, a framework based on Wenger's model of a community of practice with features of a community of learning provides a theoretical and evidence-based approach to robust and sustainable professional development. This approach provides the relevant scaffolding which facilitates and supports construction of knowledge, and the development of enhanced reflective practice and transformational learning.

Lastly, the authors, in highlighting the diverse and complex issues that underpin interactions in online education, have made significant contributions in broadening our understanding of the concept of interactivity and interactions. However, they have also raised more questions than they have answered. Some of the questions point to areas needing further research. These are:

- how students learn within a group and which interactions are key in motivating and sustaining the students' engagement in deep learning;
- which learning designs engage students in deep, reflective and transformative learning;
- how the regulation of scaffolding can be used to move the learner from novice towards gaining mastery of learning;
- the role of context and activities in promoting effective interactions and meaningful learning.

References

Dewey, J. (1938) *Experience and Education*. New York: Macmillan.

Hartley, J. R. and Ravenscroft, A. (1999) Supporting exploratory and expressive learning: a complimentary approach. *International Journal of Continuing Engineering Education and Lifelong Learning*, 9(3/4), 275–91.

Juwah, C. (2003) Using peer assessment to develop skills and capabilities. *Journal of the United States Distance Learning Association*. January, 39–50. Online. Available at: http://www.usdla.org/html/journal/JAN03_Issue/article04.html.

Kolb, D. A. (1984) *Experiential Learning: Learning as the Source of Learning and Development*. Englewood Cliffs, NJ: Prentice Hall.

Vygotsky, L.S. (1978) *Mind in Society*. Cambridge, MA: Harvard University Press.

Wenger, E. (1998) *Communities of Practice: Learning, Meaning, and Identity*. Cambridge: Cambridge University Press.

Index

action xiv, 1, 9, 13, 16, 17, 19, 24, 28, 128, 129, 130, 174, 184, 211, 214, 226,
activity ix, 1, 15–18, 24, 33, 34, 38, 47, 60, 76, 77, 79, 82, 84, 87, 93, 97, 102, 108, 111, 124, 127, 131, 152, 158, 161, 162, 173, 177, 179, 197, 209, 214, 216, 233, 234
affordances 16, 30, 98
Agostinho, S. *et al.* 105, 106, 107, 109, 113, 114,
Allen, I. E. 158, 158,
Anderson, T. xii, 2, 66, 105, 109, 114, 141, 142, 143, 145, 152, 153, 155, 156, 169, 170, 172, 173, 188, 208, 209, 215, 216, 225, 226; and Boud, D. 172, 188; and Elloumni, F. 143, 153
ARCS model of motivation
assessment 17, 28, 55, 94, 99, 100, 102, 127, 151, 163, 165, 173, 176, 179, 180, 183, 185, 193, 222, 225, 230, 235, 247, 250,
assessment criteria 165, 193,
asynchronous 168, 175, 179, 181, 184, 192, 201, 202, 232, 235, 238, 249,
attitudes 2, 17, 53, 68, 91, 92, 156, 194, 233
authentic viii, 3, 14, 73, 91–101, 122, 131, 132, 137, 172, 177, 178, 180, 218, 225, 243, 247–50

Bakhtin, M. 176, 188,
Barab, S. S. *et al.* 94, 101, 208, 210, 225,
Bates, A. W. ii, 67, 68, 157, 159, 168, 232, 244
behavioural xiii, 1, 7, 73, 237,
behaviourist 13, 49,
benefits 11, 147, 167, 179, 232, 236
Berg, Z. L. 55, 59, 68, 157, 159, 162, 168, 206, 207, 209, 225, 232, 244
Biggs, J. 23, 24, 174, 188, 213, 225,
Bonk, C. J.: and King, K. 48, 51, 53, 68; and Reynolds, T. H. 48, 68

Booker, Di 167, 168
Bormans, J. and Hill, K. 112, 114
Boud, D. *et al.* 118
Brady, E. and Bedient, D. 143, 153
Brennan, R. *et al.* 167, 168,
Brown, J.S. *et al.* 93, 94, 101
browsers 163,
Bruner, J. 14, 24, 94, 102, 172, 188,
Buford, J. A., Jr. and Lindner, J. R. 233, 244
Buzza, D.C. *et al.* 108, 114,

capability 16, 79, 216, 233
case study 29, 40, 148, 180, 184, 187, 198, 222, 250
chat sessions 162, 238,
Claessens, M. *et al.* 135, 136
co-construction 161,
Coffield, F. *et al.* 22, 23, 24
cognitive ix, x, 1–4, 11, 14–16, 18, 20–2, 31, 49, 20, 56, 75, 76, 86–9, 92, 93, 123, 135, 159, 168, 175, 177, 212–20, 228, 241, 243
cognitive presence 175, 215–17, 220
collaborative 3, 7, 18, 30, 48, 54, 56, 67, 68, 70, 75, 77, 78, 80, 81, 83, 86, 89, 132, 141, 142, 145, 149, 151, 153–5, 159, 161, 162, 172, 175, 179–85, 187, 189, 193, 195, 197, 198, 201, 202, 204, 215–18, 220, 221, 228, 232, 234, 239, 241, 250
Collison, A. *et al.* 238, 244,
competence 18, 159, 171, 173, 184, 211, 224, 242, 244,
competency 233, 235, 244, 249,
computer aided instruction 157,
computer mediated conferencing 175, 205, 228
concept xiv, 1–14, 9, 12, 16, 21, 23, 24, 36, 38, 77, 104, 105, 107, 117, 120, 129, 130, 134, 135, 137, 139, 143, 157, 158, 161, 168, 176, 179, 182, 239, 251

conceptualisation 108
conference 26, 68, 114–16, 136, 143, 146, 153, 160, 162, 168, 169, 188, 199, 203, 204, 244, 245
conflict resolution 187
construction xvi, 1, 2, 4, 10, 12, 15, 20, 26, 29, 35, 38, 51, 99, 110, 113, 114, 148, 161, 176, 177, 180, 181, 18, 193, 195, 202, 204, 209, 210, 212, 213, 214, 215, 217, 218, 221, 251
constructivism 14, 24, 51, 71, 77, 94, 117, 122, 136, 172, 178, 188, 193, 214, 215, 226, 248
content 1, 2, 10, 14, 18, 29–32, 36, 38, 39, 46–50, 52, 53, 57, 58–60, 62, 64–6, 73, 82, 87, 88, 92, 98, 99, 101, 105, 108, 112, 114–16, 118, 141–52, 157, 158, 160, 168, 172, 175, 178, 180, 181, 185, 186, 193, 194, 196, 202, 207, 209, 215, 217, 219, 220, 235–7, 239, 240, 248, 249
context 3, 4, 17, 19, 24, 27, 29, 31, 32, 35, 38, 40, 43, 51, 55, 56, 57, 66, 77, 79–82, 84, 96, 104, 105, 107–10, 114, 142, 144, 146, 156, 157, 158, 165, 171, 173–6, 178, 179–81, 185–7, 190, 195, 207–9, 211, 214–18, 221, 228, 243, 247, 248, 250, 251
contextualised 2, 112, 132, 247, 249
continuing professional development x, 207, 215, 217, 220, 222, 227
conversation xiv, 10, 14, 38, 48, 82, 83, 113, 133, 143, 144, 60, 161, 175, 176, 192, 193, 204
Corno, L. 49, 50, 69
cost effective 141, 148, 151, 162
course ware 9, 10, 12, 13, 19, 25, 127, 133, 134
Coventry, L. 191, 193–5, 198, 200, 203
Craik, F. I. M. and Lockhart, R. S. 11, 24
critique 18, 40, 163, 185
cultural 1, 24, 49, 76, 86, 123, 164, 174, 178, 179, 185, 193, 210, 219, 226, 238, 242, 248
Cyrs, T. 232, 234, 240, 244

Damon, W. 145, 153
database 19, 145, 15, 16, 182, 190
Department of Defense 48, 69
design i, ii, vii, ix, xiv, xvi, 2–4, 7, 14–17, 19, 20, 24–6, 28, 29, 30–2, 34, 39, 40, 43–6, 48, 50, 51, 53–5, 58–70, 73, 75–9, 86, 87–9, 91, 93, 94–6, 98–103, 105–17, 123, 124, 131, 135, 136, 147, 151, 152, 170, 176, 177, 195, 203, 207, 208, 215, 216, 219–21, 226, 234–41, 244, 245, 247, 249

Dewey, J. 9, 17, 24, 211, 215, 226, 248, 257
dialogic 178, 179, 185, 188
dialogue vii, 1, 3, 10, 13, 14, 17–20, 22, 24, 66, 68, 75, 90, 144, 147, 158, 162, 164, 166, 172, 175–8, 182, 186, 188, 219, 223, 229, 232, 237, 243, 247
digital ii, xii, 3, 75–8, 86, 89, 99, 102–7, 111–13, 115, 116, 118–20, 122, 124, 134, 135, 136, 144, 184, 194, 203, 232, 245, 250
digital natives 119, 136, 250
disability 184, 242
disputational 176
Dolittle, P. E. and Camp, W. G. 172, 188
Downes, S. 105, 114, 146, 154
Dublin Core 106

elearning 3, 7, 9, 46, 52, 67, 68, 89, 209
Elton, L. and Johnston, B. 180, 188
emotional 175
empathic 175
encounter theory vii, 3, 7, 27, 40, 66
encounters ix, 2, 3, 7, 10, 28, 29–43, 47, 249
Engestrom, Y. 15, 24,
Entwistle, N. J. iv, 23, 46, 54, 60, 61, 73, 88, 89, 96, 109, 127, 152, 163, 169, 177, 180, 187, 189, 211, 214, 229, 234–7, 243
evaluative 211, 224
facilitating 4, 20, 53, 59, 78, 170, 177, 180, 205, 208, 210, 212, 216, 217, 219, 222–4, 226, 230, 239, 242, 244

facilitators i, viii, x, 2, 4, 30, 31, 40, 70, 165, 167, 172, 207–10, 215–17, 219, 220, 223, 224, 241, 242, 249
faculty xii–xvi, 34, 149, 151, 159, 181, 184, 187, 204, 205, 237, 242–5, 251
formative 64, 183, 186, 188, 189, 237
Forsyth, I. 165, 168
framework ii, viii–x, xiv, 3, 4, 9, 10, 12, 21, 24, 25, 34, 40, 44, 46, 48–50, 55, 58, 66–70, 77, 80, 88, 89, 92, 95, 101, 102, 105–7, 109, 111–14, 135, 168, 172, 173, 205, 207, 208, 211–18, 220, 222, 251
Fulford, C.P. 141, 154, 159, 168

Gage, J. et al. 195, 203
games and simulations 73, 248
Garrison, D. R. et al. 46, 70, 156, 157, 169, 175, 189, 215, 216–18, 226
generation 68, 129, 146, 154, 201, 211, 231, 232, 245
Gipps, C. 179, 188
Greer, J. et al. 105, 115, 147, 154
Greller, W. and MacKay 198, 204

Griffiths, S. *et al.* 172, 173, 188
Griffiths, S. *et al.* 188
Gunawardena, C. N. *et al.* 161, 169, 215, 226

Hannafin, M. J. *et al.* 53, 69
Harper, B. and Hedberg, J. 180, 188
Harper, B. *et al.* 107, 109, 115
Hartley, J. R. and Ravenscroft, A. 176, 188, 250, 251
Henke, H. and Russum, J. 1, 5
Herrington, J. xii, 73, 92–5, 102, 109, 113, 116, 210, 216, 226
higher education 25, 27, 28, 43, 91, 94, 95–100, 102, 103, 106, 109, 113, 114, 116, 156, 169–71, 180, 188, 191, 193, 198, 199, 201, 203, 225–7, 229, 234, 241, 244, 246
Hillman, D. C. *et al.* 29, 44, 47, 50, 69, 157, 169
Hirumi, A. xii, 47, 50, 54, 55, 56, 69
Holmberg, B. xiv, 160, 169
hypertext 13, 133, 157
hypothesis 127, 128

ICT xii, 1, 109, 114, 116, 136, 204, 228, 232, 243, 250
IMS 107, 108, 113, 115, 151
interaction vii, viii, xi, xvi, 1–4, 7, 9–14, 16, 19, 20–2, 26, 29, 30, 32, 38, 39, 42–8, 50, 53, 55, 58–63, 65–71, 75–90, 92, 103, 108, 139, 141, 142–62, 168–70, 175, 178–80, 186, 193–9, 203–5, 209, 214, 217, 219, 220, 221, 224, 227, 237–41, 243, 248, 249
interactivity i, vii, xiv, 1–3, 7, 9, 13, 19, 21, 23, 24, 26, 27, 29, 36, 44, 47, 48, 66, 68–70, 91, 92, 103, 139, 157, 169, 171, 189, 192, 193, 195, 210, 251
interface ix, 1, 29, 30, 38, 39, 47, 5, 60–2, 64, 65, 70, 80, 82, 88, 92, 96, 97, 123, 134, 17, 152, 154, 155, 158, 159
InterLoc ix, xvi, 3, 75, 76, 79–84, 86–9
International Board of Standards for Training, Performance and Instruction (IBSTPI) 5, 233, 244
internet relay chat (IRC) 162
IGNOU xii, 229, 244

Jonassen, D. H. 15, 24, 25, 27, 43, 44, 51, 55, 70, 89, 93–5, 102, 213, 215, 226; and Grabowski, B.L. 22, 25
Juwah, C. i, v, vii, viii, xii, xiv, xvi, 1, 51, 66, 119, 136, 156, 166, 169, 171, 177, 180, 188, 189, 207, 212, 226, 228, 244, 247, 250, 251

Kearsley, G. 238, 244; and Shneiderman, B. 40, 44
Klemm, W. R. 175, 176, 189
knowledge i, iii, 2–4, 10–14, 16, 19–21, 23, 32 38, 44, 46, 51, 52, 54, 56, 62, 73, 75, 78, 81, 87, 88, 92, 94, 98, 99, 101, 103, 104, 107–9, 114, 117, 122, 123, 124, 126, 127, 130–2, 141, 145, 150, 156, 157, 161, 169, 171–82, 184, 185, 187, 189, 193, 195, 197, 202, 204, 208–18, 220, 221, 226, 228–30, 232, 237, 241–3, 245, 247, 248, 250, 251
Kolb, D.A. 9, 23, 25, 174, 189, 250, 251
Koper, R. and Olivier, B. 108, 115
Kukulska-Hulme, A. and Traxler, J. iii, 146, 154
Laurillard, D. 12, 14, 25, 26, 109, 115, 169, 180, 189; and McAndrew 109, 115
Lave, J. and Wenger, E. 14, 16, 17, 19, 20, 94, 171, 178, 213, 215, 216
learned 10, 12, 13, 50, 105, 122, 127, 130, 145, 154, 173, 177, 185, 189, 248
learning i, iv, viii, ix, xii–xiv, 1–4, 7, 9–57, 62, 63, 66–71, 73–138, 141–59, 162, 164–80, 182–230, 232–8, 251
learning communities 16, 20, 89, 99, 146, 149, 150, 152, 154, 159, 208, 210, 216, 227, 232
learning objects iii, viii, 2, 3, 21, 41, 66, 73, 104–16, 142, 148, 150, 151, 154, 187, 248
legal 249
levels of interactions 48, 66
linguistic 1, 77, 155, 164, 242
Listproc 162
Listserv 162, 181
Lowell, N. and Persichitte, K. A. 179, 189
Lukasiak, J. *et al.* 113, 115
lurkers 163

Majordomo 162
Marton, F. and Säljö, R. 23, 25, 186, 187, 213, 226
Mayes, J. T. vii, xii, 9, 10, 14, 19, 20, 23, 25, 26, 51, 66; and Fowler, C .J. H. 9, 10, 23, 25
mentor 153, 167, 210, 214, 219–25, 228
meta-cognitive 21, 185, 186
meta-communicative 185, 186
Min, F. B. M. viii, xiii, 4, 117, 118, 120, 126, 128, 130, 131, 135–7
Mishra, S. viii, xiii, 66, 162, 169, 237, 245
moderator 18, 162, 163, 165, 196, 224, 238
monologue 176, 202

Moore, M. G. 29, 44, 46, 47, 50, 51, 59, 69, 70, 141, 153, 154, 157, 159, 160, 168, 169, 204, 226

Oliver, R.: and Herrington, J. 109, 116; *et al.* 110, 116
Olivier, B. 79, 89, 108, 115, 116,
online education 1, 2, 5, 7, 89, 91, 99–101, 104, 116, 161, 175, 205, 226, 228, 242–4, 247, 248, 250, 251
operation 1, 12, 16, 17, 31, 40

Pallof, R. M. and Pratt, K. 220, 227
Panda, S. iv, viii, xiii, 66, 207, 212, 213, 221, 226, 227
paradigm 32, 69, 70, 77–9, 101, 157, 159, 178, 229
parallelism 134, 135, 137
Parer, M. S. 158, 169
Pask, G. 193, 204,
Paulsen, M. F. 49, 71, 157, 158, 169, 232, 245
Pawlowski, J. M. 108, 116
pedagogical perspective viii, 2, 4, 33, 115, 154
pedagogy i, iii, 1, 2, 13, 15, 16, 23, 24, 88, 99, 108, 122, 129, 149, 180, 185, 187, 191, 194, 202, 203, 222, 243, 247
peer learning i, viii, xi, 4, 19, 139, 171–9, 184–8, 219, 223, 247, 250
peer-to-peer technologies 187, 250
Perry, W. G. 23, 26, 68
phenomena ix, 1, 120–2, 124, 125, 128, 132
phenomenon 2, 7, 120, 123, 128–30, 172, 178, 211, 247
Piaget, J. 14, 18, 26, 122, 137, 172, 189
Plowman, L. *et al.* 13, 26, 38, 44
political 28, 137, 218
professional development i, viii, x, 2, 4, 66, 165, 168, 184, 189, 201, 205, 207–23, 225–37, 242, 250, 251
psychological 1, 20, 24–6, 28, 69, 77, 90, 170, 190, 196, 198, 202, 204, 229
Purnell, K. *et al.* 176, 189

radio 160, 182, 205, 228, 229, 231, 240
Ragan, L. C. 159, 170
Ravenscroft, A. xiii, 76, 78, 79, 81–3, 86, 87, 89, 176, 188, 250, 251
reflection i, x, 1, 10, 14, 17–19, 22, 77, 127, 129, 166, 172–4, 176, 178–83, 185, 186, 188, 189, 192, 205, 207, 208, 210–27, 235, 238, 243, 247, 248, 250
reflective xiv, 17, 68, 77, 79, 83, 87, 99, 157, 174, 176, 189, 211, 212, 213–16, 218–20, 224, 227, 243, 248, 251

reflective practice 211–13, 219, 225, 243, 251
reflective practitioner 189,
Reigeluth, C. M. and Moore, J. 50, 70
RGU 200, 222, 229, 245
research ii, ix, xii xiv, xvi, 1, 3–5, 7, 12, 13, 15, 19, 21–6, 29, 29, 30, 38, 44, 46, 53, 55, 57, 66–71, 78, 83, 86, 88, 89, 91–3, 95, 98–103, 113, 115, 116, 118, 119, 146, 149, 152–6, 169–71, 173, 182–4, 187–90, 193, 198, 202, 203, 204, 224, 225, 227, 234, 235, 237, 238, 247–9, 251
Robertshaw, R. 145, 158
Rose, E. 9, 26, 92, 103
Rosenburg, M. J. 238, 245
Rourke, L.: and Anderson, T. 145, 155; *et al.* 175, 189
rubric xi, 58, 63, 165, 166, 169
Rump, N. 111, 116

Saba, F. 46, 70
Salmon, G. xiv, 18, 26, 30, 31, 44, 152, 155, 161, 162, 170, 208–10, 215, 227, 237, 245
satellite 71, 159
scaffolding 14, 16, 17, 32, 98, 118, 121, 175, 177, 185, 186, 224, 248, 249, 251
Schiller, J. and Mitchell, J. 193, 204
Schoenfeld-Tacher, R. and Perschitte, K.A. 235, 245
Schon, D. 4, 174, 189, 205, 211, 215, 227
SCORM 151
semantic vii, 4, 11, 66, 139, 141–3, 153, 209
Sharma, R. C. vii, xiii, 228, 238, 245
Shirkey, C. 142, 146, 155
Simonson, M. *et al.* 46, 70, 232, 245
Sims, R. vii, xii, 2, 27, 29, 30, 32, 38, 44, 47, 66, 69, 92, 103
simulation viii, ix, 4, 13, 54, 56, 70, 73, 89, 117, 119, 120, 121, 123–37
skills 2, 3, 14–16, 24, 29, 46, 49, 51, 52, 56, 58, 62, 65, 67, 73, 75, 76, 79, 86, 87, 91, 92, 97, 98, 117, 118, 127, 132, 146, 165, 167, 168, 171–4, 177, 179, 180, 184–7, 189, 205, 209–11, 222, 223, 228–30, 232–5, 237, 238, 240–5, 247–51
social i, vii, 1, 3, 15, 17–20, 24, 26, 42, 49, 51, 56, 69, 75–8, 87, 88, 123, 142, 145, 146, 149, 151, 153, 154–61, 163, 169, 171, 172, 174, 175, 177–80, 186, 189, 190, 193, 208–21, 223, 225, 229, 236, 247, 248, 250
social presence 156, 175, 178, 189, 215, 216, 220
socio-cultural perspective xiv, 2, 7, 73, 247

Springer, L. *et al.* 145, 155
stakeholders 2, 27–31, 33–6, 38–41, 43, 201, 243, 249
Stein, D. 178, 190
Sternberg, R. 15, 26, 93, 103
Stevenson, K.: and Sander, P. 234, 245; *et al.* 229, 245
student iv, ix, 4, 12, 14, 20, 21, 24, 25, 32, 34, 44, 47, 48, 50, 54, 56, 58, 68, 69, 71, 98, 100, 102, 104, 123, 125–7, 131, 132, 134, 141, 143–53, 156, 161–3, 171–3, 179, 188, 189, 195, 198, 200, 201, 203, 204, 209, 212, 227–30, 232–4, 237, 240–2, 245, 247
summative 183, 186, 237
synchronicity 203
synchronous xiv, 4, 17, 43, 57, 59, 60, 79, 82, 83, 89, 139, 142, 153, 159, 160, 162–4, 168, 170, 175, 181, 182, 184, 192, 202, 231, 232, 235, 238

task 10, 12, 14, 15, 17, 18, 20, 21, 23, 29, 30, 34, 41, 54, 57–9, 61, 63, 70, 79, 93–7, 127, 151, 162, 177, 209, 229, 233, 235, 238
Taylor, J. C. 232, 245
teaching presence 175, 177, 215, 216, 220
technological xvi, 2, 32, 75, 79, 87, 99, 118, 179, 192, 202, 209, 209, 234, 243
technology iii, ix, xi–xiv, 1, 4, 10, 13, 17–21, 23, 24–6, 32, 38, 43, 44, 51, 53, 68–71, 89, 93–5, 99, 101–3, 105, 107, 109, 113–16, 118, 124, 130, 134, 137, 139, 150, 153–5, 157–64, 167–71, 173–5, 177, 179–81, 183–5, 187, 188, 191, 192, 194, 195, 197, 199, 200, 202–4, 209, 222–4, 226, 227, 230–2, 235, 238, 239, 241–6, 248–50
technology-mediated 158
tele-teaching 240, 241
television 118, 119, 142, 155, 159, 169, 196, 197, 229, 244

temporal 2, 4, 91, 139, 141
Terry, N. 1, 5
Thach, E. C. 50, 71, 232, 234, 246
threaded discussion boards 177
Tognazzini, B. 38, 45
Topping, K. 172, 190
tool 3, 17, 47–50, 52, 55, 57, 59, 62–6, 71, 75–77, 79–81, 84, 88, 89, 106, 111, 114, 119, 121, 124, 126, 130, 152, 154, 159, 162, 164, 169, 181–4, 187, 191, 192, 195, 200, 202, 232, 234, 238
transformational 19, 226, 251
transmissive 180
Tuckman, B. W. 174, 185, 190
two-way technologies 159, 160, 161, 168
types of encounters 43
types of interactions 7, 248

Vetro, A. *et al.* 112, 116
videoconferencing viii, x, 4, 191–205, 228, 231, 240
virtual learning environments 203, 249
von Glasersfeld, E. 51, 71
Vygotsky, L. S. 14, 16, 26, 51, 71, 76, 77, 90, 117, 122, 123, 137, 156, 170, 172, 177, 190, 193, 204, 210, 223, 227, 249, 251

web-based ix, 1, 16, 26, 59, 68, 69, 70, 97, 101, 102, 118, 121, 124, 144, 146, 160, 161, 168, 169, 191, 195, 203, 208, 219, 228, 232, 237, 238, 245
Wenger, E. 14, 16, 17, 19, 20, 25, 26, 94, 102, 171, 178, 189, 190, 210, 213, 215–17, 226, 227, 251

zapping 133, 136
Zimmerman, B. J.: and Martinez-Pons, M. 49, 71; and Paulsen, A. S. 49, 71
zone of proximal development 16, 24, 123, 177, 186